When We Were Invincible

---■---

Life Lessons from the '80s
that Defined a Generation

Becky Kliss

invincible
press

Copyright 2024 by Becky Kliss / Invincible Press

All rights reserved. This book or any portion thereof may not be reproduced or used in any manner whatsoever without the express written permission of the publisher except for the use of brief quotations in a book review.

Invincible Press
P.O. Box 946
St. Joseph, MI 49085

www.beckykliss.com

Softcover ISBN: 979-8-9885798-8-5

Hardcover ISBN: 979-8-9885798-7-8

eBook ISBN: 979-8-9885798-9-2

Dedication

To Generation X:
Find your people, Gen Xers—those who bring out your youthful spirit. May we appreciate where we've been, how far we've come, and that we grew up in the best decade ever!

To my best buds from NBHS class of 1986:
Mikey, Lisa, Rennie, Terry, Wayne, Bob, and Dave—and my BFF of fifty years—Robin, thank you for having my back on this wild ride of writing my first book and for putting up with my never-ending questions. May we keep ourselves *in* motion and invincible as long as we can, lifting each other up along the journey. I love you all!

To my mom, dad, and brother Jeff:
As wacky, dysfunctional, loving, traditional yet nontraditional, and crazy as our household was, I wouldn't trade it for anything. Love you all forever!

Table of Contents

Foreword - Don't Talk to Strangers

Introduction - East Bound and Down

Section One

Ch. 0 - (Don't You) Forget About Me: Prologue — 01

Ch. 1 - Walk This Way: Where We've Been and Where We're Going — 15

Ch. 2 - True Colors: Values — 31

Ch. 3 - Welcome to the Jungle: Technology — 47

Ch. 4 - Call Me: The Telephone — 65

Ch. 5 - Turn Up the Radio: Music — 81

Section Two

Ch. 6 - Under Pressure: Time — 101

Ch. 7 - Should I Stay or Should I Go: Choices — 117

Ch. 8 - Private Eyes: Social Media — 133

Ch. 9 - Video Killed the Radio Star: Screens — 149

Ch. 10 - The Finer Things: Treasures — 167

Section Three

Ch. 11 - Another Brick in the Wall: School — 185

Ch. 12 - Working for the Weekend: Work — 199

Ch. 13 - Money for Nothing: Money — 217

Section Four

Ch. 14 - We're Not Gonna Take it: Rules — 235

Ch. 15 - The Safety Dance: Risks — 253

Ch. 16 - Somebody's Watching Me: Fears — 271

Ch. 17 - Invincible: Perseverance — 285

Epilogue - Crystal Ball: That's all she wrote...for now... — 299

About the Author | Acknowledgments

Don't Talk to Strangers

Foreword

We all have that ONE friend, right? The crazy one who is always suggesting outrageous ideas, has no filter, and leads us down a path we wouldn't willingly take ourselves. Becky has always been that friend for me, my BFF since my earliest memories. I don't know what drew us two strangers together all those years ago on that school bus taking us to first grade, but the universe couldn't have paired two more opposite souls together, and I couldn't imagine my life without her. I've always said she kept me from being too boring, and I kept her from going to jail (even though she reminds me regularly that her dad offered her one "get out of jail free" card). We managed to grow a strong friendship out of our differences. Honestly, when I look back at all the notes we wrote—evidence of all the ridiculous things we fought about—I'm not sure how we did. We were just pure stubborn about staying friends through our teen years, and when we made it through those, it was (mostly) smooth sailing through the adult years.

Yes, you read that right. I can still read all the notes we wrote because Becky kept EVERY one from back in the day. She still has just about everything from the '80s, even her prom dress. She's taken a lot of flak for her packrat ways over the years, but who doesn't secretly love reading through those old, cringeworthy polls and notes while walking down memory lane? She is laughing at us all now as she uses her ancient treasures as research and visuals for this book. I hope you'll enjoy a good laugh at our expense here as you find them throughout the book!

Because of our many differences, I think we spent a lot of our youth trying to change things about each other. Fortunately, we are both strong-willed enough to stay true to ourselves, and with time, we realized that we worked best together as the opposites we are.

I know that at some point around age thirty, I began to appreciate Becky more for her differences and began to really see the characteristics that drew me to her friendship. She is one of the best-spirited people I have ever known. You could say she is a walking Murphy's Law; whatever could go wrong usually does with her, and she always rolls with it and gets through with a smile and a good story. She is a great storyteller (which you are about to discover) and can make you smile with her unique perspective on life situations. She is not afraid to talk to anyone and asks a lot of questions. (I admit this one can still be irritating at times.) Her curiosity and desire for knowledge are what drive her to do better and be better. You can't ask for more than that. Whatever she does, she gives it 200 percent. If she sets her mind to it, it's going to happen, like our first concert experience at fifteen years old. From how she won two concert tickets to see Rick Springfield in 1983 in Chicago, to us getting to the concert and screaming our heads off the minute we saw his shadow on stage.

Her determination and resourcefulness were already top-level at this point! She has gotten better with age, and I absolutely love that she decided to write a book that combines the decade she loves most with her drive to improve herself and make life better, not just for herself but for anyone she is able to affect.

Becky has always helped her friends and has a very loyal friend base. The biggest thing she does is keep us all connected and in touch. I think there should be another love language inspired by her called "throwing parties" because she knows how to get everyone together to have the best time. It all started in the '80s in her basement. She had some great parties back then and continues with them even today with her BecFest parties. She has these parties so she can get all the people she loves together and create the best memories with them.

When Becky started this book, it had the same concept, but a completely different format. In true Becky fashion, she has been absorbing all the knowledge on writing she can through research, seminars, and coaching. She has surrounded herself with people who are experts to help her through a new process. It is hard to describe her passion for this project. While she does LOVE her '80s music and all the feel-good stories and memories from that decade, this is more about making TODAY better by utilizing some things from our past to bring balance into today's crazy world.

For as long as I can remember, Becky has utilized advice, methods, and techniques learned from experts to improve her mental and physical health. In this book, she'll share some wisdom from her travels and experiences for all of us to learn from. She doesn't have a Ph.D., but I believe life experience is most often the best teacher. She's talked me into countless things I wouldn't have otherwise tried, and I can always say it was worth the learning experience. Of course, I'd never turn down any time spent with my BFF, either!

Becky really wanted Rick Springfield to write the foreword for her first book, but he doesn't know her like I do, so I won the job. I know *When We Were Invincible* will give you some good laughs and bring back your own memories, but what I truly hope it does for you is what it did for me: make you stop and think about what you really want out of each day, and how to get there if you haven't yet. If nothing else, I know it will make you feel good and inspire you to be happy in each moment.

I am so excited to get you started on this journey with Becky. I know you will not be disappointed!

YBFFL,

Rob

East Bound and Down

Introduction

When We Were Invincible is the first book in *The Invincible '80s* series.

It's the first book I've written since I scribbled out a novel in multiple-colored markers when I was seven years old. The series will delve into the milestones of growing up in the '80s, from our first concerts, first loves, first kisses, first jobs, and first cars, as well as our unforgettable summers, notorious school days, and cherished mixtapes.

When We Were Invincible kicks off the series by reflecting on the risks we took, the rules we broke, and the choices we made as adolescents, while brimming with excitement about what the future might hold. It also examines how we, now middle-aged, navigate decisions about work, money, and the value of our time. We'll key in on how screen time—cell phones, computers, television, and social media—impacts our lives.

While our experiences in the '80s may have been unique, I believe you'll find much of this book relatable.

Writing this book has empowered me to slow down and enjoy life more. My hope is that reading it will do the same for you.

So many of us struggle with some of the same things:

- Keeping up with the technology and endless choices thrown at us daily
- Coping with the life sandwich of caring for aging parents while raising good kids and enjoying our own life
- Contemplating retirement, downsizing, and ways to simplify your life
- Knowing that your body is aging faster than your mind
- Trying to understand today's crazy world and how we fit in
- Wanting your '80s carefree lifestyle, culture, and iconic music back!

As you read on, my wish for you is to be able to **STOP** and **REWIND**. Replay what your mixtape of life looked like back then and **PAUSE** to reflect on what you remember. Take those life lessons and **FAST FORWARD** to today. Then hit **PLAY/RECORD** and turn your mixtape into the solid-gold version to live your best life today.

THE GENERATIONS

I'm just a small-town girl from New Buffalo, Michigan. I'm a Gen Xer. We are known for our independence, sarcasm, ingenuity, and creativity. I'm also a strong-minded Aries who came out of the womb in March with the word "stubborn" stamped on my forehead. You are going to see a lot of things in this book. Sometimes I make up words. I may get a little bossy. I'm an overachiever wanting to get every topic imaginable in one book, along with banging out a few cusswords here and there.

Wait, did I mention I'm also ADHD? That's a fun one when trying to write a book!

I owned a successful cleaning business with a staff of hundreds of employees. I invested decades in personal growth and coaching to step up my management game and my roller coaster of a love life. I often sought answers without even starting with the right questions. My struggles have inspired self-discovery. My endless curiosity and drive led to new experiences, relationships, and a refreshing new outlook on life. In writing this book, I've learned so much about Gen X and I'm excited to share those lessons with you.

Before moving on, let's cover the seven living generations chart and what their ages are as of 2024:

The Greatest Generation: born between 1900 and 1924 (at least 100 years old)

The Silent Generation: born between 1925 and 1945 (most of our parents, 79 to 100 years old)

Baby Boomers: born between 1946 and 1964 (60 to 79 years old)

Gen X: born between 1965 and 1980 (44 to 59 years old)

Gen Y (Millennials): born between 1981 and 1996 (28 to 43 years old)

Gen Z (Zoomers): born between 1997 and early 2010 (14 to 27 years old)

Gen Alpha: born in early 2010 and will continue through 2025 (younger than 13 years old)

Although most people reading this book are likely to be Gen Xers, Baby Boomers in their early sixties and Millennials in their early forties can relate to a lot of what Gen X is going through. We're all in this middle-aged club. *So, if* we're going to be in a club, we need a name for it. Let's call it the CD-55 Club, and I'll add it to my very own "Bec-tionary." Here's my definition of it:

CD-55 \ *noun* **a** : a **C**an-**D**oer who has a birth year ranging from 1960 to 1984 **b** : could be a Gen Xer, a young Baby Boomer, or older Millennial [one who is approaching or just past double nickels in age] **c** : one most often in their fifties [give or take] **d** : one who experienced the '80s in their youth **e** : someone who <**C**an't **D**rive> 55 and or a Sammy Hagar fan.

CD-55ers \ *noun pl* **a** : <**C**an-**D**oers> **b** : group community or club consisting of cool people on a quest to enjoy life [to its fullest].

This "club" is mentioned often in the book, and I hope you'll join—whether you're part of these generations, or just relate to the Gen X lifestyle. If you're younger and reading about your CD-55 parents, buckle up and have some fun with this—there's a reason we are the way we are!

RESOURCES

Typically, nonfiction books have appendices in the back. I've chosen to not include one. Instead, my sources are mentioned within each chapter or in the Chapter Rapture sections.

The amount of information the internet provided at my fingertips was invaluable—I couldn't have written this book without it. I did my best to fact-check everything and choose credible sources; however, the amount of data and options that Google blasts out is way more than any game of Asteroids ever did. My friend Mike Gathright, lead teacher at Storyline Church, humorously says, "If you find it on the internet, it's gotta be true." It is *impossible* to trace all the information on the internet back to determine what is 100 percent accurate and what is not. Should someone want to challenge me on a stat in this book—like whether the top-selling movie soundtracks of the '80s were *Dirty Dancing*, *Fast Times at Ridgemont High*, or *Top Gun*—I'm probably going to let you win.

What's *not* on the internet are all the vintage diaries, stories, polls, and stacks and stacks of notes my BFF and I saved—these are unique treasures you will never find online or see in any other book. The notes inserted are authentic and original, dating back as far as 1978, are sprinkled throughout the book in a handwritten style. I insisted, despite my editor's recommendations (and pleas!), to leave in all the misspelled words from the notes for your reading enjoyment!

The thirty-some polls referenced in the book are invaluable; memories may fade, but the forty-year-old documentation lives on. I created these surveys for my classmates, asking hundreds of questions from favorite foods to all-time fantasies to favorite cars and singers and recent thrills. The polls began in junior high in 1980 and continued until after graduation in 1988. The answers offer a snapshot of '80s life without distortions—and provide blackmail fodder that I'm saving for our fifty-year class reunion—*I joke.*

This book also features more than four hundred quotes collected over the past four years, 95 percent of them from Gen Xers. I have thousands of quotes from interviews, conversations, and responses on Gen X social media sites, including my *Invincible '80s* Facebook group. I wanted to include them all, but a five-thousand-page book wouldn't fly—and that's why two more *Invincible '80s* books are in the works.

I've interrogated, interviewed, and pestered so many people during my research that I've lost count. (I'm sure they'll remind me.) If your quotes or stories aren't in here, know you're not off the hook completely. I already have a stash saved for books 2 and 3 and will continue to rally for more. One key discovery I made was that our memories change over the years—for one story, I interviewed eight people and received eight different versions!

CHAPTER RAPTURES

Remember those activity sheets we used to do in school? In the spirit of CD-55ers, '80s music, and Blondie's song "Rapture," I've included a two-page Chapter Rapture spread at the end of each chapter. These modern-day activity sheets offer fun ideas and advice to revive '80s playtime, corresponding to each chapter's theme.

Pick something that resonates with you and explore! Most non-movie items can be found on YouTube or by searching the internet using the title listed. Each chapter features its own mixtape playlist with the top ten songs. There is a link and QR code to access the full playlist with even more tracks. *The Invincible '80s* mixtape playlists and the soundtrack for *When We Were Invincible* are on Spotify, and by scanning the QR code in the Chapter Raptures, you can listen to them almost instantly! If you have a Spotify account, you can play and save the playlists; if not, just sign up for a free account to reconnect with those iconic tunes. Having a rough day at work? Putting in too many hours? Play *The Invincible '80s* "#12 WORK" playlist.

Trying to use your time more wisely? Play the "#06 TIME" playlist.

BEST READING EXPERIENCE

Burt Reynolds once said, "All you really have in the end are your stories." At this stage in our lives, we've accumulated lots of them. As you read this book, consider taking in just *one* chapter a day to let it truly resonate. We've all weathered a lot over the years. Take the time to process it and enjoy the songs, memories, and lessons that emerge. Dive into each Chapter Rapture page and listen to the corresponding *Invincible '80s* mixtape playlist before moving on to the next chapter. If someone from your past pops into your mind, give them a call and reminisce about those crazy times you shared.

Join *The Invincible '80s* group on Facebook to share your thoughts and experiences as you go through each chapter. Let's celebrate and honor our generation and support one another with where we've been and where we're going. We're all in this together, so let's make our journey as Invincible as possible!

~XOXO
Becky & The Invincible '80s

section one

Purple Rain

Be Invincible with a Simpler Life

(Don't You) Forget About Me

Prologue

> *"You ought to spend a little more time trying to make something of yourself and a little less time trying to impress people."*
> ~Principal Vernon, The Breakfast Club

A long time ago, in a neighborhood in the '80s far, far away…

The GE clock radio flips to 6:30 a.m. and begins playing "Flashdance…What a Feeling" by Irene Cara on WLS FM radio out of Chicago. I roll back over, not wanting to get out of the heated waterbed as the cold November 1984 air slides through the cracks of my bedroom windows. *Man, I wish Mom would turn up the heat.* In his husky voice, disc jockey Larry Lujak announces they're giving away concert tickets to Prince's *Purple Rain* tour to the fifteenth caller later that day. *Free concert tickets? Okay, now I'm awake!*

A Bud Light commercial with Oingo Boingo singing "This Bud's for You" plays before Duran Duran's "Hungry Like the Wolf" spins across the airwaves and over Lake Michigan, shooting down into my wire antenna that's Scotch-taped to my windowsill.

I hear my mom yell through the thin walls and into my younger brother's room. "Jeffrey, do I need to bring a wet washcloth in there and rub on your face to wake you up?" Then Mom pushes open my door and scolds, "You stayed up way too late last night, young lady!" *Yeah, yeah. How'd she figure that out? I had a flashlight on with a shirt shoved under the crack of my door. Whatever. I had to finish writing a note to Dave and finish making a new poll. I'm not tired. I'm fine. Parents just don't understand.*

I began creating polls in seventh grade for my classmates to fill out. Using my yellow, plastic ruler stamped "Rebecca's Ruler," and my fine-point colored markers, I would draw columns on notebook paper. Each column featured a question at the top, with about one hundred and fifty questions per poll. My inquisitive brain was always in overdrive, conjuring up new questions for each poll, such as:

- The person that makes you most happy?
- What do you like to do most on your own?
- Most Romantic?
- The Sleaziest? (*Yes, inconsolably, there was no holding back in the '80s*)

New questions mean *new answers*, yielding critical data for developing teenagers craving social interaction. Classmates who participate pick a number between 1 and 35, then flip through the stapled notebook paper and answer each question in the columns on their assigned line. Those who fill it out have the luxury of reading everyone else's answers, too—who likes who, who hates what (and whom), and what everyone has going on—or at least what they are willing to divulge. When someone secretly likes someone else and wants to know more about them, they say to me, "Get Jill (or whomever) to do the poll." Classmates who fill it out ask to borrow it back later so they can peruse the new answers from everyone. I circulate a new poll every three months or so, or whenever it is time for blistering, new data. This is our "social media" mechanism—before we even knew what social media would become.

Swinging myself out of bed, I scream, "I call the bathroom!" and bolt for the only one in our moderate, ranch-style house with pink and avocado-green, mini-tile shower walls and clashing wallpaper. I look in the mirror and do my best to force my bangs to feather in the right direction after my pillow did a holy number on them last night. A splash of water and a sizzling Conair curling iron appears to help. Blue eye shadow and rosy-red blush are a must as I throw on my rainbow sweater with built-in shoulder pads and large, red, diamond-shaped earrings.

Mom's been up since 6:00 a.m. preparing a hot breakfast. At least three times a week, we get eggs and pancakes or French toast with plenty of real maple syrup. It is important to her that we never go without breakfast; what's important to us is the extra load of sugary goodness.

My last stop before leaving the house is to hang over the pink "warsh bowl" (as Mom calls it), and brush my metal mouth. I wince as the inside of my mouth reminds me of the orthodontist trip after school yesterday, cranking the wires another painful notch. *Man, I hate canker sores.*

I yank on my canvas, turquoise-stripe Nikes and shove my purple, curvy, big-tooth Goody comb in the back pocket of my Lee jeans with the handle strategically sticking out. *Gotta hurry. I'll die if Mom has to drive me to school in her big, yellow "Woody"* (wood-grain station wagon). As I fly out the door behind my brother, coat unzipped, running to catch the school bus, I hear Mom yell, "Zip up your coat! You're gonna catch a cold!"

The brakes squeal as bus number seven stops abruptly on Maudlin Road, lights flashing. The bus driver, Dorothy, has a voice you can hear a mile away. She shoves the big handle forward and the doors flap open, welcoming the small group of country kids at our bus stop. Kids pumped up on sugar-infused cereal are bouncing around—my little brother will soon be one of them and, of course, I pretend not to know him. I head to the back of the bus acting all "big" and cool, plop down on an empty, maroon vinyl seat, slouch, and put my knees up on the back of the seat in front of me. I start organizing my notes and papers in my Trapper Keeper. *I can't wait 'til we get to Rob's stop.*

Rob—short for Robin—is my BFF. We met on the school bus in first grade and have been BFFs ever since. We were the perfect match from day one; she is the shy, sensible one who behaves, and I am the rule-breaking, irrational one who keeps her voice of reason in practice with "we shouldn't do that," "that's not a good idea," or the infamous "I wouldn't do that if I were you." We've had more fights and make-ups than any married couple I know, but it's been the perfect imperfect balance.

◇◇◇◇◇◇◇◇◇◇◇◇◇◇◇◇◇◇◇◇◇◇◇◇◇◇◇◇◇◇◇

Meanwhile, other classmates are preparing for their route to New Buffalo High School (NBHS).

On the other side of town, Denise, nicknamed "Shorty" because she never grew an inch taller than 4'9" after eighth grade, is hopping on bus number two. Shorty is a peppy, fun, do-first, think-later kinda girl. Today, she is feeling presumptuously badass with the contents she secretly packed in her trumpet case last night, hocked from her dad's liquor cabinet. As she prepares to board the bus, she turns and shoves her little brother out of her way and yells, "Have a nice life, jerk!" as her mom smiles and waves goodbye.

The "in-town kids" have their own morning routines. Terry's house doesn't have a shower, so he takes a bath the night before. In the morning, he bathes instead in Ralph Lauren Polo cologne—extra splashes to drive the girls his way. Terry, over six feet tall, with blond hair parted in the middle and feathered back, turned sixteen two months ago. Having his driver's license is a chick magnet, and he knows the importance of dressing the part. He tosses on his white Izod shirt and pops the collar up. After downing a bowl of Frosted Flakes, he heads to meet Wayne, his best friend. As they cut through the ravine and arrive at the back of the school, one of the class pranksters (aka the class Spicoli), Mikey, is pulling up on his moped without a helmet, wearing a Loverboy concert T-shirt from last night. His parents make him wear a helmet, but once he gets a block away from his house, he stops and whips his helmet into the ditch because it doesn't look cool.

Terry looks at him and thinks, *How'd that fu%#er get lucky enough to go to a frickin' concert? I'd kill to see Loverboy.*

Bob C, just a block away, jumps into his zippy, hunter-green Toyota Celica to pick up his girlfriend. His lead foot has already gotten him into trouble with a speeding ticket in the first month of having his license. But the thoughts of risk are nowhere in his brain at the moment as he puts the pedal to the metal. Tall, skinny, with medium-length, dishwater-blond hair, he's self-conscious about his looks, yet confident knowing he gets along with the jocks, geeks, stoners, brains, and artsy kids. He's looking forward to band class today, knowing Shorty is bringing a treat for sixth hour.

Lisa, "Miss Pretty in Pink," lives on the opposite side of town. She is self-sufficient. She prefers waking up early, skipping breakfast, and focusing on ramping up her "cute factor." She makes sure every curl is aligned and Aqua-Netted into place. Her pink shirt matches her pink belt, which matches her pink pearl necklace, pink socks, and pink everything else. She's looking as adorable as possible and can't wait for her older boyfriend Bruce to pick her up for school in his muscle car, a blue Laguna S3.

Rennie, "Mr. Independent," lives a couple of miles out of town at Judy's Motel, a family-owned business. He can't find a ride to school and refuses to ride the bus, so he decides to drive his grandpa's spit-polished, two-tone maroon Chevy El Camino to school. After all, he is *almost* sixteen. Tall, skinny, with naturally curly blond hair, cute dimples, and big glasses, Rennie is on the shy side and kind of a loner since his parents divorced. He is learning how to process it all by replacing his feelings with as many parties at the motel as weekends allow.

In Union Pier, the next town over, a handful of NBHS students are in the middle of their morning routine. Dave, who most call "Tink," is lifting weights while listening to The Loop out of Chicago. Disc jockey Johnathan

Brandmeier's morning show is playing "(You Can Still) Rock in America" by Night Ranger. Trying to fight for the only bathroom with four older sisters isn't a good use of Dave's time; building his biceps is, however. Tink resembles the dark, curly-haired John Oates of the singing duo Hall & Oates. His early mustache enhances his manly image with the girls. He puts on a black muscle T-shirt, Levi's, and white Nike high-tops with the signature black swoosh and struts out the door. He turned sixteen in September and was at the DMV **on** his birthday to get his driver's license. Finally, he can legally drive his '77 silver, four-wheel drive, short-bed Ford truck to school. Most who drive to school like Tink cruise the beach first, *or cat-the-drag*, with their smokes and the tunes cranked up, listening to Van Halen and feeling rebellious before they are required to succumb to the structure of the day.

Six miles later, Dorothy, who has two sets of eyes—one on the road and the other looking in the bus's overhead rearview mirror—bellows at the top of her lungs, "Sit down and shut up before I come back there and put my shoe up your rump!" as bus number seven turns down bumpy Bell Avenue, coming to a stop in front of Robin's house. My BFF gets on, hair curled, no make-up other than eyeliner, with her skin-tight, maroon corduroys and NB Bison softball jacket. We slouch down in the bus seat, trying to be inconspicuous to the nosey little humans, and pull out the poll results from yesterday. We're zeroing in on Whit's answers since he's our latest infatuation.

Who are you going with? "Toni J"

Your present main worry: "Grades"

Your latest disappointment: "Friday night"

What are you looking forward to most at present: "Weekend"

If you were granted a wish, what would it be? "To have my parents leave for a week"

We agree he's up to something, but the bus ride doesn't give us enough time to theorize what could've happened to him Friday night or what he expects to happen this weekend. We add him to the long list of boys to investigate. Our daily agenda really has nothing to do with getting an education. We exit the bus and head into the fifty-year-old, brick, two-story building where we spend 20 percent of our adolescent life.

Mr. Hart at NBHS already has a jump on all of us, though. As of last year, Hart is the new sheriff in town, coming on board as assistant principal and athletic director.

All hell breaks loose around 7:30 a.m. when students whisk in any door like it's the Wild, Wild West with God knows what drama and excuses they thought up overnight. Hart is ready and mentally armed for their hijinks.

⁂

Robin and I hit our locker, twisting the built-in combination lock four notches backward and opening the door. The shelves are crammed with thick, heavy books, and pictures of the Chicago Cubs, Rick Springfield, the San Francisco 49ers, and BJ and the Bear are taped to the inside of the door. As the bell rings at 8:00, Mr. Hart stands in the hall on guard, reminding any lollygaggers that first hour starts in five minutes. He knows the usual troublemakers will be wandering the halls after the bell. Hart belts out, "Hey, where are you supposed to be?"

Mrs. Grant sends the student aide around to pick up the handwritten attendance slips hanging on the clipboard outside each classroom door. Some teaching staff have assigned seats, while others prefer to handle roll call the "Bueller? Bueller? Bueller?" way. Word on the street is Rennie's grandpa's car is sitting in the school parking lot. Hart is like an old hound dog; when something smells suspicious, it usually is, so he mentally adds another item to his morning to-do list: find Mr. Burian and have a talk with him.

As everyone scatters to first hour at the prompt of the 8:05 bell, classes kick into motion.

In home economics, it is sewing week, and Mrs. Mann is teaching how to put a zipper in. Miss Pretty in Pink is excited about finishing her new cute pink skirt. Tink shouts out, "Hey, Mrs. Mann, can we make those ice cream-infused brownies again? Those are better than Mountain Dew!" Shorty scowls and thinks, *This is so stupid. I wish they'd teach music or bartending in this damn class. I hate school.* She is sitting, bored, thinking about the liquor bottle she has stashed in her trumpet case that she'll sneak a drink from during sixth hour.

In Mr. T's English lit class, Terry walks through the door feeling his stress level elevate a tad. Mr. T is strict. You have to be on your game and best behavior, or you can count on being called out for it in front of the class. Terry spent time at the New Buffalo Public Library last week, buried in the Encyclopedia Britannica's thirty-two volumes, doing research for a report that was due in a few days. He can't wait to turn it in and be done with it.

It doesn't take Wayne long to get a hall pass to leave accounting class so he can go down to the pay phone outside the office and call his mom to bring him lunch money. Someone stole his lunch out of his locker already, and he suspects the girls from the softball team *again*. As he passes by Mrs. M's typing class, he hears the sound of the noisy IBM typewriters billowing out into the hall and stops. While digging in his pocket for two dimes for the payphone, he looks up and bursts into a jumping jack to get the attention of Fatty, who is sitting by the glass door pecking on the keys. Fatty, as everyone knows him, glances up in the hall to see his friend Wayne's shenanigans, loses his place, shakes his head, and mutters, "What an asshole."

In algebra class, Bob C is busy crushing one adult dosage of ex-lax tablets ("The Overnight Wonder") into a fine powder on a piece of paper on his desk. He rolls and tapes the paper into a tube for easy transportation to the lunchroom in preparation for his prank on longtime frenemy and rival Stan the Man.

Bob's plan is extremely well thought out. He knows what a mooch Stan the Man is, so he will buy himself a milkshake, put the ex-lax powder in his *own* shake, and then sit at the opposite end of the table from Stan. When lunch is half over, he'll claim to be full and say, "I don't know why I got this shake; I'm not going to drink it. Does anybody…?" Stan will yell, "Yo!" and snatch the shake before Bob can even finish his sentence. And Bob's plan will go precisely as predicted.

Unbeknownst to Bob, across the hall in shorthand class, two other classmates are busy plotting to TP Bob's house this weekend. *The concept of what comes around goes around hadn't entered our minds back then.*

In Spanish class, Robin and I are passing a note back and forth, cussing up a storm. Mrs. Brooks, soft-spoken and sweet, is *not* teaching a lesson about how to cuss in Spanish, but that's how we use the class time. In one swift motion, Tommy tries to grab the note from us to see who we're hot after now. He gets a hold of it and runs to the pencil sharpener, where he can read it. He comes back and throws the note at us. "What the fu%#, fish code names now? Who the fu#& are Coho and Salmon?" And this is how we learned to outsmart the note-stealers—alias fish names.

In between classes, the bell screams, granting us the social lives we crave. Our schedules are much busier in the six 5-minute bell breaks than during the fifty minutes of each class. Agendas consist of strutting the hallways, looking cool, and arranging spy missions next to drinking fountains, hoping for your secret crush to be thirsty. The boys hang at their lockers, eyeballing girls' chests, comparing the older girls' size "racks" to the younger "flat-sos." Boobs and trying to get laid take precedence over any textbook for these hormonally imbalanced boys. Rennie's gawking gets cut short as Mr. Hart walks up and gives him the finger motion that says "follow me to the office."

Rennie knows what's up, but his best hope is to play dumb. "Are you kidding me? What'd I do now? I'm just here to learn and get good grades. Geez."

But Mr. Hart doesn't play games. "Mr. Burian, do you think it's wise to be driving without a license to the public school system? I think your grandpa would appreciate being informed that you aren't a legal driver in the state of Michigan yet." And that is the last we see of Rennie that day. *Don't worry, he'll be back.*

<hr>

When the 2:50 p.m. bell rings, everyone scatters in different directions to our late afternoon routines.

Tink pulls into football practice with his Marlboro Lights cigarette pack sitting on the dash. Earlier in the week, Hart had cornered him. "Mr. Bragg, would you do me a favor and please get the empty kegs out of the back of your truck?" Tink knows he has to be a little more careful because Hart doesn't pull any punches. If he crosses the line too far, his charm and star player status won't work on Hart. At practice, the team is pumped for the upcoming game, except for Stan the Man, who isn't feeling well.

After practice, Tink goes straight to work at Little Bohemia, where he is a cook. He looks forward to it because he has a crush on the waitress, who is almost twenty-one. He munches on food from the kitchen while he works and sneaks off to do homework when it's slow. He walks in the door at home at 9:30 p.m. and yells, "Hey!" to his mom and dad, heads straight to the shower, then watches *M*A*S*H*. He is the only one in the house that has a TV in his room. It doesn't matter that it is only a 14-inch black and white with rabbit ears and no remote. What matters is that it is *his very own* he bought with his hard-earned money.

Shorty normally has to be home after school to watch her little brother, but today she is off the hook. Still buzzed from her sixth hour sips, she walks down to the arcade after school. The older boys hangout there; plus it is the coolest place to go in town. She knows, though, that if she isn't home by dinnertime, she'll be grounded *again*.

Terry heads to his back patio to shoot some hoops. He loves playing with Wayne and Fatty at lunchtime in the gym, but this time gives him a chance to cool his thoughts before his dad gets home from work and his parents expect him to be seated at their regimented family dinner at 6:30 p.m.

Bob C has been thinking of his packed after-school schedule since the morning. As a latchkey kid, he has abundant responsibility, including juggling after-school band practice, working at Redamak's (along with Mikey), and getting home to care for his autistic brother, since his mom, a single parent, won't be home from work until 7 p.m. One thing is certain: He'll make time for his Dungeons & Dragons game, even if it means staying up late.

Miss Pretty in Pink walks home to change and puts on her black-and-white, pressed restaurant uniform before hoofing it a few blocks to start her job at Little Bohemia bussing tables. These aren't her colors by any means, but she likes it there, and the rules are the rules at work. When she gets home, she stretches the phone cord into her room until there aren't any curls left in it and talks for hours to her boyfriend, until she falls asleep. She is *so* in love and excited about their date tomorrow night. They'll start out at Pizza Hut, then go to the movies and see *The Terminator*, but she's dreaming about what else the night might bring in the back seat of his car.

Rennie heads to his dad's party store to work, still sulking. He had to catch a ride since his grandpa now knows his real age. He hopes he won't be too busy ringing up booze for customers so he can practice playing Hacky Sack and work on building his back-door stash for the party at the motel he is having this weekend. Tonight after 9 p.m., when his grandpa is sound asleep, he'll be hopping back in the El Camino to secretly "borrow" it again and cruise the beach as part of his nightly routine.

Robin's parents divorced when she was fourteen, and her mom works full-time. Robin and her brother come home from school, let themselves in, and fend for themselves. *Also latchkey kids*. Her brother makes a box of mac and cheese but doesn't share it, so they have a brawl, and then Robin huffs to her room and slams the door. She'll bury her life in Harlequin romance novels or Danielle

Steel books. She'll dreamily fall in love within the pages, escaping the day's immature boys until her mom gets home to make dinner.

I walk five blocks to the NB Public Library to go to work my short shift, but first I stop at the NB Savings and Loan to withdraw $10 from my savings account so I can buy Bryan Adams' new cassette, *Reckless*, at the record store this weekend. When the library closes at 5:30 p.m., my mom pulls up at the curb to pick me up in the "Woody" while wearing her big glasses and jean overalls from working in the yard. She quizzes me about any tests I had, while finishing up the home-cooked dinner she makes for us nightly. The neighbor kid, who's teaching me chess, stops over for a competitive game before watching *Magnum P.I.* in the living room with everyone. I am secretly frothing over what a hunk Tom Selleck (aka Thomas Magnum) is, before escaping to my room to listen to my radio, write some notes, start a new poll, or create something new before my clock radio goes off tomorrow morning to start a new day's adventure all over again.

This is how my classmates and I remember life some forty years ago on a slightly embellished day. The scenes described here are reflective of those found across America. Some of us have good memories of our upbringing and some not-so-good. Most of us had sprinklings of dysfunction in our families, but here we are, alive and holding this book, knowing that our cherished '80s life is behind us.

The ten of us who you just met—Rennie, Mikey, Terry, Robin (my BFF), Shorty, Wayne, Bob C, Tink, Lisa, and me—were part of the class of '86, with a graduating class of fifty-six. These NB peeps remain close friends to this day and were instrumental in recalling stories of how it was then. My hope is that this book inspires you to reconnect with those special people in your life, those who accept you for who you are—you know, those people you haven't seen in ten years and can pick right back up where you left off. Those are the ones I'm talking about.

More importantly, by reading this book, my wish is for you to reconnect with *yourself*.

What did we learn from that time in our lives?

In the coming chapters, we'll reflect on the thirty to forty years behind us and explore how Gen Xers, the kids of the '80s, have evolved in this thing called life.

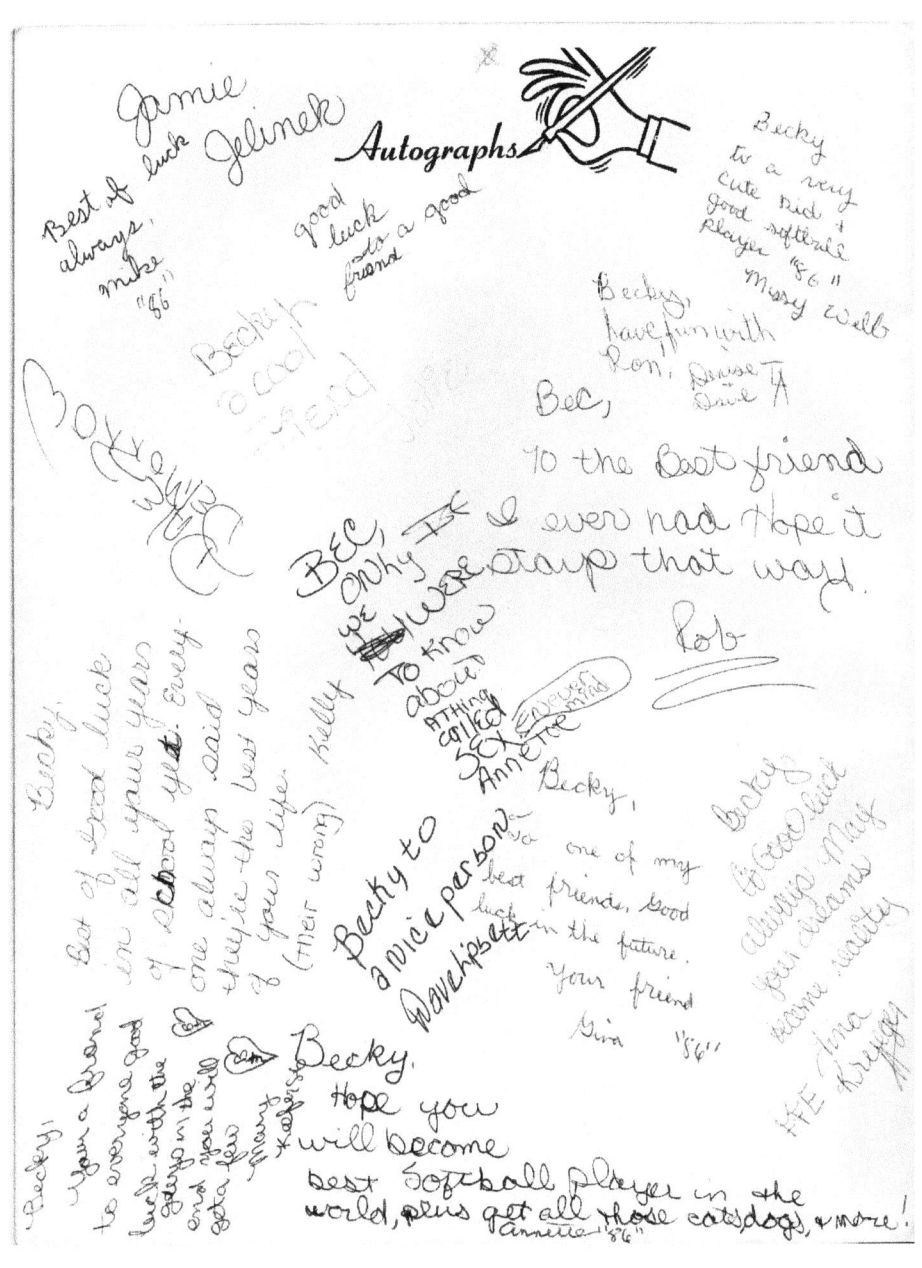

A classic signed yearbook page from
New Buffalo Junior High, 1980.

Prologue - (Don't You) Forget About Me

Chap. One

Walk This Way

Where We've Been and Where We're Going

"Sometimes things happen, we live with their result, and then, occasionally, a long time distant, we try to make sense of them."

~Andrew McCarthy

I turned fifty-five last year.

I knew what I wanted for my birthday: to play the *Name That Tune* trivia game at the New Buffalo American Legion with my closest peeps. I took some razzes on the night of my birthday about how I'd planned my own "surprise" party, but I laughed it off with a hint of embarrassment. When someone teased me about it again at the end of the night, without thinking, I shot back, "Hell, yeah, I did. If you know what you want, why wouldn't you?" Everyone stopped and nodded their heads. Suddenly, there were high-fives all around, and my friends were yelling, "Yeah!"

For most Gen Xers like me, this is exactly where we are in life. We've realized that if we keep hesitating to pursue the things we want, they might never happen. But it's more than that. We've begun to contemplate our mortality. We've learned what we like, what we don't, and what irritates us. We know who isn't healthy for us, even though we may be afraid of making a change. We're comfortable, more set in our ways, and our energy level isn't quite what it used to be. We all want to live our best life, but the curve balls keep coming while life is whizzing by.

The big question is, what are we doing about it?

I've always felt a bit out of balance, almost like I was missing something. Nothing was ever blatantly wrong, so I rolled with the days, weeks, months, and years as they came, feeling like I was on a hamster wheel trying to accomplish everything. I chased the next big and best thing, but never felt really content. And I was my own worst critic.

But through it all, I loved the '80s. I always have. The music, the creativity, the amount of time we made for play. All of it. And, yes, part of it was being young without major responsibilities.

There were rules we lived by, yet we had the freedom to roam. We formed friendships by playing Little League together, writing to our pen pals, talking to our BFFs for three hours on the phone at night, and sitting on the school bus together. We craved adventure and time with our friends. Our families—even the dysfunctional ones—instilled values in us. Our amazing music was often our one and only therapist.

The '80s were so much more than a time period to me; they were a state of mind.

A state of mind I never want to forget.

In 2020, I began to write about the decade that brought me cherished memories and shaped me into who I am today. When the pandemic hit, like the rest of the world, I struggled with isolation, but I kept writing.

In 2022, when concerts returned, three of my closest friends and I went to see *The Stadium Tour* at Wrigley Field. Joan Jett and the Blackhearts, Poison, Mötley Crüe, and Def Leppard headlined. I was ecstatic to be back in the social scene and talking to everybody. By the next night, I was sick. And by the next morning, I couldn't move. I had COVID-19. I thought the first week of misery was the worst, but it wasn't. It was week two—when I *could* move again—and was still isolated and unable to think straight. I didn't want to watch TV, Google a damn thing, talk on the phone, or listen to music—for the first time *ever*. With my notebook on my lap, I'd try to write, but nothing came out. *Literally, nothing.* One day, I sat in my sunroom for hours staring at the walls, battling an anxiety attack.

I had no choice but to take a close look at my life.

Where had my life brought me so far? I spent my childhood outdoors, riding my bike all over the countryside, hanging out in my tree fort, organizing clubs with friends, creating polls to survey classmates, writing stories with my BFF about the boys we liked, and planning parties full of shenanigans. Life was all about my friends and my latest crushes (*yes, that's plural*). In my twenties, it was about surviving evening college classes while working multiple jobs, partying whenever I could, running up my bills, making new friends, and shacking up with my boyfriend.

By my thirties, my career was my life. While many of my friends became parents and raised kids, I started my own business, got married to the wrong person, and became a successful entrepreneur in the building maintenance industry.

My life was focused on supervising employees, keeping clients happy, and growing my business. I spent years learning how to manage people, discovering what unhealthy relationships looked like, and figuring out how to do things faster and better. My life became a procedural manual with checkboxes and a perpetual to-do list. Family and friends were viewed more as an obligation than people I appreciated and valued in my life.

And even with all the awards I'd won and the industry certifications I'd earned, I never gave myself credit for my achievements.

In my early forties, I realized I needed to escape the stress of managing hundreds of employees. I sold the company that I had nurtured like my own child for almost fifteen years. In exchange, I got my life back. I started a nonprofit focused on sustainability initiatives for businesses, and my marriage ended.

But something started to change in my late forties. Social media helped link me to friends from the '70s, '80s, and '90s and brought us closer. I reconnected to my roots, and it felt good. My career was in exploratory mode—it was now based on my passions—and I *thought* my relationships were getting sparingly better.

So, as I sat in my sunroom unable to write while reflecting on five decades of life, I wondered if I had made the right choices. Was I truly content? Was I happy with who I was? Why didn't I feel more grateful? Where was I headed?

The universe forced me into a screeching halt with these questions.

I realized I had forgotten what gratitude looked like. I might have said "thank you," but I didn't necessarily feel genuine appreciation in my heart when I said it. I would tell myself what I wanted to hear, but not what I *needed* to hear. I realized life wasn't about being bigger and better anymore. How enjoyable is life if we're living it at 90 mph, anyway? It wasn't about my bank account, pleasing others, my calendar, or checking boxes on my to-do list anymore. It was about being in the moment, being grateful, and being a best friend to myself before anyone else.

For me, like so many of us, it took a wake-up call to understand what I wanted in life.

After that day, my attitude, appreciation, pace, and values shifted. Suddenly, I knew this book was my mechanism to sort out my life. I had a purpose.

Now, after finishing the book, I see things like I did when I was younger,

'80s-style. More carefree, playful, confident, and with less stress. Walking my dogs doesn't feel like a task anymore; it's a source of joy. When I'm outside with them, I focus on the sky and trees and breathe in the fresh air. As I watch their tails wag and their curious noses sniffing away, my heart grows. I see people as human beings who, like me, have their own obstacles to overcome. When I say "I love you" to those close to me, they are not just words, I actually feel love in my heart. I've learned to pick my battles and let go of things that take away my inner peace and precious time. This may sound like I've perfected everything, but I haven't. I'm still learning and growing each day. But it's so much easier to learn and grow if we like who we are and are honest with ourselves.

That's my story.

We all have a story, don't we? As we journey through this fast-paced world, juggling massive amounts of information we never imagined we'd need to process, including endless posts of everyone else's lives on social media, is it possible we've forgotten to look at our own story of how we got here?

That day in the sunroom taught me to slow down. I discovered an inner peace I didn't know existed. The crazy thing is that at fifty-five, I feel like I'm just getting started, like I'm seeing everything through new eyes. Eyes that aren't so critical or judgmental, but more open and receptive. I'm living life at a pace that is actually relaxing! I'm aware of my mortality and see the importance of making each day count. I don't want to lose this feeling or go back to the way I was.

I believe the answer is *uncomplicating* our lives. Toss that youthful approach to life we once had into a blender, mix in the carefree, unplugged lifestyle of the '80s, and pour it abundantly into our lives today.

Remember taking the time to write notes to our closest friends when we were kids? We shared everything we thought, felt, wanted, or needed. We took our time when we were young because we *had* the time. Now we have to work so much harder to find time to truly connect. Ask yourself: Could the things you view as burdens actually be important? The phone call from your long-winded mother, the friend who wants you to take a day off to go gallivanting, the significant other who wants you to lay on the couch, cuddle, and watch a movie with them. In the '80s, we had time for all those things—*well, except a long phone call from your mother.*

"Things were carefree with minimal responsibilities when we were kids,"

Robin, my BFF, says. "No mortgage, no bills to pay, no pressure of raising good children and maintaining better health."

Chandra from Georgia adds, "Best friends, slumber parties, roller skating. Living life before the hard lessons, before seeing what adulting was all about."

Robin and Chandra are two of the sixty-five million people classified as Generation X. As of 2024, Gen Xers are between 44 and 59 years old.

Of the seven living generations, Gen X is perfectly positioned with three generations before us, and three after—we are the true center of it all. The youngest Baby Boomers and oldest Millennials who sandwich our generation can relate to much of what Gen X has experienced. *Hence the CD-55 Club.*

Gen X is a generation of firsts and lasts: the first to experience a high number of moms working outside of the home, divorced parents, and friends coming "out of the closet." The first to browse a Blockbuster or Hollywood video rental store and take a movie home. The first to play video games like *Pong* and *Pac-Man*. The first to write term papers on computers and the youngest to use the internet daily.

Gen X was the last to use rotary phones, typewriters, encyclopedia sets, and cameras with film (except for photographers). The last to spend a largely unsupervised childhood on dangerous playground equipment and running the neighborhoods until the streetlights came on. And my favorite: the last to make prank calls without being identified. Little did we know we'd be the last generation to have an analog childhood.

While pop culture, MTV, music, movies, and style unite us, what deeply connects our generation is that most of us relate to coming from a time when we lived a more carefree, less complicated life.

In her book *Generations*, Jean M. Twenge says, "Gen Xers came to adolescence early and hardened, thus experiencing a shortened childhood and a fast-life strategy early in life." She adds, "Schools and society were slow to recognize the new reality that most school children no longer had a stay-at-home parent—thus the rise of Gen X latchkey kids was not a cyclical pendulum swing."

We are known for our common sense and independence because, yes, we were the latchkey kids. We're also self-reliant, individualistic, and resourceful.

"We were a generation that knew how to roll up our sleeves and work our asses off," Pat from Canada says. "Then we'd turn around after work and party like there's no tomorrow, just to turn around and do it again the next day."

Jeff in Windsor sums it up well, "Our best trait, hands down, is adaptability." Jeff's right—how many of us were expert DIYers?

Undoubtedly, there's something special about Gen X as the middle child of the generations. We've seen both sides. We've noticed a shift in values, experienced technological advances, and witnessed musical styles change after the '80s.

Many of us lack political correctness but love sarcasm and inappropriate humor. "We're like the honey badgers of generations. We don't give a shit," Heather from Wyoming says.

Many Gen Xers identify with characters in the popular 1985 movie *The Breakfast Club*. Were you the brain, princess, jock, criminal, or basket case? Or maybe you were the preppy, the rebel, or the recluse? If you didn't fit into one of those categories, you knew people who did.

My hometown, New Buffalo, Michigan, was no different when it came to having *Breakfast Club*-like cliques. NB may have been small, but our experiences and life lessons were universal.

Aren't we all in *The Breakfast Club* of adulthood now, pigeonholed into cliques? The empty nester, divorcée, retiree, workaholic, homebody, or social butterfly. When asked to name our generation's stereotypes today, some Gen Xers have said the couch potato, the blue-collar dad, the get-off-my-lawn grouch, or the plain, old, tired and cranky one. The most popular Gen X answer? "Whichever clique is up to their eyeballs in debt!" At this point, we might feel more like the janitor or Vernon, the high school principal in *The Breakfast Club*, than any of the students.

After leaping from *The Breakfast Club* to *St. Elmo's Fire*, all of a sudden we're starring in *The Big Chill*, reuniting at funerals and questioning why we did what we did when we were younger and asking what's important to us now.

"In the past, I've made it through one day to the other just fine, but I think about big things now," Steve of Wisconsin says. "My parents aren't in good health. What's going to happen when shit hits the fan? Who's going to be there? Is coping really living?"

Steve asks some thought-provoking questions that so many of us are silently exploring. What truly matters to us now? What's *important*? I've found that reflecting on where we've come from and what we've learned, and acknowledging what no longer serves us, is crucial to moving forward with a purpose.

As we navigate this middle-aged chapter, quality of life is paramount.

While our mental maturity has (hopefully) increased with age, our body's invincibility level is flagging. For many CD-55ers, we're enduring achy kneecaps, sleep apnea, heart conditions, tinnitus, poor eyesight, and spotty memory. And we don't dare bend over and twist the wrong way or we end up in physical therapy! Needless to say, we can't do many of the things we used to.

All of us have experienced trauma, battled internal demons, and hauled around emotional baggage for years. Maybe you had your wake-up call much earlier in life than I did—maybe you've lost a loved one or have experienced illness, cancer, or abuse. Sadly, you most likely know classmates who are suffering from a disease or have passed away.

How weird does it feel to wake up with aches and pains when mentally you still feel like you're in your twenties?

Not only are we aging physically, but we're also juggling elderly parents while helping our kids get acclimated to the world. We are planning for retirement knowing we crackle and pop just walking up the stairs, wondering, "Well shit, how's this going to work for our plans to travel and be more active now that we will finally have more time?"

"We are the sandwich generation," June in Florida says. "Taking care of kids and aging parents. Some of us have to subsidize our parents' expenses and our kids' educations. It really leaves little for us."

June is right. We're going through a lot, *but we've also been through a lot.*

Gen Xers can sometimes struggle to identify with today's younger generations and shake our heads at how things have become so different. We're now the generation that says, "Kids these days don't understand." Think of the major events in the world since we've left high school: the Oklahoma City bombing, the Columbine shooting, the 9/11 terrorist attack, the wars in Afghanistan and Iraq, the George Floyd murder and riots, the Black Lives Matter protests, and the Trump/Biden presidential race. Then there was the trainwreck of 2020 and 2021 from COVID and the related lockdowns, which turned many against each other, causing a massive, heartbreaking divide because of personal choices and opinions.

Of course, the '80s were far from perfect. There was the HIV/AIDS crisis, the crack epidemic, rampant homophobia, the Cold War, trickle-down economics, the expansion of the national debt, and the lack of environmental awareness.

"We probably damaged the ozone layer with all that Aqua Net," Lyn in Texas says.

Despite the negatives—including shoulder pads, mullets, programming the VCR, and having to memorize phone numbers—the '80s were simpler.

Tara in Wisconsin summarizes Gen X this way: "We had pride in our country. We believed in hard work and earning the good things in life. We kept the values of our parents while learning critical thinking and common sense from a young age by practically raising ourselves and our siblings while our parents worked. We were chill—just having fun—and full of optimism, but we also understood responsibility, and that it's primarily our choices that make our lives. We were not victims. We knew not to talk back to our parents and that the world didn't revolve around us. In fact, sometimes we wondered if the world even cared that we were alive."

We've all been on a journey. And there is something to be said about looking back to look forward.

"I love the idea of taking what we know, think, and hope from our past to find peace now," Kristen in Minnesota says. "Actually, that might be everything."

So, what *did* we know back then that we didn't realize were the real, hidden treasure troves?

Three fundamental things have changed for us—other than our aging bodies, of course. I call them the "Gen X Trifecta"—the umbrella over everything that permeates this book: values, technology, and music. Let's look at a snapshot and then we'll explore them further in upcoming chapters.

VALUES

In the '80s, most of us had to earn what we wanted, and we never passed up the chance to make a buck. While we were provided with a roof over our heads, clothing, and either home-cooked meals or TV dinners, if we wanted anything extra—say, designer clothing, or a TV in our bedroom—we had to earn our own money to buy it. If we wanted a car, we had to get a job. Except for a Malt-o-Meal, Sanka coffee, and a McDonald's Quarter Pounder, things took time. Our neighborhood pals pretending they were Evil Knievel was the only thing to binge-watch—not our favorite TV show. We had to wait a whole week to see that next episode!

If someone asked us what "instant gratification" meant, we would've been like, "What's that?" You had time to think, process, and respond, and, most of all, time to create and play. We appreciated and took care of what we had because we had worked for it. We would ride our bike down the country roads miles from home without wearing a helmet and not think twice. Most of us weren't afraid to talk to strangers. The rules of not talking about politics or religion applied, and we weren't divided because of our sentiments. People couldn't judge everyone to the nth degree like they do today because of social media. And, most importantly, **we knew the word "respect" and the consequence of not showing it.**

TECHNOLOGY

Remember when technology didn't consume us? In the '80s, there were only a handful of TV channels to choose from, and generally only one TV per household. The never-ending, 24-hour news cycle didn't dominate our TVs. We trusted the news because we trusted the familiar news anchors; today, it's hard to have confidence in all the sources on the internet. Back then, word on the street was that the only questionable news source was the *National Enquirer*.

Communication wasn't dependent on technology, other than our hooked-to-the-wall phone that we spoke on for hours and hours. We weren't intimidated by eyeball-to-eyeball conversations. We entertained ourselves by going outside, building forts, riding bikes, and playing games. We started a band in the garage and worked on our cars. We had rowdy sleepovers, choreographed our own dance moves, and wrote stories. We were all like little MacGyvers, creating and inventing. What one of us didn't think of, the other one did. If we wanted drama, we had to create our own. Today, drama finds us and follows us through our messaging and apps, yet we are dependent on them for communication. Ultimately, **we didn't depend on technology to enjoy our lives.**

MUSIC

In the '80s, we had pop. We had sexy, bad-boy hair bands, disco, and hip-hop. We had the *Thriller* craze. And of course, we were the first decade to experience music videos, *period*.

MTV and VH1 arrived on the scene scorching hot, blasting posters off our walls and album covers off our shelves, then transforming them onto our TV screens—a new sensation that infatuated us from the start.

Lyrics connected us to our feelings and gave meaning to our world. Music helped us through difficult times; it was our friend and spoke directly to us. Many of us spent endless hours on push-button tape recorders making mixtapes of all our favorites. When we bought an album or cassette, it was a big deal, and we listened to it repeatedly until we knew every song by heart. Stopping to flip the tape over was something we could do on autopilot. We made up dance moves and drove with our music blasting.

Going to a concert and wearing an authentic concert T-shirt to school the next day was a status statement. Remember piling eight friends in a car and hitting the road, driving for hours to see our music icons explode out of our radios and onto a stage, larger than life? There wasn't access to millions of songs because there was no streamed music. We appreciated, prioritized, and loved our music endlessly, every single day. In so many ways, **music was our therapist.**

LET'S FIND OUR WAY BACK

The speed of technological change and the way the world interacts on social media can cause real pressures. It's easy to lose focus on what's important, and it can be frustrating trying to keep up with it all. I don't know about you, but sometimes I need a little ass-kicking to unplug from all the gadgets and give my brain a break. The problem is, I'm the one who has to kick my *own* ass.

There is a video on YouTube by Ze Frank called "The Time You Have (in Jellybeans)." In the video, one jelly bean represents each day of your life, assuming you live until you're seventy-nine years old. After removing a jelly bean for each twenty-four hours you spend sleeping, eating, working, doing chores, commuting, bathing, and watching TV (and other mundane things), the jelly beans remaining are what you have left for enjoyment. When I first watched it, I had a "holy shit" moment—there aren't as many days left for enjoyment as you think.

The CD-55 Club is becoming increasingly aware that the years ahead of us are fewer than the ones behind. We're asking, "Where did it all go?" Every time we lose a classmate, friend, or family member, we're reminded tomorrow isn't guaranteed.

I'll ask a lot of questions in this book, like what will *you* do with the days you have left? It can help start a conversation with yourself where you discover things about your life, just like I did in the sunroom that day. It will invite you to explore answers that work for you. Do you live with intention, or are you on autopilot? Is it time to rethink your habits, values, choices, and priorities?

This book invites you to wonder…and wander. Have exploratory discussions with those close to you, especially other CD-55ers. No one has all the answers. If you find someone who says they do, we need to have an "I call bullshit" Gen X intervention with them!

We're all figuring things out as we go. Each month, year, and decade throw more changes at us and more things to navigate. Even at eighty, my parents say they haven't figured it out. That's the reality—we'll be figuring things out 'til the very end. That's how life works.

Boston may have sung "Don't Look Back," but I agree with Jefferson Airplane, who advised "Find Your Way Back." Let's find our way back to making the most of every day.

So buckle up, put on your X-ray glasses, neon shades, red plastic Devo hats, jelly shoes or Air Jordans, and *Walk This Way*. Let's look at life through an '80s lens. Let's find our way back to simple, to a place of inner peace. Let's *de-complicate*, declutter, and decompress. How? By reimagining our relationships and reinventing our schedules. By examining our priorities. By figuring out how to be at peace with our choices and laugh about where we've been.

Remember when I asked earlier if we've forgotten to look at our own story? It's time to go on that journey. On our way, we'll relive some of the greatest '80s songs that are nothing less than therapy for the soul.

Let's find our way back to *When We Were Invincible.*

Chapter Rapture 01
Your story is being written every day

Sixth Hour Bell

Burt Reynolds once said, "Sometimes you have to lose yourself 'fore you can find anything."

In today's fast-paced world, overloaded with information, have we lost sight of ourselves and our own journey? Have we forgotten to look at our own story on how we got here?

Take a moment to watch the YouTube video "The Time You Have (In Jelly Beans)" or search "Life in Jelly Beans video."

It's a powerful reminder to ask yourself, what truly matters now? Reflect on where you've been, the lessons you've learned, and what no longer serves you—these reflections are essential for moving forward with purpose.

Extracurricular Activities

- For your next birthday, plan your own adventure doing something out of the ordinary, such as a roller skating or bowling party that takes you back to your youth!

- Take the Enneagram Personality Test at enneagraminstitute.com. For $20, you'll get a full report that's often surprisingly accurate and a useful tool.

- Explore how growing up in different eras shaped us by reading *Generations* by Jean M. Twenge.

After-School Specials

- Rewatch *The Breakfast Club* and reflect on your days of youth and how far you've come.

- Watch *Generation X*, a six-part documentary narrated by Christian Slater, exploring the decade and the 65 million people who define Generation X.

- *My So-Called Life* starring Claire Danes was a television series in the early '90s about a realistic portrayal of adolescence that's still relatable for many Gen Xers.

Passing Notes in Class

"One of the best books I've ever read is *The Five People You Meet in Heaven* by Mitch Albom, along with his first book, *Tuesdays with Morrie: An Old Man, a Young Man, and Life's Greatest Lesson*."
~Fran in Florida

"My dad always used to say, 'The world owes you nothing.'"
~ Eric Levy, keyboardist for Night Ranger

"The decade of the '80s was the best decade to be alive. We had the best TV shows, cartoons, movies, toys and music. We were able to see TVs change from black and white to color and then cable TV, and MTV. We saw everything change before our eyes. We saw the beginning of arcades and then home video game systems and computers. Long live the '80s."
~Shawn in Wisconsin

Field Trips

- Find a trivia or music trivia night, round up your friends, and have some fun tapping into your memory instead of Google.
- Take your dog for a walk someplace new. A park or trail and leave your phone behind or silence it and enjoy the moment.
- Travel the backroads of America just stopping along the way to meet people and hear their stories. (Advice from Shawn in Michigan)

Chapter Mixtape

- "Walk This Way" – Aerosmith
- "My Life" – Billy Joel
- "Check It Out" – John Mellencamp
- "Kids in America" – Kim Wilde
- "Solsbury Hill" – Peter Gabriel
- "Pop Life" – Prince
- "Find Your Way Back" – Jefferson Starship
- "I Still Haven't Found What I'm Looking For" – U2
- "Heartbeat City" – The Cars
- "Back on the Chain Gang" – The Pretenders

Shortcut to Spotify Playlist: beckykliss.com/CR01

Chap. Two

True Colors

Values

"I'm trying to find the truth in myself. To play somebody else doesn't interest me."

~Neil Diamond

When I was ten years old, I'd ride my bike to my cousin Kelly's house, and we'd hang out in her tiny upstairs bedroom, hiding from the adults. We'd play Neil Diamond's album *The Jazz Singer* on her all-in-one, state-of-the-art Zenith stereo. When that big, square, electronic box with shiny silver knobs and robust wood-grain cabinet speakers pounded out the first song, "America," my entire being felt uplifted. I'd ask Kelly to play it over and over again. One day, I made up my mind; I had to have my *own* Zenith stereo.

With my hair flying behind me and bike tires squealing, I pedaled home faster than usual that day, on a mission to convince my parents that I needed that same stereo—one with a hefty price tag of $300. As expected, the answer was, "Money doesn't grow on trees at this house." My relentless pleading persuaded my dad to cut me a deal: raise a calf and earn the money. I'd have to get up early in the morning before school, mix the calf milk, tromp out to the barn to feed the baby cow, and wait until he sucked the bottle dry; then I'd have to repeat the process each night. If I were responsible and held my end of the bargain twice a day for eight weeks, I would earn $300 to buy my very own Zenith stereo.

And I did.

Playing my Neil Diamond record on my *own* stereo checked so many boxes for me—accomplishment, self-worth, and pride. Listening to my first records and cassettes of Shaun Cassidy, The Village People, and Billy Joel put me in a happy place—and I'd even made a new friend in the process (even if it was a cow named Alex).

I treasured that Zenith stereo for the next eighteen years until it was regretfully left behind at an ex-boyfriend's house, and I was unable to get it back. At the time, it didn't matter anymore, though. I was approaching thirty and other things had become more important—like my career. My values had shifted.

Our foundational values are formed in our youngest years. They are our "True Colors" and they come from our parents or trusted adults. As we mature, churches, schools, guidance counselors, books, friends, work, and relationships influence those values.

When I was chasing boys around school, I valued what I thought was love. I believed having a boyfriend equaled *being* loved. I had no clue that respect, connection, and acceptance should be the real goals in relationships.

Today, outside factors, such as social media and the internet, can influence our values immensely. For example, when I peruse Gen X social media groups about Madonna, I see comments describing her anywhere from an icon to "a grandma in fishnets." Some say she's amazing, "epic and untouchable," influential, or idiotic. Others "love her courage" or characterize her as "just a caricature now." One comment was short and cocky: "Meh." If I didn't know who Madonna was, these comments might sway my opinion of her. It's the same in real life—if I were reading comments about relationships, I might be affected by people who've been scorned or others who've been in love forever and happily married. It would be so easy to have my values influenced by reading all the comments, stories, and opinions out there.

People who jump on bandwagons that don't align with their core values can become overwhelmed, indecisive, and miserable. There's a saying, "If you don't stand for something, you will fall for anything." I make my shittiest decisions—ones that I later regret—when I do what I think others want me to, instead of sticking to my moral compass, which is based on my values. Those values give me boundaries. This happens to many of us; we lose direction amidst all the noise in life and just agree to whatever, thinking it will go away.

We are constantly at crossroads, faced with umpteen million choices daily, juggling what's most important to us. The truth is, our willpower is challenged constantly. When it comes to midlife challenges, like retirement, relationships, and societal expectations, what are we basing our decisions on? How do we get that roadmap to success that's sustainable and personally rewarding? How do we balance wealth, health, success, serenity, fame, bravery, security, fun, responsibility, adventure, and achievement? Or are these even priorities for us in the long list to choose from? The truth is, sometimes we get it right and sometimes we don't.

When we make choices based on our fantasies, desires, and wishes over our core values, it skews things. Remember that cute boy in school? *Yeah, you know the one.* How many times did you change your priorities over him? *I plead the fifth.*

When I was ten and tromping out to the barn in two feet of snow with a warm bottle of calf milk, I would've rather been in the comfort of my warm bed. Instead, I stayed focused on my value of responsibility over comfort, *and being stubborn and hellbent on having that stereo helped.*

Amy in Dayton says, "My values have changed over the years because my life has changed. Back in the '80s, I valued the friendships I made and valued my job because it gave me a paycheck to put gas in my car. As I grew older, I valued *how well* I did my job. I continually learn to value my family in new and different ways as we age. I value my husband for teaching me that life doesn't always have to be serious."

"I value compassion and inclusion," Eric in Canada adds. "I was ostracized a lot as a kid because I was shy and introverted, so I show compassion to those different from the norm. I also value curiosity. When I see a kid interested in science, be it nature, physics, chemistry, or whatever, I go out of my way to encourage them." Eric is right. We can cultivate deeper connections with others who share similar beliefs and priorities and build a support network that offers mutual understanding and encourages personal growth.

Exploring our values—where they've come from and why—can be illuminating.

"Maybe our boundaries were tighter, or our manners were stricter," Kristen in Minnesota says. "It was bad manners to speak about religion or politics. Didn't those manners really lead to societal norms that kept us all a lot more civil to others? You couldn't hate someone for politics if you didn't know their views."

Knowing our values is the path to bringing our lives back to "'80s Simple." How many of us have let ourselves be twisted, warped, pulled, and yanked like Stretch Armstrong into what someone thought we should be? It took me fifty-five years to realize that's *not* how it's supposed to go. How can we truly be content if we look to the outside world for answers instead of finding them in our hearts? The answer is we can't.

In the '80s, we didn't have the long list of resources today's kids have, such as counseling services, life coaches, YouTube videos, value apps, vision boards, assessment quizzes, and value cards. We had to work to achieve self-awareness. Strangers on social media weren't questioning why we said or did something, or what we thought about something. It was us and our intuition.

For the longest time, I believed that a checklist or spreadsheet could solve any problem. In my thirties, I purchased an e-book with a worksheet on values. Each month, I sat down and filled out the worksheet with the things in my life that were important and associated with each of my core values. For a year, it helped me balance my life.

My values then were: 1) peace and happiness; 2) adventure; and 3) purpose. Each of these values was broken down into subcategories. For example, for peace and happiness, I needed to be healthy mentally and physically, and to stay organized. To be healthy mentally, I needed downtime to read and do breathing exercises. To be healthy physically, I needed better meal planning and to stop eating out so much. To stay organized, I needed to define my work schedule, follow a routine, and balance my finances in QuickBooks. Those became my goals for that month. The next month, those goals might shift a little as my needs did. I realized that aligning my schedule and habits around my values gave me a roadmap to what was personally rewarding.

If you type the word "values" in the Amazon search bar, it returns more than ninety thousand products. How is that even freakin' possible? Could all these options be playing into our anxiety? Sure, I want to understand my core values and know what's driving me, but that answer doesn't come from a product I buy on Amazon. Yes, it may take using tools like a worksheet, cards, or going to therapy to help sort it out. The method you choose doesn't matter, as long as you are true to your authentic self.

Let's talk about some of the common Gen X-taught values that shaped us in the '80s.

VALUE 1: "YOU WANT IT? YOU FIGURE IT OUT"

I loved playing with Barbie dolls, but the Barbies at the Kliss residence weren't cruising in shiny pink Corvettes or swanky Star Traveler motorhomes, getting their nails done at the plastic salon, or buying extravagant new outfits at Kmart. My mom designed original patterns and sewed Barbie dresses for me, often from scraps of repurposed material. She was crafty, so going the homemade route was viewed as the only way. She made me Barbie-size furniture: a couch, bed, fridge, kitchen, dining-room cabinet, and even a fireplace with grouted mini bricks. I had the whole kit and caboodle, and it *didn't* come from a store.

We were taught to appreciate what we had and take care of our possessions because they weren't plentiful. If we wanted something for our Barbie dream world, we'd either make it, buy it with our allowance money, or hope it landed in our birthday or Christmas gift pile. When my BFF and I wanted Barbie and Ken to live in a townhouse, we'd round up some cardboard, game boards, and Lincoln Logs and build one. When the time came for my Barbies to get a swimming pool, we simply went to the kitchen and confiscated one of my mom's mixing bowls, filled it with water, and next thing you knew the Barbie girls were at a pool party, waiting for Ken to strut in, crash the party, and take a dip.

As kids, we were forced to be resourceful, which proved rewarding. We tapped into the creative side of our brains and used our imagination. Have we gotten lax with our resourcefulness? Do we still tap into our creative imagination?

VALUE 2: "IF YOU WANT IT, GO EARN YOUR OWN MONEY"

How many times did we hear our parents say, "If you want it, find a way to earn it?" A parent's response guaranteed to piss us off every time was, "If I let you have (or do) that now, what will you have to look forward to?" Remember their annoying responses like "you'll live" or "because I said so" when we'd resort to pleading? Sometimes that led to our retaliation of "but Mommmmm," only to have that fall on deaf ears. Sure, we wanted things, but we didn't *expect* to get anything, ever! We wished, hoped, pouted, and, yes, even begged, but if we'd acted as if we expected it, we would've been read the riot act.

How much do we give our kids today? Do we keep anything out of reach so that they long for it and can earn what they desire?

Jason in Wisconsin says, "I got all the stuff for Christmas no kid ever wanted. Socks, underwear, new clothes, etc. I got an Atari 2600 around 1978 and that was the only fun gift I'd gotten as a kid." How many of us have wrapped up iPads, computer games, or Amazon gift cards for Christmas gifts to our kids instead of socks and underwear? *Exactly.* We all want our kids to have a better life than we did—to have the fun things that we didn't have. But dare we ask the question: Is our approach causing Gen Zs and Gen Alphas to struggle to find their way?

"Nobody ever offered me a 'chance of a lifetime,'" Pat from Canada says. "I had to slog my way through to achieve everything on my own. I financed my own education. I paid for my cars, the TV in my room, clothes, food, and living quarters without help from anyone." This approach has served Pat well in life.

He owns his own home and says, "I have no regrets growing up this way despite the hard days. I have great pride in my life and who I am and have become. I appreciate the difficulty and determination that got me to this point."

There was no such thing as entitlement or instant gratification for us Gen Xers.

VALUE 3: "STOP CRYING BEFORE I GIVE YOU SOMETHING TO CRY ABOUT"

For Gen Xers, manners and respect were nonnegotiable. Here are some of the things our parents said that kept us in check:

"Stop crying before I give you something to cry about!"

"Don't make me pull this car over!"

"Wipe that smile off your face, or I'm gonna wipe it off for you."

And we were supposed to feel sorry for our parents as they were whipping our butts while saying to us, "This hurts me more than it hurts you!" *I don't think so!*

The dinner table was where most of us were taught respect.

"We washed our hands, kept our elbows off the table, and always said 'please' and 'thank you,'" one Gen Xer says. For most of us, if we didn't eat what was given to us, we went without. It was called the "Take It or Leave It Menu."

Gen X kids weren't angels by any means. We broke rules, pushed limits, and talked back on our boldest days but *knew* there'd be consequences. We learned the boundaries and knew our parents didn't bluff. If we were disrespectful toward our elders, we had it comin' like clockwork.

VALUE 4: "BE HOME WHEN THE STREETLIGHTS COME ON"

Gen Xers played indoors during hurricanes, tornados, floods, and tsunamis; otherwise, we were outside every chance we got. We very much focused on the outdoors; we had woods to explore, miles to pedal, forts to create, creeks to fish in, combat sports to play, and neighborhoods to terrorize.

When those streetlights came on at dusk, it was our generation's cue to hightail it home from wherever we'd meandered off to.

A note to my BFF in junior high about going camping in her backyard reads:

> Welp, you'll be the big 14 tomorrow! Now your mom's getting the frozen pizzas for supper, right? That way we'd at least have something solid in our stomachs (we could eat while watching Knight Rider and then ship out to the woods). I hope you know we're going to freeze our butts off. Do you know how cold it was out this morning at 6:30? There was steam to the very top of every window in the house, and believe me, it wasn't from the heat! Maybe we can buy a portable incubator to keep us alive. Let's just hope it doesn't rain too.

We were more focused on the adventure—even if we froze to death. We explored, created, and were resourceful; we worked from the limited options we had, and knew it was up to us to make the best of it.

We didn't know how to articulate our values at that age, though.

J.C. in California says, "It's like our values were FAFO (fu%# around and find out)."

"Things that were so important to us back then aren't anymore," Robin says. "Things that we thought were the be-all, end-all, we don't even remember now. We grow, and our priorities and needs change."

At fifty-five, I know the only person responsible for my happiness is me. That requires me to be genuine, up-front, and authentic to myself. Otherwise, I'd still be chasing boys around, hoping one of them decides to marry me and solve all my problems—*like the fairytale, right?*

In my forties, I attended a counseling session at Canyon Ranch in Tucson. Ann, my counselor, asked me, "What are your top three values?" I was pretty sure it still wasn't boys, boys, boys, but honestly I didn't know. I had gotten way off course with knowing my values.

To help me find the answer, Ann gave me a little deck of "value cards." Each card described something important: relationships, love, kindness, persistence, security, achievement, and so forth. She told me to take them home and sort them in order of priority. It was easy to sort out the top ten but narrowing these down to the top three required a real inward look.

My top three were: physical security, responsibility, and relational pleasure or connections. Once I understood and accepted that feeling physically secure kept me grounded, putting responsibility before play gave me self-worth, and connecting with people brought me joy, my decisions became clearer and my boundaries were more in check.

Earlier this month, I didn't leave the house for three days. Why? Because I'd wake up each morning, throw on my bathrobe, grab my coffee, and practically run to the computer to write about all the ideas I'd woken up with. Next thing you know, it'd be 2 p.m., then 10 p.m. *And we won't talk about whether the bathrobe was still my daily attire or not.*

I had taken my job of writing a book to a hyper-responsible level, and while that fulfilled my responsibility value, it tanked my need for relationships and being social. The end result was by day three of my bathrobe binge, I actually felt more *irresponsible*, in that I hadn't gone outside, connected with my dogs for a walk, or had human interaction. It was almost like a form of mini depression because I was out of balance and didn't feel good about myself. How many of us get in a rut like this and find the longer it goes on the harder it is to pull ourselves out and get back to a healthy mental place? Guess what? Our values *are* our secret decoder sheet to get us back on track.

It really comes down to asking yourself these questions: When do you feel your best? When are you most at peace? Are you making decisions about things that truly matter to you?

In 2022, my ex-boyfriend lost his battle with cancer. He was fifty-eight years old. There was an estate auction at his house, which was my home for eight years. I made a few calls, inquiring if a stereo was still in the garage. I was told, yes, there was one resembling my description. It was difficult for me to return to that place on the day of the auction, but low and behold, there sat my Zenith stereo up on a high shelf in the back of his garage, buried under layers of dust. I looked at it and it looked at me; it was like reuniting with a long, lost love.

I figured the old stereo probably wouldn't even work after thirty years of sitting in a Michigan garage that wasn't temperature-controlled, but it had enormous sentimental value to me. The auction began, and, with a winning bid of $25, the stereo was being loaded into my SUV. I was so excited; I could barely sit still to drive home.

Yes, the Zenith stereo is just a material item, but it represents my deep-rooted value of responsibility. My parents taught me more than to simply work hard for the things I want; they taught me to take care of and appreciate those things, too.

◇◇◇◇◇◇◇◇◇◇◇◇◇◇◇◇◇◇◇◇◇◇◇◇

Pay attention to your mood. The other day I caught myself dancing in my kitchen while making scrambled eggs. Where did that come from? Maybe it was because I was having a balanced, productive morning fulfilling my values. *And listening to the song "Maniac" by Michael Sembello helped.*

Debbie in Ohio says, "I make myself take time *for me* with music, wine, and traveling. It helps *me* reconnect with *me*."

"My life felt pretty empty and insignificant for many years. Now, at fifty, I'm seeing there's a whole new way of existing and peaceful living," Deanna in Missouri shares. "I've had shit hit the fan and people I thought I could count on bail. You can only count on yourself. I had to learn that it's not my job to make sure everyone else is okay. I need to be okay, too. Learning what it actually means to put yourself first and why it's important *is* a big deal."

How many of us were raised to think that it was selfish to put ourselves first? *The truth is it's not.*

As we age and have more life experiences, our values will shift. A married person's values may change if they get divorced—maybe they divorced *because* their values changed. Valuing our career may shift to prioritizing time with loved ones over long work hours. If we begin valuing our health more, we may quit drinking or stop smoking. I know I place greater value on health and well-being than I used to. My values are still shifting and balancing, especially after writing this book—and will continue to long after.

We are always changing, evolving, and learning, and must recalibrate and realign with our values continually.

The worksheet in the e-book and cards from my therapist were tools that helped me sort out my values. So I'll ask you: What are *your* values?

Following is a list to help you choose from if you're unsure. After you've picked your values, prioritize your top five to ten from most important to least. Then drill down on each value. Ask, "If someone took this value away from me, what will I miss?" If your relationships went away, what would you miss? The loss of loyalty, compassion, respect, or appreciation? What's important to you about family? Is it a sense of belonging or connection? What does money give you? Security, power, or freedom?

"It might take a couple of weeks or months to stabilize your top values," Irina Cozma, Ph.D., said in a *Harvard Business Review* article titled *How to Find, Define, and Use Your Values*. "It's important to come up with your own definition for the broad nature of the words." She stresses having short, precise, and personal definitions. For example, happiness is one of her values, and to her the definition is simply "the joy in the process of what you are doing." As you explore the values most important to you, Dr. Cozma suggests evaluating your values when there are mood shifts. For example, when you're frustrated, ask yourself, "What is lurking behind my frustration? Are my values not being met?" The same goes for recognizing when you *are* balancing your values—those "making scrambled eggs while dancing in your kitchen" moments.

When I got that 45-year-old Zenith stereo home, for just a second I couldn't decide what to do first: clean it up, or just plug it in and push play. But since I'm a **FAFO Gen Xer,** *and an Aries,* I took that plug and went right for the outlet and that baby fired up. After a good tune-up, it works like a charm. I can always count on my old stereo to do the job if I need to get out of a funk or get in a positive head space. I'll play Journey's *Escape*, put in a Bryan Adams or Rick Springfield cassette, or even pop in John Denver's "Take Me Home, Country Roads" 8-track (yes, that's right, 8-track). But, for sure, playing *The Jazz Singer* will always take me to a happy place.

Commit to the values that define your True Colors, and reflect on them often. It will help you navigate what's important for living a more purposeful and fulfilling life.

Authority/Lawfulness
Independence
Challenge
Togetherness
Caring/Kindness
Cleanliness
Popularity/Fame Influence
Connections
Boldness
Stability Relationships
Service Health
Loyalty Adventure Growth
Wealth
Integrity Compassion Contribution
Well-Being Selflessness
Recognition
Beauty/Image Knowledge
Respect
Achievement/Success
Justice Family Wisdom Peace Faith
Status Acceptance Success
Optimism

Value List

Autonomy Spirituality Humor Love Hope
Accuracy Efficiency
Accountability Determination Bravery
Balance Creativity
Harmony Calmness/Peace
Pleasure Forgiveness Curiosity
Clarity Honor Happiness Fairness
Honesty Religion Gratitude
Sincerity Courage Appreciation
Inner Openness Competency Kindness
Authenticity Community
Prosperity Reputation
Resourceful Trustworthiness
Responsibility

Chapter Rapture 02
Values are your compass

Sixth Hour Bell

Knowing our values is the key to bringing our lives back to '80s Simple. How many of us have let ourselves be twisted, warped, pulled, and yanked like Stretch Armstrong into what someone thought we should be? Our values are the secret decoder to getting back on track. Be genuine, up-front, and true to yourself. Ask yourself: When do you feel your best? When are you most at peace? Are you making decisions that truly matter to you?

Pay attention to your mood—where is it coming from? Commit to the values that define your True Colors.

Extracurricular Activities

- Identify your top three to five values. Write them down, tape them to your bathroom mirror or above your desk, and revisit them often, at least quarterly.

- Consider a session with a life coach, or utilizing a workbook to explore what's most important to you.

- The original value eBook mentioned in the chapter was by www.Teresia.com/goal-setting.

After-School Specials

- Watch *The Outsiders*, which features the famous line "Stay gold, Ponyboy," urging you to hold onto your innocence and values as you age.

- The movie *The Jazz Singer* starring Neil Diamond has a great mix of music and themes about finding yourself.

- If you need more assistance choosing your core values, check out Adriana Girdler's YouTube video "How to Find Your Core Values: 3 Easy Steps."

Passing Notes in Class

"At the end of the day, you always have to live with yourself. Always be true. If you're not, you'll know—it'll bug you. Change it and be true."

~Terri in California

"Maintain your integrity. Understand who you are and don't compromise what you believe for the sake of others' approval."

~Kerrie in Minneapolis

"Some of my favorite childhood memories I value were with my family. Sitting down together every day with the whole family for dinners. Trips to Chicago to visit family and Cubs games. Summer vacations to Wisconsin Dells, Mackinac Island, and Florida. Camping with my siblings."

~Pam in Texas

Field Trips

- Go on a solo adventure—a road trip, yoga retreat, or wellness resort such as Canyon Ranch in Tucson. Choose a destination for a soul-searching journey, with no expectations except to go with the flow and explore who you are.

- Plan a family dinner night where everyone disconnects from their phones. Enjoy meaningful conversation. Ask questions and take the time to learn something new about each other.

Chapter Mixtape

- "True Colors" – Cyndi Lauper
- "All About Soul" – Billy Joel
- "The Logical Song" – Supertramp
- "A Life of Illusion" – Joe Walsh
- "Hearts On Fire" – John Cafferty
- "Cult of Personality" – Living Colour
- "Hole In My Soul" – Foreigner
- "Life's What You Make It" – Talk Talk
- "Passion" – Rod Stewart
- "You Don't Know Me at All" – Don Henley

Shortcut to Spotify Playlist: beckykliss.com/CR02

Chap. Three

Welcome to the Jungle

Technology

> *"The dreamers give us the technology, and sometimes that technology curbs our own dreams. Just remember, the best science fiction stories have the most dire warnings about civilization and the future. Most of them are cautionary tales. Well, society will pay a price for that."*
>
> ~*Steven Spielberg*

When my grandma was in her fifties (which seemed like her eighties to me at the time), my Uncle David thought it would be funny to throw her into my cousin's above-ground pool during a family gathering. He told my Uncle Quennie what he was going to do, and Quennie replied, "Okay. I'll get the camera."

Uncle David scooped Grandma L up, catching her off guard. Her arms flailed and her legs kicked as he tossed her into the pool. What my Uncle David didn't know was that my grandma was terrified of water. Most of the adults knew this and were in shock watching it all go down. For us kids, we thought it was funny—and, of course, Uncle Quennie was laughing with us, as he filmed the entire episode with his movie camera.

At family functions for years to come, Uncle Quennie would whip out the 8mm home projector for movie night. There was no sound except for the *whizz* of the spinning projector while we watched the grainy film on a portable, roll-down projector screen.

My cousins would get so excited when Uncle David appeared on the screen with his triumphant grin, getting ready to douse Grandma L in the pool. Uncle Quennie knew this scene in particular entertained us kids way more than the footage of Uncle David getting reamed out *after* the toss. When the reel was rewound, you could actually watch the movie in reverse, so he'd stop the film and purposely play that scene forward, then backward—Grandma getting thrown into the pool, then flying back out into David's arms. Grandma flying into the pool; Grandma flying back out. In, then out. It was hysterical. My cousins would laugh 'til they cried.

That was what we used technology for back then: entertainment.

TECHNOLOGY IN THE '80s

Let's take a walk down Nostalgia Road and take a look at the gizmos and gadgets we had in the '80s.

There were boxy TVs, VCRs, VHS/Beta tapes, clunky cable boxes, and laser discs. And let's not forget all-in-one stereo systems! Video games and computers began to show up everywhere: Atari 2600, *Pac-Man*, *Pong*, Commodore 64, Intellivision and Colecovision, Apple Macintosh, IBM PCs with the DOS and early Windows operating system, TRS-80, and those floppy discs. We could venture to the arcade in the mall or sit and play *Pac-Man* in Pizza Hut.

Atari assured us, "We take fun seriously" and "Don't watch TV tonight, play it!" and we did. We also loved handheld games like *Merlin*, *Mattel Football*, *Donkey Kong*, and *Speak & Spell*.

"I vividly remember wishing for all these things in the '80s, knowing they kept improving them, yet they were super expensive," Amy in Florida says.

But if we couldn't afford to buy the latest and greatest gadgets, at least we could experience technology in the movie theater. *War Games*, *Star Wars*, and *Star Trek* were monumental! *Tron* was one of the first CGI films to use computer animation combined with live action, along with *The Last Starfighter* and *Flight of the Navigator*.

Eric in Canada says, "In the movie *Electric Dreams* from 1984, a computer was competing for the affection of a girl. In *Short Circuit* in 1986, it was about a robot trying to survive being disassembled. They all have some CGI and VFX but had nothing on *Tron* in 1982—that movie was literally taking place inside a computer."

Admittedly, not all '80s technology was for fun or entertainment. We had everyday electronics like typewriters (Smith Corona, IBM Selectric), Casio and Swatch watches, Ti35 Trig calculators, fax machines, and our made-like-a-tank clock radio combos. We communicated with touch-tone phones, pagers, and intercoms—and we had the first brick-like mobile phones, carried in a suitcase. And let's not forget when microwaves were thrown into the mix, bringing home the excitement of cooking our own popcorn in a bag, topped with a sprinkle of fear of radiation.

For most of us, though, it was exciting to get our hands on these new and exciting tech gadgets.

So much was ramping up in the '80s in the tech world: space shuttles (NASA had thirty-two launches in the '80s), Radio Shack, *Popular Mechanics* magazine, the Sony Walkman, tape recorders, and boom boxes—even our cartoons.

As kids on Saturday mornings, we'd lie on our stomachs, eating our giant bowls of cereal and watching *The Flintstones* and *The Jetsons*. That's right, we're the generation whose brains were soaking in the stone age and the space age at the same time. It's no wonder we're so damn versatile!

In 1987, Hanna Barbera Productions merged the two cartoons and released a movie called *The Jetsons Meet the Flintstones*. In one scene, Barney Rubble is in the air, test-flying a Jetsons rocket strapped to his back.

"But how do I get down?" he yells to George Jetson and Fred Flintstone, who are standing on the ground watching the experiment unfold.

"Your usual way—by fallin'," Fred shouts.

George yells, "Just push the button that says 'down.'"

Fred turns to George and says sarcastically, "Don't make it too complicated for him, George." Some of us felt like Fred Flintstone—that technology *was* complicated even in the '80s, from programming the VCR, to making a mixtape, to taking photos.

Whether or not we found the technology in the '80s complicated, processes were certainly involved. Kris in Kalamazoo describes it painfully. "Buy film. Load film in camera. Turn the dial until the film clicks. Decide if you need a flash. Load flash bulb. Take one picture. Turn the dial until the film clicks. Repeat. Once you have maxed out the roll of film (could take days, even weeks), drive to the drugstore with the roll of film. Fill out a paper envelope with a pen. Place film in envelope, seal, remove tab, wait in line, and remit to cashier. Put your receipt tab in a safe place. Wait one week. Drive to the bank to withdraw money from your savings account, then go to the drugstore, give the cashier the tab, and pay. You tear that envelope open right there in the middle of the store, only to find that half of them didn't turn out. They were either out of focus, over or underexposed, crooked, or eyes were closed. It was a crapshoot. Snapshot photos from the '80s are truly miraculous treasures today."

Now it seems the '80s way is viewed as old-fashioned, difficult, or complicated. *Really?* Come on, how hard was using a paper map, looking up movie times in a newspaper, or finding a service or product in the Yellow Pages with our fingers "doing the walking"?

But while technology advanced, Gen Xers got more savvy along with it.

TECHNOLOGY TODAY

We may not have lived as primitively as the Flintstones, but most of us didn't predict the Jetsons' uber-techno world we live in now.

Today, the number of features, filters, and equipment options we can use to take something as simple as a video or photo is endless. Light rings, selfie sticks, tripods, rear cameras, front cameras, increasing megapixel counts, black-and-white filters—I could go on and on. The number of videos and photos stored on my phone and computer is more than I have time to ever sort—and it just keeps growing.

Even Gen Xers who felt our systems worked fine in the '80s actually love and totally rely on some of the cutting-edge features now available.

"Without GPS, I couldn't find my local 7-Eleven now," Don in New York jokes.

Kim in Bridgman concurs. "I'm surprised I'm still not out there lost using that big atlas."

"I always hated the stupid card catalog and Dewey Decimal system trying to find what I wanted to know," Rebecca in Pennsylvania says. "I love online shopping and information."

Julie in Oregon agrees. "Access to instant information via the internet is like an encyclopedia, dictionary, and thesaurus at my fingertips, but better."

And Gen Xers are dabbling in AI. Some are using it to write documents and property descriptions for real estate, or for enhancing photography, making their work easier, or as pure entertainment. Students are using it to help research reports and essays.

"AI does our meal planning and organizes our shopping lists," James in Chattanooga says. "We both have dietary restrictions and are ballin' on a budget and AI is great at deduction."

Some Gen Xers I polled said they can't live without the internet, online shopping and banking, iPads, cellphones, and Apple watches.

Susan in Los Angeles jokes, "You aren't gonna trick me into saying something bad about my iPhone! If I hurt its feelings, it will tell my Alexa, who will tell my Firestick, who will tell my Roomba, who will tell my Tesla and they'll all go on strike!"

Alternatively, some of us despise advancements in technology.

"Outsmarting the algorithms when you're trying to get a job now is insane," Terry says. "Companies have software that screens resumes, and without the right keywords in it, resumes are electronically funneled into the resume graveyard. What happened to the days of getting a face-to-face interview?"

Technology not only affects *getting* a job, it might also affect *keeping* one, too.

Last year I was in a grocery store with my dad, and there were carts with built-in devices to scan each item as we put it in. Then, when we were done, we whizzed through the checkout lane and paid in less than two minutes. My dad watched the process in dismay and said, "They're gonna lay someone off for this." He might be right. At the same time, though, an IT developer may be getting some extra hours or landing a new job. The question is this: Is technology eliminating jobs or replacing one job for another?

Julie in Madison says, "I think a lot of people are going to lose their jobs. They can make anyone say or do anything and it looks real. Plus, you won't be able to tell a lie from the truth."

Creatives inherently realize this. During an interview on the 80s Cruise (an annual themed cruise I attended), Bob Mothersbaugh, Devo's guitar player, said sarcastically, "We're going to let AI show us what a Devo song sounds like." *As if.*

I have a friend who was toying with an AI program that can create images of people. I could give him any two people's names—like *Twins* (1988) co-stars Arnold Schwarzenegger and Danny DeVito—and next thing I knew, he sent me a picture created using AI of a man that looked like Arnold and Danny combined. Crazy! It's probably a good idea to view any picture of someone you don't know on the internet with a little Nancy Drew skepticism.

Despite the mixed feelings of Gen Xers on technology, the most popular answer our generation gives when asked what they'd do if they could go back to the '80s? Buy Apple and Microsoft stock. *We just didn't know what we didn't know.*

How did we get to this point?

TECHNOLOGY BACK THEN

When I think of technology in the '80s, I think of my little 110 camera and the excitement of picking up an envelope of photos from the drugstore, or I picture my grandma L flying out of the pool backwards. I think of making mixtapes, watching *The Empire Strikes Back*, or playing Atari. Watching TV was our way to get local news; viewing VHS tapes was our family's entertainment. The family camcorder was considered high-tech, not to mention having our very own electronic typewriter at home! Of course, video games with our friends were the bomb. Talking on the phone was something we looked forward to—we loved hearing it ring, hoping it was for us.

In the '80s, I'd guesstimate about 80 percent of the time our generation used technology for fun and entertainment, and 20 percent of the time for work and efficiency.

What does that percentage look like now? Today, technology is ingrained in our everyday lives: preordering Starbucks coffee on their app, checking in for a flight at airport kiosks, scanning our own items at the grocery store, paying for gas at the pump or a meal with a handheld device, and using a QR code to access a menu. Even at our small-town public library, there is a self-checkout kiosk.

The list is endless, from big-ticket items like being able to electronically sign a contract for our next house on our phone to using three remotes to control our TVs.

We need so much brain power just to pay for something these days. Checking out at a store with a credit card can be confusing. I went on vacation with my mom and gave her the rundown on how to use Tap to Pay and she proceeded to ask twenty questions. *Mom, just try it.* In the '80s, this was all done eyeball-to-eyeball, without trying to figure out how a machine worked or stressing about remembering complex passwords. Zelle, Venmo, PayPal...what's next?

We are flooded with communication sources and options. Seeing the person we're talking to on the phone via video chat is no longer the stuff of *The Jetsons* or *Blade Runner*.

Kerrie in Minneapolis says, "My mom prefers to talk on the phone, my boss is all about Zoom, my child is sending DMs, my sister is texting me, and, of course, my dentist expects me to show up in person. How do we keep up with the various methods that are preferred for each situation?"

I'm guessing that for many of us, the percentage of what we use technology for has flip-flopped. We're relying on technology for efficiency, communication, and work 80 percent of the time and only 20 percent of the time for entertainment and enjoyment.

In one scene in *The Jetsons Meet the Flintstones*, George's alarm clock wakes him up by saying, "Rise and shine, George! It's time to face the world." Do you think this was Hanna Barbara's way of implying that we are in for a real ride when all this techno mumbo jumbo takes over?

Meanwhile, Fred's pet dinosaur, Dino, licks his face to wake him up.

Where is the balance between The Flintstones and The Jetsons?

Dina in Delaware observes, "We're losing our tactile joys—a book, a greasy menu, the joy of counting paper money. My eyes feel like they're worsening daily, and having to do everything on a phone isn't helping."

In a 2020 article published in the *National Library of Medicine*, Dr. Gary Small et al. say, "Our brains are wired for immediate gratification. The big issue is technology. We've changed how our brain processes information, how we use memory. We're not paying enough attention to what's going on because we're checking our social media feed all the time and that kind of mental repetitive activity doesn't really stimulate the mind as well as good conversation."

We're being forced to adapt to technology.

It's even apparent in the words we use. In the '80s, viruses made us sick and worms lived in grandma's garden. Today, viruses and worms are synonymous with malicious cyberattacks. "Hacked" meant cutting something off in shop class while "cloned" reminded us of science class—neither one implied someone was trying to steal our identity.

We're almost *required* to upgrade our gadgets regularly—especially our phones—because technology outdates itself so quickly.

I believe three things make today's technology especially challenging for us CD-55ers:

1) The need to process a large amount of information daily,
2) The speed at which that information is coming at us, and
3) The assumption that we are available 24/7.

THE AMOUNT OF INFORMATION

Think about the amount of information we process every day—or the sheer number of features our electronics now offer. Notifications pelting us on our devices are at the forefront of this problem. We're alerted when there is a traffic jam even if we're working in our yard. Inclement weather notifications pop up on multiple devices. A new email, a new text message, a new social media interaction. We have access to hundreds of different versions of what's going on in the world, but we still have to decipher which is true. If we're watching TV, it takes an hour to click through our options and another hour to research them because we've never heard of 75 percent of the shows.

I went on the '80s Cruise in 2023. Mark Goodman, an original MTV VJ, was one of the celebrities on the ship. In an interview he said, "We have access to the entire world of music—*it's too much.*" What does Mark mean? Is the amount of data really too much?

I think he makes a valid point. When I tried to add "Someday" by Glass Tiger to my Spotify playlist, I typed "Someday" in the search bar. More than one thousand songs came up in the search. Ironically, I never found the one by Glass Tiger until I typed "Glass Tiger." *Are you kidding me?*

Where does all this information fit into our overflowing brains? For me personally, I feel that my ADHD has gotten much worse the more I'm on my screens. I have a sign that sits in my office that says, "My brain has too many tabs open." And, apparently, I don't pay attention to it, because I just counted the number of Windows tabs on my dual monitors I have open—28. Twenty-eight sources of information I have open simultaneously. Why? *Because I can.* Technology is giving us more and more options to tap into. Back in our day, that'd be like having twenty-eight encyclopedias open in front of you. There's a reason we were outside all the time!

Maybe this is why one of my most productive places to be is on an airplane, squished in a small seat with a less-than-adequate folding tray. Because I don't use any technology other than my iPod, which isn't different from an old Sony Walkman in my mind. I listen to my downloaded airplane playlist on my earbuds. It's just me, my music, and my notepad; it's my time for creative thinking. Why should this just happen on a plane, though?

How do we start making room for these time-outs in our day to tap into our creativity? Things like sitting with our morning coffee and a notepad, mowing our lawn, spending fifteen minutes a day stretching, meditating on our yoga mat, or playing tug of war with our dog on the floor—anything where we can close our brain tabs down and focus on our thoughts.

THE SPEED OF INFORMATION

How many of us have gone for our internet provider's jugular while demanding a faster download speed? We want our information downloaded as fast as we can get it. No one wants to go back to when the World Wide Web was beginning to percolate and we were doing our first dial-up, listening to the R2-D2 beeps, buzzes, and whines coming from our computer modem as it rigorously searched for a connection. It was painful!

In this day and age, no one wants to be the last to learn, hear, or know it. Think of how fast news spreads on our devices when someone dies or a story breaks. It's practically instantaneous.

I'm guessing even George Jetson would be overwhelmed by the speed of things today.

How many of us are struggling to keep up with communicating, learning, researching, shopping, social media, gaming, emailing, and messaging—and what, still have a life *off* screen? It is literally impossible to keep up with it all. And where's our quality of life if we're trying to?

Kindra, a Gen X parent in Michigan, says, "One of my teenagers will flat out tell me that they can't sit still long enough to watch a movie with us. I think all the TikTok videos and shorts have lowered the younger generation's attention span to two minutes."

What are the long-term ramifications for our attention spans?

24/7 ACCESS TO EACH OTHER & EVERYTHING ELSE

Think about how available we are 24/7. If ten people want to tell us something at the same time, they can. And it's *our* job to keep up with what each one is telling us (and process and manage all the information, too).

Kevin in Texas says, "It was a much better world when you could leave for the day, and no one knew where you were or what you were doing."

Do you ever feel like Kevin? Or that you feel obligated to respond quickly or share what you are doing? Maybe you're being asked why you can't respond in a timelier manner.

"When we were in school and had a spat with someone it was usually put on hold once we went home, until the next day back at school," Kelly in Tallahassee adds. "My daughter comes home and carries her daily issues with her friends long into the night and it actually gets worse because there's no time to let issues rest."

In the '80s, we had to leave home for almost everything. Hell, even if we wanted to send someone a note, card, letter, or picture, we had to get off our asses and walk to the mailbox. If we wanted to send an instant message, it was called "go talk to that person."

Access to the internet has made it easy to not leave our homes anymore. We have virtual doctors and veterinarians, grocery delivery, online banking, and remote jobs. More than three hundred million households have Alexa or Siri helping them become more hands-free and to not leave home. We can command our gadgets to make calls, send messages, order products, and tell us our schedules, weather, and virtually anything else. Are you connected 24/7?

WHOA, NELLIE: HITTING THE BRAKES

In the early 1900s, Albert Einstein said, "I fear the day that technology will surpass our human interaction. The world will have a generation of idiots." Is this where our future is headed? Einstein wasn't a Gen Xer, but I think he was spot on.

We all depend on technology for efficiency, productivity, knowledge, communication, and entertainment. I couldn't have written this book without twenty-eight tabs open for research. You probably couldn't have bought this book without using some sort of technology.

The information our devices provide is mind-blowing. When I asked fellow Gen Xers what they've recently googled, they responded: who was in the band Faces, how do you raise meat rabbits, what are the "Love Removal Machine" song lyrics, what you need to know to purchase a pontoon boat, how to bake bread from scratch, what is a fire rainbow, what are the health benefits of castor oil, what are the best cities in Greece to visit, and how to distribute an e-book. *Yes, that last one was me.*

Brandi in New Mexico says, "Being able to google the bizarre questions my brain generates at 3:00 a.m. is magical."

But where does it stop?

"I disconnect from my phone at night when the Vicodin and vodka kicks in," Donald in New York jokes.

Another Gen Xer adds, "I never disconnect. My phone is surgically attached to my eyes 24/7."

The reality is that most of us are probably on our gadgets more than we realize. It might even be to the point where it's arguable if it's a pro or con in our lives.

We simply need to pause more and examine how, when, and why we interact with technology. With any new electronic device you bring into your life, there are benefits and compromises. Do you know the price you will pay in time? Have you considered the learning curve to transfer your information, integrate it with your other gadgets, and understand all the features? What about the time to spend with tech support if the gadget doesn't work like it should or you encounter problems? How do the benefits of the gizmo help you in your daily life? If the benefits don't outweigh the price you'll pay with your time (and money), why not skip it and stick with what is working for you already? I used to think I had to have the latest and greatest gadgets, but not anymore. I believe in going for what adds value to my life and brings me the least amount of stress.

"Change is inevitable," Joe in Texas says. "Some of us don't want it because we love the world we grew up in. The evolution of technology has made things simpler for us not to have to think things through, and that starts to take away from the beautiful world we were used to."

Ironically, when I asked Gen Xers what things are most important in their life now, it wasn't their electronic devices. It was family, friends, health, pets, God, peace, respect, self-esteem, joy, and contentment; others said traveling, staying fit, relaxing, and taking care of their mom; still others said their farm, house, and garden. One Gen Xer nailed it with "comfortable shoes!" Only one answer of many had to do with a machine—a motorcycle.

Eric in Colorado reflects, "When I was growing up, most summers we stayed in a cabin on a lake. We had no phone and a 13-inch TV that had two channels. I had some of the best times of my life there."

So, if we know what's important, why does the techno BS consume us so much?

FIND THAT ANALOG BALANCE

Never forget that we were analog kids. We weren't raised on digital devices, and we survived. However, we don't live in that old-school world anymore.

How much lust for life are we missing because we are engrossed in technology? I'm not referring to electronic gas pumps or Tap to Pays that are out of our control; I'm talking about the devices we *can* control.

It's impossible to scramble our way back to using technology 80 percent of the time for entertainment and 20 percent for work. But think how good a 50/50 balance between the two would feel! If we want to have a joyful life, we must try to balance those numbers more evenly. *Piece of cake, right?*

I can sit and tell myself all day long that I need to decrease the amount of information I'm taking in and unplug more, but until I actually alter my habits, it won't change.

Gen X is the last generation to navigate life before the tech boom. Isn't this to our advantage? We know what analog life was like, and we've been doing a pretty good job trying to keep up with the high-tech stuff for decades. But now, as many of us are trying to simplify, downsize, *de-complicate*, and even retire, do we still feel like we have to keep up with technological advancements? AI, robotics, self-driving cars…some of us Gen Xers might be ready to bow out of keeping up with the Jetson's because we believe simpler is better at our stage of life.

Do we start thinking like Uncle Quennie, and make decisions to whip out our camera or phone for play, instead of the things that might not add quality to our lives?

Technology surfaces in damn near every chapter in this book, because it affects every aspect of our lives. So let's start shifting our habits to using technology more for fun and entertainment. Appreciate those things or people in your life like Uncle Quennie who bring laughter and entertainment to your world through technology.

The first step is to begin recognizing what brings value to our lives and what doesn't. When using technology, simply ask: Is this adding value or enjoyment to my life?

SONGS ON TAPES

A

1. A LITTLE MORE LOVE — OLIVIA NEWTON JOHN — #18 C #28 E
2. ABACAB — GENESIS — #11 B
3. ABRACADABRA — STEVE MILLER BAND — #12 C
4. AFRICA — TOTO — #71 C
5. AFTERNOON DELIGHT (oh what a night) — FOUR SEASONS — # 9 C
6. AFTER THE LOVE IS GONE — EARTH WIND & FIRE — #28 C
7. AGAINST THE WIND — BOB SEGER — #39 B
8. AH LEAH — DONNIE IRIS — #55 C
9. ALL NIGHT LONG — AC/DC — #24 B 38 B
10. ALL OF MY LOVE — — #26 B
11. ALL OUTTA LOVE — AIR SUPPLY — #15 B 42 B
12. ALL OVER THE WORLD — ELO — #39 B
13. ALL THOSE YEARS AGO — GEORGE HARRISON — #55 B
14. AND YOU SAY YOU LOVE ME — — #10 C
15. ANOTHER ONE BITES THE DUST — QUEEN — #42 B
16. ARE YOU READY? — — #23 E
17. ARTHURS THEME — CHRISTOPHER CROSS — #55 C
18. AS THE BEAT GOES ON — THE — #40 B
19. Affair of the Heart — Rick Springfield — #22 E # 73 E

B

20. BABY COME TO ME — PATTI AUSTIN — #71 B
21. BABE — STYX — #23 C 42 C
22. BAD CASE OF LOVIN YOU — BLUES BROTHERS — #27 B 28 B
23. BAD GIRLS — DONNA SUMMER — #14 B 29 B
24. BAKER STREET — GERRY RAFFERTY — # 5 C
25. BE A STAR — VILLAGE PEOPLE — # 8 C
26. BE GOOD JOHNNY — MEN AT WORK — #11 C
27. BETH — KISS — # 9 C
28. BETTE DAVIS EYES — KIM CARNES — #56 B
29. BLACK BETTY — — # 9 E
30. BLUE COLLAR MAN — STYX — # 1 B
31. BOOGIE NIGHTS — — # 7 E 9 C
32. BOOGIE WONDERLAND — EARTH WIND & FIRE — #26 C
33. BURNIN — — #23 B
34. BURNIN FOR YOU — BLUE OYSTER CULT — #54 C
35. Beat it — michael Jackson — #72 E 73 E

C

36. CALL ME — BLONDIE — #12 B 15 B 24 C 42 E
37. CAN'T CHANGE THAT — RAYDIO — #26 B
38. CAN'T SMILE WITHOUT YOU — BARRY MANILOW — #10 C
39. CAROLINAS COMIN HOME — SHAUN CASSIDY — #15 C
40. CARS — GARY NUMAN — #38 B 72 E
41. CAR WASH — — #10 B
42. CAUGHT UP IN YOU — 38 SPECIAL — #11 B
43. CELEBRATION — KOOL & THE GANG — #43 B 55 B
44. CENTERFOLD — J. GEILS — #53 C
45. CHARLIES ANGELS THEME — — # 9 B
46. CHUCK E'S IN LOVE — RICKI LEE JONES — #25 B
47. CLOSE ENCOUNTERS — JOHN WILLIAMS — # 2 B
48. CLOSER I GET TO YOU — R. FLACK + D. HATHAWAY — # 4 C
49. COLD AS ICE — FOREIGNER — #10 C
50. COLOUR MY WORLD — CHICAGO — # 9 C 18 C 67 C
51. COME ON EILEEN — DEXY'S MIDNIGHT RUNNERS — #69 B
52. COME SAIL AWAY — STYX — # 3 E
53. COMING UP — PAUL McCARTNEY & WINGS — #24 C 41 C
54. COPA COBANA — BARRY MANILOW — # 4 C

The analog method I used to track my mixtapes; when rolling paper into the typewriter crooked, without corrector tape, felt state-of-the-art!

Chapter Rapture 03
Never forget we were analog kids

Sixth Hour Bell

What does your current tech usage look like—how much is dedicated to fun and entertainment versus work and efficiency? Strive for a 50/50 balance.

To live joyfully, we need to manage our tech use and embrace the peace that comes from unplugging.

Close your brain tabs and focus on your thoughts—where can you find the time and space to do this?

Begin creating moments in your day for these time-outs to tap into your creativity. Reflect on what truly adds value to your life and what doesn't. When using technology, consider: Is this bringing joy or adding value to my life?

Extracurricular Activities

- Convert your '80s photo albums and video libraries to digital formats for long-term preservation and easy access from your phone or computer.
- Dive into *Atomic Habits* by James Clear for practical strategies to build better habits, especially related to your gadgets and screen time.
- Use apps such as Google Keep or Todoist to organize your tasks and streamline your to-do lists.
- Missing your '80s gadgets? Visit Retrospekt.com to shop for retro tech items like Sony Walkmans, Nintendo Game Boys, vintage Polaroid cameras, and more nostalgia!

After-School Specials

- Watch Hanna-Barbera's two-hour classic cartoon special: *The Jetsons Meet the Flintstones*.
- For your '80s technologies movie fix, watch *Tron, Short Circuit, Flight of the Navigator,* or *War Games*.
- Watch *Weird Science* and get a good laugh about how creating the perfect woman on a computer isn't a thing of the past anymore.

Passing Notes in Class

"Setting up and connecting Wi-Fi nowadays can be a big time waster: to new cars, phones, printers, ovens, vacuums, TVs, glucose monitors, computers, speakers, washing machines, lights, alarms, doorbells, apps where you shop/eat/work/breathe...But hey, sooo happy having 2-factor authentication to "protect my privacy" and prevent "someone" from paying my electricity bill!"
~ Cori in Oklahoma

"We are giving up our privacy for efficiency and simplicity using electronics."
~ Dave M in Michigan

"Passwords and password recovery procedure requirements 'new password must contain at least 12 letters, 4 numbers, 2 special characters, 6 ancient runes, the blood of a virgin pygmy goat, and the first 10 years of your life as an interpretive dance.'... Oh, and the new password can't be the same as the old password."
~Eric in Canada

Field Trips

- Have a video call with someone who lives in a faraway location and take advantage of one of the best technological advancements for connecting with others across the world.
- Plan a family movie night featuring old home movies and share stories about the good ol' days.

Chapter Mixtape

- "Welcome to the Jungle" – Guns N' Roses
- "Computer Blue" – Prince
- "Round and Round" – Ratt
- "Mr. Roboto" – Styx
- "She Blinded Me with Science" – Thomas Dolby
- "Mr. Speed" – KISS
- "No Reply at All" – Genesis
- "We R In Control" – Neil Young
- "Breakaway" – Big Pig
- "Weird Science" – Oingo Boingo

Shortcut to Spotify Playlist: beckykliss.com/CR03

Chap. Four

Call Me

The Telephone

> "'Call Me' is about longing and the need for connection. It's about the urgency and desire to reach out to someone, whether it's for love or companionship."
>
> ~Debby Harry

When my brother was a baby, he was given a finely crocheted green and white "blankie" by our great aunt. He dragged that thing everywhere. He wouldn't sleep without it, and it was crisis central if it went MIA. When my brother was six, it was left in a hotel room in Mackinaw City during our family vacation, and by the time he realized it was missing, we were ninety miles away. Talk about pandemonium! My parents stopped at a payphone, my mom called the hotel, and the tattered blankie was found; the hotel agreed to mail it to our house. Every day until it finally arrived, my little brother would stalk the mailman worse than Yosemite Sam hunting down Bugs Bunny. He was attached to it for more years than he's going to appreciate me telling you. Let's just say the term "security blanket" was invented by my brother.

Aren't our cell phones our security blankets today? The blankie we are dragging around that gives us some sense of assurance? How often have you had a panic attack when you can't find it? How many times have you turned around and driven miles out of your way when you've forgotten your phone?

If there is any topic in this book that has the greatest potential to impact our lives positively, it's this one, because the mobile phone has transformed every aspect of life since the '80s.

Let's rewind our phone habits back to the days when they were permanently part of our houses. That sucker was *never* leaving home because the damn thing was tethered to the wall (or so we thought).

That clunky telephone had to be plugged into a phone jack in the wall to even work. It could be heard across the land when it rang and could double as a lethal weapon because it was so big and heavy. And mobility? Sure—about as far as we could stretch the twenty-five-foot, rubbery, curly cord past its QC rating. We had to get as far away from the "big ears" listening in the house as we could. When I was talking on the phone, I'd sit in the laundry room among my brother's dirty underwear for privacy, if that tells you anything. I still think my mom has a permanent kink in her neck from holding the receiver with her chin while maintaining hour-long conversations with my Aunt Lindy and cooking dinner. What took that damn speakerphone so long to become mainstream, anyway?

Most families had two phones in their house, but generally there was only one telephone number, unless our parents footed the bill for a second line and number. One phone line, one phone number, *per household*. If we were in a big family and needed our phone time, we were screwed! Hearing those dreaded words from your mother, "Your dad is expecting a call," put you into a tailspin because that meant everyone had to stay off the phone.

In a note to my BFF I wrote:

> My brother went to the neighbor's, and mom went up to Rex's. I have to stay here and listen for the phone to ring because my dad is supposed to call at 2:00.

You knew your super-important conversations with your BFF would have to wait and a five-page note would have to suffice. Talk about sulking!

An address book was a staple item, but many of us worked hard to memorize all our friends' phone numbers. You probably can still recite your BFF's phone number by heart because you had to physically dial each digit every single time. A fun Kliss family fact: My parents have had the same phone number and landline for fifty-four years now—they have definitely contributed their share to keep AT&T in business. Just think, one of the most famous phone numbers of all time, 867-5309, came from an '80s song by Tommy Tutone. In 2004, a popular New Jersey DJ bought the number but eventually sold it because he received more than thirty calls a day from fans who dialed the number as a joke. *Maybe Jenny should have changed her number.*

As phones advanced from rotary to push button, we could dial a little faster. But if we got that *meep-meep* busy signal, it wasn't uncommon to dial ten more times to try to get through while on the verge of a meltdown theorizing who the person on the other end was talking to...like that would make you feel better.

When the paid call waiting option became available, it alleviated the prison sentence of staying off the phone because our parents were waiting for a call.

And the caller ID feature was like a James Bond spy mission come true, because we finally knew who was calling before we answered. This feature also meant our parents would know who was calling us. Once we discovered we could dial *67 and place a call anonymously, we were back to making prank calls again.

God forbid we had a friend in the next county or state with a different area code than ours, because that meant a long-distance call. That would cost us part of our hard-earned allowance! Yes, it's true; our parents were most often billed for every "stinkin'" minute of calls outside our area code.

Remember when everyone left the house and we didn't have caller ID? You'd never know if the "hoodlum" (as my Grandma L called the boys) you were hoping would call actually did. I recall overanalyzing and debating this critical issue many times with my BFF. That is, until the answering machine became popular in the mid-'80s. Yes, one electronic box for the entire family's messages for *everyone* to hear. *Suuuumbitch.*

Our dinosaur telephone had a few whopping capabilities back then: making phone calls, providing directory assistance, and telling the time. If we didn't know the phone number we wanted to call, we had a couple of choices. You could grab the microscopic-print phone book that would require +3.00 readers now, or we could dial "0" for directory assistance and get a live, non-recorded *real* human whose job was to look it up for you. (To the younger generations: this is no lie.) We could call 555-1212 and get an automated voice recording telling us the exact time. This was a big help when we were setting our windable watch or wanted to ensure our watch battery was keeping good time. Yes, I tried that number recently, and no, it does not work; it is very much extinct.

That was as smart as our phone got in the '80s: it could do *three* things for us.

Recently, I calculated that my Android smartphone does no less than FORTY-ONE things for me. It is my alarm clock, portable jukebox, to-do list, personal set of encyclopedias, mini TV, camera, video camera, photo album, travel planner, map, bank, journal, notepad, library, calendar, social media link, meditation assistant, boarding pass, retail store, gaming center, address book, GPS tracker, home security hub, thermostat, weatherman, parking spot guide, portable doctor, food barcode decoder, and calorie tracker. It allows me to complete stock market transactions, reminds me to workout, helps me shop, identifies constellations, birds, and plants, and remembers all my loyalty reward programs. And what, seriously, it functions as a flashlight, too? (Yes, and surprisingly, a pretty good one!) Of course, it does email, texts, messages, searches the web, and—oh, yeah—makes calls. Forty-one things compared to *three* in the '80s. No wonder it's our security blanket.

The smartphone is here to stay and replaces at least sixteen gadgets we used to use. The number of things it can do will only multiply.

My dad, the conventional flip-phone user, received a letter from Verizon saying his cell phone was no longer being supported and he'd have to upgrade. Talk about all hell breaking loose! He made it clear, saying, "I don't want one of those g-damn computerized phones," and off we went to Verizon to give them a piece of his 79-year-old mind. Thank goodness they still make newer flip phones; otherwise, I'm certain his walker would've turned into a weapon that day.

One of my dad's friends says, "My flip phone does everything I need it to."

God bless them and their fight to keep it simple in this high-tech world.

But it's more than the number of things our cell phones can do; it's the time we spend on them. Have you ever tracked how much time you spend on your phone each day? Or have you considered what you might be missing in your life when you're absorbed in your phone? Probably not, because most of us don't *want* to know. I'm going to argue we *need* to know. Chances of face-to-face, feel-good, serendipitous interactions in your life are slim to none if you are always staring at your phone.

Part of the process of writing this book for me included experimenting and trying new things. So, the last few times I've been at the airport waiting for my flight, I've made it a point to eat, grab an adult beverage, and *not* be on my phone. Let me tell you, doing this the first few times was painful. Sitting in a public place by yourself and not using your security blanket as a crutch feels like being the kid in the corner everyone is staring at.

The first time I sat at an airport bar, I looked around. Almost everyone was focused on their phones, including the kid sitting next to me who was probably twenty-five. *Ahhh, I just realized I called a 25-year-old a "kid."* The girl next to him was on her phone but glancing up from time to time. I caved and got on my phone. Then I realized this was stupid; we weren't afraid to talk to people in the '80s, and I needed to walk the talk of what I write about. So I started talking to the guy next to me. Within minutes, the girl next to him, Beth, was engaged in the conversation, too. Turns out the guy is an Elvis impersonator, Jimmy Holmes [IG- @Jimmyholmes_eta], and travels all over the country to gigs. The three of us had such a fun conversation. Beth and I ended up being so engrossed in chatting about our Gen X similarities that we nearly missed our flights.

Maybe the reason they call it a "cell" phone is that we've all become prisoners to it.

In 2023, I went to Paisley Park in Minnesota to tour Prince's estate, which is now a museum celebrating his music and art. Before the tour started, the group was lined up outside and each of us was handed a thick sponge bag with a sharp magnetic needle at the top. We were told to shut off our phones, put them in the bag, and turn off our watches. Then the bag was closed, and the magnetic needle locked into the buckle. Unless we had a hacksaw or happened to be carrying a big-ass magnetic device, we weren't getting that baby open. We were allowed to keep our bag with us, but it didn't matter because our cell phone was locked away like a felon.

I looked at my friend and said, "Okay, this is like giving me a minor panic attack."

She made a face and gasped, "Ohhhh, me, too!"

When the tour ended, they brought out the magical mystery magnet and unlocked the bag, giving us the world back in our hands. We both admitted that the tour was a completely different experience without our phones (although I won't lie, I was ecstatic to be able to take pics again). Once the initial shock of not having our phone was absorbed, we really paid attention to the sensational details of Paisley Park because we were truly in the moment.

∞∞∞∞∞∞∞∞∞∞∞∞∞∞∞∞∞∞∞

When we were growing up, "Don't Leave Home Without It" was drilled into our heads every time we'd hear American Express commercials featuring famous people such as Roger Daltrey, Stephen King, and even Jim Davis's Garfield, the big, fat, orange cartoon cat. The ad was cute and funny. Now, it's relatable.

"We used to have to take magazines and newspapers to read in the bathroom while doing our business," Palmer in Hawaii says. "Then there was the printed toilet paper with jokes on it to read. Now, we can't use the shitter without our phones."

Admittedly, I have a knack for leaving my phone in public restrooms. Just the other week, I did it again at Trader Joe's. The lady working in the produce section saw the whole episode play out: me picking out avocados, my sudden panic attack, and me feverishly digging through my bags, pocket, and purse, then the "oh, shit!" moment, and me running back to the bathroom. Sure enough, I found it sitting on the toilet paper dispenser right where I left it. Relieved, I came out holding it up and said "found it" to her (like she cared). Then something new flew out of my mouth. "I hate this thing."

So, is it the phone we hate or the feeling it gives us? Is it the realization that the more it does for us, the more we can never be apart from it? Whether it's to snap a picture, check our bank balances, or send a message? How many of us left our landlines in the dust and are 100 percent dependent on our cell phones now?

Julie in Massachusetts says, "We still have a landline because it's a bundle through Comcast and ironically more expensive to drop it. Seriously, I don't even know the phone number. Once in a while it will ring, and we'll all crack up laughing."

I asked Gen Xers on social media what they would call their cell phone if they had to name it. The answers I got were pretty telling: pocket spy/NSA tracking/government surveillance device, toilet Nintendo, The Interrupter, tumor, slave, tether, Mr. Belvedere, a necessary evil, and Go-Go Gadget. The most entertaining answer was "a vibrator." David in Arizona had the most popular answer, "Electronic Leash." The majority implied they hate the ball and chain feel of the phone, yet they know they need it.

One Gen Xer says, "Every answer I ever need is on my phone. What could be simpler?"

But do we really understand the impact of being held hostage by it?

While most of us have a love-hate relationship with our cell phones, some find ourselves in this conundrum: We don't want these constant interruptions or intrusions, *yet we do*. We want to know if it's an emergency with one of our kids, an elderly parent, or a loved one. In this crazy world, we want the reassurance that those we care about are not in harm's way.

However, is that worth the trade-off of jumping to every ding or vibration? Is that adding peace of mind or more anxiety?

The majority of time, the ding or vibration is related to a decision I need to make, an answer to a question someone is asking, or something I'm being reminded of that I had forgotten. These all may be good things, but they often derail my day from what I originally was trying to accomplish.

This is your brain on ~~drugs~~ your cell phone. The number of interruptions it can bring into your life is like a cracked egg in a hot pan, frying our brains.

In a way, we knew this torment when we were teens. If we were sitting down for dinner and the home phone rang, we might've heard our parents say, "Let it ring." It would kill us not to know who was calling. We couldn't help wondering if it was that cute "hoodlum" we were hot to trot after. However, in retrospect, wasn't that the simplicity of the '80s? Whoever was calling had no clue if we were on vacation, outside mowing the lawn, at Kmart, or just busy. We weren't accessible 24/7. *Period.*

Pat from Canada recalls, "If you were home, the proverbial answering machine was a blessing because you could screen the calls you didn't want to answer, like those from your boss calling on your only day off work to ask you to come in."

Consider that in today's context. How many of us find that our employers' access to us blurs the line between work and personal time?

Think of the Gen Z and Gen Alpha generations. Those kids will never experience a world without cell phones or know what it's like to not be connected 24/7.

For most of us, the best way to change a habit is to change how we think about it. I suggest we do that with our cell phones. Maybe we don't call it our "cell phone" anymore, but instead our "electronic toolbox (E.T.)." Toolboxes are useful when we need something to fix something else. (We also know E.T. was an extraterrestrial that could make magical things happen.) However, we need to be efficient with the time we have in this busy day and age—to use our apps as the trail of Reese's Pieces, as young Elliott did in the movie, to lead us where we need to go, not drop us into more chaos.

In a real toolbox, there's a small assortment of hardware most commonly needed to fix a problem; otherwise, it'd be too damn heavy to carry around. It's the same with your E.T. Do you need five exercise apps, or can you live with one or two? More importantly, do you even use them? Do you ever dig around in your toolbox when you don't need a hammer or screwdriver? Of course not. Why should it be any different with your phone? Why give it the power to suck you into randomly rummaging for things that take time away from something more important?

Changing how I view my phone has helped me to stay on task—just by stopping before I randomly grab it and asking myself, "What tool do I need?" I get the information I need, deal with the issue at hand, and then I get back to my regularly scheduled program. Remember, if you wear a mini-me E.T. wrapped around your wrist, every time you look at it when it vibrates is an intrusion.

Think about how you feel when you are with someone you enjoy spending time with, and they get on their cell phone and you become second fiddle. One of Passion Restaurant Groups' establishments in Miami has little boxes in the middle of each table that say, "By placing your cell phone here, we promise that you will have a more enjoyable dinner, an improvement in your relationships, and definitely a better gastronomic experience." When my friend and I saw the sign on the box, we chuckled at first, but we put our phones in "time out" and went on to share a meaningful evening of truly enjoyable conversation.

In a way, isn't that how family dinners were when we were kids? There were no toys or gadgets at the table; we were there, seated as a family, sharing our day together. And, technically, if our parents wanted a true, interruption-free meal, it was called "taking the phone off the hook."

We can laugh and poke fun at a rotary telephone attached to the wall now, but remember, it did the job—it connected us with people. Yes, our E.T.s are here to stay, but should we consider adopting part of this mentality again? The telephone was never meant to replace the people or relationships that meant something to us; it was supposed to bring us together. AT&T was spot on with their slogan, "Reach out and touch someone."

One Gen Xer says, "We all know we need to put our phones down more. It's like our parents telling us to clean our rooms—in one ear and out the other. We need new solutions. Out of sight, out of mind. Maybe it's putting the thing in a drawer with a timer on it."

Whether we hide our phones somewhere or put them in airplane mode, we each simply need to find what works best for us. Is your phone set up to ding every time you get an app notification? I've been working to master my DND mode on my Android. I've discovered all sorts of features I didn't even know I had—for example, I can choose the people who can bust through DND. So parents or kids could be set up so that their calls or texts always come through. How fabulous is that? We all could use this when we are at work, trying to focus, or relaxing.

Make the commitment to think of your cell phone as your E.T. Only use it when you actually need a tool. Don't compromise your in-person relationships with phone intrusions. Keep them meaningful. For example, you can use your E.T.'s modern-day features for our '80s principles, like sending a greeting card, only now it's a text of a picture of your granddogs or an inspirational meme.

Pat from Canada says, "Don't allow your whole life to rest in your pocket."

Why not make those '80s sensibilities work for us again? Unplug. Whether it's during family dinners or golf, nature walks, sewing, or going to a dog park—whatever you choose as your unplugged or quality time. Even when in DND or airplane mode, you can still use tools like your camera or flashlight.

And, yes, you *can* leave home without it. I asked my brother the other day,

"Hey, do you still have that blankie?"

"Hell, yeah, I do!" he said. "There isn't much left of it, though."

Not necessarily wanting to know the answer, I had to ask, "Do you still sleep with it?"

To my relief, he said, "No, but I know right where it's at."

TAKE CONTROL OF YOUR E.T. (ELECTRONIC TOOLBOX)

Pick a length of time each day and be mindful every moment you interact with your cell phone (and computer.) I'd say do this every time you touch those devices, but that's not realistic. I suggest doing it once a day, say, every morning or evening.

Whittle down the items you see that are of no value to you. Consider unsubscribing to the emails you don't need, unfollowing groups, pages, or people who aren't adding value. Send that needless clutter and noise to a galaxy far, far away. For everything you eliminate from repopulating, you give yourself the gift of time.

Make your E.T. work for you; don't work for it. And always remember, cell phones can bring you closer to people far away, but don't let them take you away from those sitting next to you.

Here are a couple of additional things that really worked for me:

- Keep only the tools and apps you need that add value to your life and delete the rest.

- Think of airplane mode or DND mode instead as quality time mode. Screw thinking that you have to be on an airplane to use this feature.

- Utilize the auto-text response or auto-reply driving feature. You can hit one button that sends an automated message, like mine: "I'm on '80s retro downtime right now. I'll hit you up when I'm back in the 21st century!" Training people that it's important for you to have downtime might rub off on them.

- Know what rings and dings are important. Set specific ringer sounds for the special people in your life, such as your spouse, kids, or parents, and special notification sounds for crucial reminders, such as taking medication or taking out the trash.

- Use the feature on your E.T. that tracks the time you spend on apps each day or week. Use it as a compass to find your way to more quality time.

- Make your own basket for the table at family gatherings or events for everyone's phones with a cute (but on-point) saying on it. Find a way that works for you and untether your E.T. at least once a day!

```
BECKY,
      This is a farwell letter. Sinse Wednesday at the game
I've relised that i've been replaced by MISSY. I dont hate
her now just because shes your best friend now in fact I
like her very much. Its really sad because you refuse to
talk to me and if you do you dont even look at me. I'll have
stop this letter now because my eyes are getting blured  if
you please,dont show this to anyone not even MISSY. This
probably sounds like a letter between lovers.( my eyes are
unblured now ive taken control dont worry)If Iam wrong
please call and te... me(i hope Iam) Are you still going
trucking with your dad? I'll be asking quit a few
questions just call or write(I'd prefer if you called)
are we still going to be trucking partners? or do you have
a new one? i'd apreceate it if we were  cause i've saved
$17.00 so far (all my money) I'll be back in a minute I
have to take a 10-100 (remember?) Im back. This must be a
corny letter one minute Im cring in emotions the next I
act as if nothing ever happened between us.there I go again
emotions.Have I done something  to make you mad? was it
because I practicly ignored you the day you made the
surprise visit? When I went home I tried to call you but
you weren't home. I called to say I was sorry for ignoring
you because I am. Every time I try to call but your never home
Before I forget I've been meaning to ask you if you've been
  watching GENRAL HOSPITAL? Remember you got me in to
watching it? By the way Monday I started a new story I'll
somehow get a copy of it to you when I finish it. By the way
did you ever rip up that story you wrote? Its about time this let
  letter ends Its longer then I expected anyway ive got to get
a few z's

                  10-4
                  ROBIN HAMANN
                  Robin Hamann
```

PS THIS SITUATION IS A
   10-33 so GET ON
   CHANNEL 25QUIKE
   JUST DONT THINK I'M
   FORCING YOU TO CALL
   ME (BUT CALL ME
   ANYWAY.)

A corney letter huh?

'80s friendship drama: wanting and
waiting for our phone to ring.
"Call me" were the magic words.

Chapter Rapture 04
This is your brain on ~~drugs~~ your cell phone

Sixth Hour Bell

Don't let your phone become your security blanket. Remember, we weren't tethered to our landlines in the '80s. Change how you view your phone: think of it as an electronic toolbox (E.T.) to be a tool you use when needed, not something to cling to.

Protect your in-person relationships from phone interruptions. Every ding or vibration—does it bring peace of mind or add stress? Make your E.T. work for you; don't work for it. While cell phones can bring you closer to people far away, don't let them pull you away from those beside you.

Extracurricular Activities

- Read *How to Break Up with Your Phone* by Catherine Price for creative tips on preventing your E.T. from taking over your life.
- Declutter your apps—keep only those that add value and delete the rest.
- Use airplane or Do Not Disturb (DND) modes as your "quality time" mode.
- Create a phone basket for family gatherings, adding a fun, meaningful saying on it.
- Organize a group video call with long-lost friends for a "happy hour" to share heartfelt reminiscing and reconnect like you were all together.

After-School Specials

- Experience the real magic in watching *E.T. the Extra-Terrestrial* again, when phoning home with your "E.T." was of utmost importance.
- Watch classic American Express commercials on YouTube and actually consider leaving home without your E.T. occasionally.
- Revisit *The Wonder Years*, specifically "The Phone Call" episode, to relive the excitement of anticipation before instant communication.
- *Saturday Night Live* "Phone Booth Confession" with John Candy and "Getting off the Phone" with Will Ferrell are classic episodes to watch.

Passing Notes in Class

"Cell phones dehumanize us. When smartphones first rolled out, I was offended when meeting friends because they would check their cells or text—we didn't do that before. The emotional connection to a voice is lost. Remember talking hours with your first love because you liked the sound of their voice?"

~Kim B from Three Oaks

"My watch is connected to my phone, so I just have to say to it, 'Hey Siri,' and I can ask away for anything. I feel like James Bond."

~Sheila in California

"My favorite function or app on my phone is mute."

~Jay in Ohio

Field Trips

- Embark on a scavenger hunt to find a still-working payphone, or buy an antique rotary phone for your grandkids to experience a piece of the past.
- Sit alone in a public place without using your E.T. and strike up a conversation with someone new.

Chapter Mixtape

- "Call Me" – Blondie
- "867-5309/Jenny" – Tommy Tutone
- "Baby Don't Forget My Number" – Milli Vanilli
- "I Just Called to Say I Love You" – Stevie Wonder
- "Telefone (Long Distance Love Affair)" – Sheena Easton
- "Don't Lose My Number" – Phil Collins
- "Telephone Line" – Electric Light Orchestra
- "Operator" – Midnight Star
- "Rikki Don't Lose That Number" – Steely Dan
- "Hanging on the Telephone" – Blondie

Shortcut to Spotify Playlist: beckykliss.com/CR04

Chap. Five

Turn Up the Radio

Music

> *"Music is everything to me. I love making music…*
> *Music is spirit, it's therapy. It makes me feel a certain way,*
> *and if played with conviction and soul, the same thing occurs*
> *in other people."*
>
> ~*Prince*

Silver Beach was the hot spot in St. Joseph, Michigan, for Jen and Karin, especially on summer nights in the '80s. They'd borrow Jen's parents' powder-blue Delta 88 sedan and cruise to the beach loop parking lot. Jen and Karin had one problem, though, despite the car being large enough to hold a party of ten: musically, it only had an AM radio. That wouldn't get the girls the "cool pick-up chicks" rating they were looking for, so they had to improvise on ways to blast music. They wedged Jen's boom box, locked and loaded with Def Leppard's *Hysteria* cassette, between the front seats. As they entered the beach loop, the boom box was queued with "Pour Some Sugar on Me" to start pounding. After every loop, they'd scramble to rewind the tape in time to play the song again as they circled to reenter the loop. The song's lyrics belted out "Hey! Hey!" and then the music blasted *do-do-do-doo-do-do-do-doo* over and over again as the girls were counting on the cute boys to notice. How could they not, *right?*

When we wanted to take our music with us, it required ingenuity. Some strapped their tape recorders to their bike handlebars to listen while pedaling down the road. Some snuck their radio or tape recorder onto the school bus, knowing darn well to make sure those big-ass C batteries were fairly new so the music wouldn't die a slow death. Then there was the classic balancing act of carrying our boom box on our shoulder *while* riding our bikes, hoping we didn't wipe out, or worse, bust our boom box.

Back then, it was much harder for us to have access to new music; we had to physically go to the store or barter with our friends—there was no such thing as streaming. Making playlists, aka mixtapes, took hours and hours.

The Sony Walkman was our first cutting-edge gadget that finally became affordable in the mid to late '80s. We were ecstatic to slap on our headphones and listen to our music while we were on the go, decreasing the risk to life and limb. Even concerts were hard to get to—they were such a big deal, they deserve their own chapter later in *the Invincible '80s* book series.

Our music was everything to us. It was the backdrop to our lives.

"Music was our map," Mark in Ohio says.

And it all started with our radios.

RADIO STATIONS

Radio stations were the bomb in the '70s and '80s. Radio DJs were known for taking calls and playing requests, and generally not running from a preplanned or prerecorded script. This was the connection to the outside world of live entertainment that we longed for.

Ross in New Buffalo says, "I remember Jonathon Brandmeier on The Loop calling phone booths and prompting whoever answered to sing 'Stairway to Heaven' on the air to win a prize."

Casey Kasem's American Top 40 Countdown was a weekend morning staple and his long-distance dedications always tugged at our heartstrings. We'd hear, "And this song goes out to…," and we'd stop and listen, hoping it was us or someone we knew.

"I had an ex-boyfriend dedicate Bon Jovi's 'You Give Love a Bad Name' to me and put the lyrics on my locker," Amy in Dayton remembers. "He knew I loved Bon Jovi and we got back together after that."

Most radio stations had giveaways with some pretty rad incentives for being the correct caller. If we heard the song or song clip of the day and were, for example, caller number nine, bam! You won stuff. How many of us can relate to having magic dialing fingers and scoring some winnings? Over the decade, I had major wins with tickets to see Rick Springfield, Triumph, U2, the Jacksons' *Victory Tour* (with Michael Jackson), David Lee Roth, Poison, and Madonna. We didn't have social media to share these good fortunes; instead, we'd hit the RECORD/PLAY button on our cassette player while we were still on the phone with the DJ while he announced, "Becky Kliss, all the way from New Buffalo, Michigan, gets herself out to see the Jacksons this Saturday at Comiskey Park." Yes, I still have the 40-year-old proof on my mixtapes!

MIXTAPE PLAYLISTS

Making a mixtape back in the day was rigorous. Our radio or jam box and tape recorder had to be ready with a blank tape. Then we impatiently waited for the DJ to play what we wanted to record. Those who strategized knew any new song they wanted would be played in the weekly countdown hosted by Casey Kasem. Everyone loved Casey's raspy voice until they were trying to record a mix tape because Casey liked to talk over the music.

Michael in South Carolina recalls, "Blah, blah, blah, long-distance dedication… come on! What's the song? My fingers are getting tired!" But, when we heard the tune we wanted, we had to pounce, ambushing the PLAY and RECORD buttons at the same time. Then we had to tiptoe around because every itsy-bitsy sound within earshot from that moment on would be heard in our recording.

When listening back to what we'd just recorded, we'd hear an array of background noises: our mom yelling "dinner's ready!" or our own voice screaming at our little brother in the hallway "don't go in there, I'm recording!" or the dog barking, or worse, the phone ringing. The one that cracks me up the most is *the background sneeze*. And let's not forget the obnoxious radio static! Do the younger generations even know how excruciating that is when you're trying to record music?

If any of the above happened, we had to start over. Once we finally scored success with one song, the process started again. Depending on whether we purchased sixty, ninety, or one-hundred-twenty-minute blank tapes, sometimes a mixtape could take a week or more to finish. But the process *still* wasn't done. We needed to create a table of contents to know which songs were on which sides of which tapes of our heaping pile. How many of us remember the tape counters on the machine, those little rolling numbers to help us know where our song was on the tape?

Note to my BFF in junior high:

> Do you know something that makes me really mad? Well, I've been going through my tapes, and you know the little tablet with all the numbers and names of songs I made? Well, I discovered that when I got the numbers to the songs I still had my old tape recorder, so now, with my new one, the numbers turn faster, so I have to re-do every tape! And I have 58 sides! Well, at least it will keep me busy.

True story, right there.

God forbid we heard a song morph into a garbled mess while being devoured by the tape player. We'd dive across the room to hit STOP in hopes of saving the tape. If *Shark Tank* was a thing back in the '80s, the inventors of cassette "splicing kits" would have never heard "I'm out!" Those repair kits that spliced our treasured tapes back together were a staple item. If the tape was broken inside the cassette, we'd pry the cassette open with a screwdriver, hoping we could fix it. Ninety-nine percent of the time, it sadly ended up in the cassette graveyard.

DECODING SONG LYRICS

In the '80s, if we wanted to sing along to a song, we had to decipher the lyrics. We replayed the song we'd recorded, and then paused the tape after each verse to write down what we *thought* we heard. Then we had to memorize what we wrote so we could sing it when we heard it. *Got all that?* Not everything from the '80s was simple!

In a note in 1983 to my BFF, I wrote:

> Geez, their playing 'Africa' on the radio again-the third time this hour. That's OK, I need to learn the words anyway.

Learning lyrics was way more important than learning our possessive pronouns.

Lyrics sheets inside albums saved us hours of time. How many of us look back some twenty years later and realize how badly we butchered the lyrics of "Rock the Casbah" by singing "rock the cash box"? *OK, maybe that was just me.* Hopefully, I wasn't the only one singing "like a douche" when it was really "revved up like a deuce" in "Blinded by the Light." By the time we discovered our mistake, maybe we thought our original "like a douche" lyrics were better anyway, so why change them now?

In a famous *Friends* episode, when Phoebe sings "Tiny Dancer" by Elton John, she incorrectly sings "hold me closer, Tony Danza." I think we can all relate!

It could even be difficult to identify the title of a song sometimes back then, whereas today Google and Shazam reveal it in a matter of seconds.

PURCHASING MUSIC

Ask any Gen Xer what they remember about going to the record store, and they probably have a memory of buying concert tickets, sheet music, or getting a glimpse of MTV on a TV screen.

In the record store, MJ in Jacksonville bought an Iron Maiden patch to sew on his jean jacket and checked out the board behind the counter for the list of upcoming concerts. Keith in Austin flipped through the poster rack to see what was new. Can you still hear the clanking of the metal racks? I can!

JW in Michigan thumbed through the record albums and did the math to see if he had enough money to buy the two he wanted while still being able to afford Sbarro Pizza. Chris in Virginia admired the 3D display of Styx's "Mr. Roboto" and the cardboard standup of Billy Idol as he purchased Mötley Crüe's *Shout at the Devil* cassette. Lance in Tulsa browsed T-shirts featuring The Cars or The Doors and picked out ones to buy. Louis in Ohio checked out the cute chicks slurping on their Orange Julius in the store, while he took his time hunting down the *Theatre of Pain* cassette by Mötley Crüe. Chad in New Orleans scoped out the girls and had to bum $5 off his friend so he could buy a Metallica cassette.

I targeted the record store to collect radio station survey sheets, on printed colored paper with the top hits and albums of the week. The bonus was on the back, where we could find the lyrics of one song. That could put us in the "cool seat" and give us an edge at slumber party sing-alongs or those first concerts!

Shorty worked at Record Town for a year at Marquette Mall in Michigan City, Indiana. She says, "We were *always* busy. Some people just came to hang out and talk about all the new music coming out. The invention of the CD happened while I was there. The first CD I ever saw when we got our first shipment of them was Bon Jovi's *Slippery When Wet*. I got first dibs on the import albums when they came in from overseas."

Buying a cassette, record album, or a single was a milestone for us. However, when Columbia House and BMG music mail order catalogs entered our world, they were game changers. We could suddenly grow our collection by buying twelve cassettes for one penny. Their offer was exclusive—only one deal per person. No problem for Gen Xers; we just signed up everyone in the house. Next thing you know, your five-year-old brother was getting AC/DC cassettes, and your mother was getting Joan Jett ones. It's not like someone was coming to lock us up for committing underage piracy, right? Every penny scotch-taped to the order card and dropped in the mail generated some serious anticipation. It was like Christmas morning when the package of cassettes arrived. You couldn't rip the cellophane off each tape fast enough and listen to them all. It was all fun and games until we forgot to mail the damn card back, declining the next month's full-price shipment.

Today, we literally have endless music at our fingertips. Whether fee-driven or free, music sources such as Apple Music, Pandora, Sirius, Spotify, and even YouTube can be streamed to our devices in a nanosecond.

On the '80s Cruise in 2022, I saw the original MTV VJ Mark Goodman interview Morris Day. Morris talked about fans in the '80s, saying, "Before, you used to have to jump through hoops to be a fan. You had to wait on a record. You had to go to the record store. You had to buy the record and actually spend money. Now the access for fans is much greater, but it's not a loyal fan base like it was. There's no emotion to buying music."

Additionally, Morris feels that streaming music makes releasing a new album feel anticlimactic for many musicians. Fans now can just download the songs they want, and the musician gets a fraction of a penny.

I often wonder if kids today have a connection to their music and its meaning like we did. Like Karin and Jen, we wanted more options for our music and often went overboard to have access to it. Why was that? Isn't music that for every generation? What was different for us?

I believe there were three reasons music seemed so important to us: 1) we used music as a form of communication and therapy; 2) the variety made us crave more; and 3) music, including MTV, was a form of education.

MUSIC WAS OUR COMMUNICATION

Our music communicated to us. It was our therapy. Crappy mood? Problems at school or home? Music rejuvenated us. We were immersed in deciphering every song lyric and dissecting every word that spoke to us. It could lift us up and show us the path out of a twisted funk.

Ken in Virginia says, "My first concert was the Violent Femmes in a small venue. I listened to every word they sang. I watched each of the band members play their part and was entranced how they collaboratively put the song together. The lyrics said things to me that I couldn't think to say at the time."

Ken's feeling is universal to our generation. We associate so many things with our music that we can look back on it now with an array of emotions.

"DJ Christopher J played 'Headhunter' by Front 242 on the '80s Cruise," Penelope in San Jose says. "It had been nearly twenty years since I heard the song. I started crying from the flood of memories that came at me suddenly. I felt like I traveled in a time machine."

For some of us, music was a form of escape. Pat from Canada remembers, "Once upon a time, all we needed to be happy was a friend, a ghetto blaster, a frisbee, and a six-pack (or joint) while hanging out at the beach."

Our mixtapes were a true form of communication. Wikipedia confirms our beloved mixtapes started in the '80s as a part of our youth culture. They became expressions and compilations of things we wanted to say, and, often, we'd name the tape per our mood. Rough day? Put in your tape labeled "Easy Listening." In the mood for a boyfriend? Put in your "Slow Romantic Music" tape. Pissed off? The "Jive Talkin'" one it is. We'd put our heart and soul into creating mixtapes to gift our BFFs or our crushes by carefully crafting which songs had the lyrics that spoke the messages we wanted them to hear.

Bob C says, "Today it's simple to share an online music mix and give it to anyone and everyone—but when we made a mixtape, from the creation of handmade covers to the workarounds we used to record and sequence the music, it took a lot of effort and time—and time equals love."

VARIETY

The second main reason music was different for us was because of the sheer number of genres, one-hit wonders, and soundtracks at our disposal. We clearly had variety—no doubt about it. We rolled into the '80s riding on a '70s musical magic carpet ride.

If you ever decide to write a book about the '80s and ask for input to try to categorize all the main bands by genre, plan on literally banging your head against the wall. Here's my makeshift answer:

"AlternativerockBritpopClassicrockDanceEDMElectroElectronicdanceElectronicaFunkGlammetalGlampunkGothHairmetalHardrockHeavymetalHiphopHouseNewwavePopPoprockPostdiscoPunkRapR&BReggaeRockSoftrockSynthpopTechnoThrashmetal."

See my point? The '80s had some serious music diversity.

Kimberly in Texas says, "I was a hard rocker on the inside and a preppy on the outside—a music chameleon." Technology was driving innovation in the music industry with new sounds and more experimentation and turning many of us into music chameleons.

"I had a lot of influences when it came to music. I loved everything from AC/DC to Duran Duran to Neil Diamond," Jackie in Michigan reveals.

Think about the impact movie soundtracks and amazing one-hit wonders had on us. Iconic soundtracks like *The Breakfast Club, Dirty Dancing, Fast Times at Ridgemont High, Flashdance, Footloose, The Lost Boys, Pretty in Pink, Purple Rain, Rocky III, Say Anything, St. Elmo's Fire, Top Gun,* and *Vision Quest*. Or one-hit wonders like A-ha's "Take On Me," Soft Cell's "Tainted Love," Toni Basil's Oh "Mickey" (*sing it!*), or Nena's "99 Luftballons." The ironic thing is many of the musicians classified as one-hit wonders were still pretty darn good; they just didn't happen to have another chart-topping hit. In each of the Chapter Raptures, you'll find the top ten songs of the chapter, along with the link to *the Invincible '80s* Spotify playlists expanding on the variety of genres and soundtracks, including one-hit wonders.

A bonus for us was to see our musicians cross over into acting—or vice versa—like David Bowie (*Labyrinth*), Shawn Cassidy (*The Hardy Boys*), Madonna (*Desperately Seeking Susan*), and Eddie Murphy (*Saturday Night Live, Raw, Beverly Hills Cop*). And what female didn't want Dr. Noah Drake calling? Rick Springfield on *General Hospital* was a must-watch, and then his movie *Hard to Hold* stirred conversation when he boldly bared his little, naked butt on the big screen.

Prince and *Purple Rain* were beyond iconic. Kerrie in Minneapolis says, "My college club was First Avenue, which was Prince's club. Watching *Purple Rain* reminds me that for a while, I was truly *in* his world and was able to experience the town, his club, and dancing to his music in a way very few did."

MUSIC WAS OUR TEACHER - MTV

Sure, we watched shows with our parents like *The Lawrence Welk Show, Hee Haw, Donny & Marie, Barbara Mandrell & the Mandrell Sisters,* and *Sonny & Cher*. Then we advanced to shows like *American Bandstand, Dance Fever, Don*

Kirshner's Rock Concert, Saturday Night Live, Soul Train, and *Solid Gold.*

But what were we actually learning from those music shows? Maybe a few conventional, square dance moves or that you really should be singing with your little brother, like Marie Osmond, instead of beating him up all the time? Certainly not about '80s culture.

On August 1, 1981, the switch flipped. We blasted off with "T-minus 27 seconds" and headed straight to the moon with "Ladies and gentlemen, rock and roll." Truly epic. Our music literally came to life on a TV screen 24/7 with the debut of music television, *aka MTV.* Those of us who had cable TV can vouch for the impact of watching a blue screen, anxiously waiting for midnight, when MTV flickered on and off, then cranked out the first music video, "Video Killed the Radio Star" by The Buggles. The original MTV VJs were Nina Blackwood, Mark Goodman, Alan Hunter, J.J. Jackson, and Martha Quinn.

If we didn't have cable to watch MTV, we had to find someone else's house who had it so we could. MTV was undisputedly the most anticipated new cable channel of its era.

"I watched it the second it came on the air and was blown away," Kelly in Austin says. "It introduced me to so much music. The variety on MTV was amazing: *Headbangers Ball, 120 Minutes, Yo! MTV Raps, Flying Circus, Young Ones,* and *Kids in the Hall.* It was genius."

"I was in middle school and the next day, it was all we could talk about," Rob in North Carolina says. "I remember knowing on some level what we were seeing was something important."

Gen Xers say they learned more than just music from MTV: Men who wear makeup are hot, people can spin on the top of their heads, zombies are good dancers, what "she bops" were, and that "we're not gonna take it anymore." We could also see what our music looked like, from Men Without Hats to A Flock of Seagulls, Van Halen to Duran Duran, and Devo to The B-52s.

MTV continued playing for twenty-four hours a day, seven days a week for more than eighteen years. It drove us to express ourselves in new ways, especially with dance moves like the Moonwalk, the Snake, the Running Man, the Cabbage Patch dance, and the Chicken dance. (*Oh, wait, that last one was our parents' hand-me-down!*)

"*Thriller* itself is a masterpiece," Eric in Canada says. "When the full video came out, the whole family stayed up late to watch it. It was quite the event! Some friends and I watched the video over and over to learn the whole choreography and re-create it in my basement."

Videos influenced our clothing styles, too: Madonna and Cyndi Lauper's lacy tops and miniskirts, decorated with multiple belts and crosses, and their stacked rubber bracelets and bangles. Madonna made crop tops a fad—and it wasn't uncommon for the cute kid working at the record store to have A Flock of Seagulls hairstyle with flips and wings jetting off his head.

Thank God when *Friday Night Videos* aired in 1983 to finally let us non-cable subscribers in on the action one night a week. Yes, that's correct, *one* time per week only. And then on January 1, 1985, VH-1 aired and jumped on the music-video train as well.

By the mid-2000s, the endless music videos on MTV were relegated to only a few hours in the morning; by the mid-2010s, they stopped altogether and the channel was changed to reality TV. This left our generation in dismay. Three of the original MTV VJs, Mark, Alan, and Nina, are now DJs on Sirius XM, hosting *'80s on 8*. Martha is still in the business as well.

We also had events that rallied us CD-55ers. While we watched the Jerry Lewis' *MDA Labor Day Telethon* each year as we were growing up, it was events like *Do They Know It's Christmas* by Band Aid (11/29/84), *We Are the World* (3/7/85), *Live Aid* (7/13/85), and *Farm Aid* (9/22/85) that taught us there was more beyond the borders of our cities and towns.

In 1985, Dave from Texas was in Italy visiting family. He heard about this thing called *Live Aid* happening at Wembley Stadium in London. At twenty-two, he became obsessed with wanting to go, but none of his friends were biting, because it was too expensive to travel to London, and tickets were sold out.

Dave didn't have the money either or a ticket, but he loved U2 and was hellbent on seeing his favorite band. He set out by himself using the *Planes, Trains, and Automobiles* approach, only with a super-slow ferry instead of a jet plane. He left two days before the event, and it was a good thing because it took so long to get there; he arrived at the stadium only an hour before the first band started playing. He met people on the ferry also headed to Wembley who offered to let him leave his overnight bag at their apartment. He walked up to the stadium and within five minutes found a guy standing outside with an extra ticket for sale at face value (£52 GBP, or around $65 USD).

Looking back, Dave says, "I just kept saying to myself, 'I can't miss this.' I was so determined. I ended up being about thirty bodies from the stage and stayed there for ten hours. It was exhausting and hot and we were getting sprayed down by hoses. I could see Princess Diana and Prince Charles escorted into their seats in the stands to the right of me and talking to band members. U2 was awesome, but Freddy Mercury is who blew me away. He owned that stage. When he sang "Radio Ga Ga," there were 96,000 people in that stadium, and 95,999 of them were clapping to the song with Freddy from the moment it started. Yeah, I was the odd American man out there who didn't know when to clap or stomp, but I learned real quick; this was a communal moment in time and I picked up on the rhythm with the crowd. In fact, Freddie didn't just own the stage; he owned that entire audience."

Dave reflects on how he thought seeing U2 would be the most important thing for him but actually it wasn't. He says, "When you are young and in college you think you're bulletproof, there is a sense of innocence. Going to *Live Aid* taught me things about being morally correct. From the bands who were doing this for free to help people starving, to those in the front rows who weren't territorial and let me cut through the crowd to the front of the stage for free bottles of water, or the strangers I met who let me sleep on their couch. It was so moving. It really felt like we *are* the world."

This was what music did for us in the '80s. It moved us in ways we didn't even realize.

How have our music tastes changed as we've aged? Is this instant access to all the music diversity we'd ever want changing our norms?

Debbie in Virginia says, "I wanted to go see Rick Springfield and Richard Marx in 2017 play an acoustic show. I asked my husband Ken to go with me and his response was, 'They're all washed up.' Well, guess what? He went with me and became a fan."

Ken responds, "I tried to get out of the concert and go to the hockey game instead. Turns out that watching the concert with Rick and Richard swapping stories on what inspired them and singing each other's songs was actually enjoyable. The crazy thing is, it changed our lives. Rick Springfield was one of many artists playing the next year at an event called '80s in the Sand' in Cancun. Since my wife had won me over, we decided to try something new again. We ended up meeting people in Cancun at the event from all over the country and had a blast. The music diversity brought us together, and it's now an annual trip with friends we met there who are forever family to us."

Is it possible we can all still create our own versions of communal experiences through music? Ones that move us and enhance our lives? Ken and Debbie think so.

Whether we're lonely, healing a heartbreak, or lost in love, music can help us through every feeling.

My Aunt Boots, now ninety-three years old and still living on her own, says, "My music is my relaxation, my entertainment, my mood and spirit lifter, and it keeps me from being lonely." She connects with music by playing her piano. "When I play certain songs, it reminds me of particular people and I feel a connection to them, especially those no longer here."

"Music is made for us to move and dance to," my mom adds. "It's not just somebody talking fast." She loves to dance to polka and country music. When we were kids, she would play country music songs like "Luckenbach, Texas" by Waylon Jennings and "Mammas, Don't Let Your Babies Grow up to Be Cowboys" by Waylon Jennings and Willie Nelson. I put them on my playlist because they remind me of when I was little and of my mom.

Kristen in Minnesota jokes, "My husband and I played 'The Rubberband Man' by The Spinners to our nieces and nephews. The kids laughed and said, 'That song is ridiculous' and my husband and I laughed, too, because they were right. So many songs like 'It's Raining Men,' 'She Blinded Me with Science,' or 'Tarzan Boy' aren't any different. They don't make sense."

"My kids have some shit that makes my ears bleed," Terry, father to four boys, admits. "Some of the lyrics have either more hidden meaning or make no sense whatsoever. They just put stuff together that rhymes with zero message. Our music was more about love and relationships, and today it's more about drugs, guns, and banging each other."

How many public places do you walk into today and hear '80s music playing because it's still widely accepted? But then you look at today's music and shake your heads about our kids' hype or fandoms over such artists as Billie Eilish, BTS, Harry Styles, and Taylor Swift? Is it possible our parents said the same thing about us when we were obsessed with the *Thriller* dance, or wearing leg warmers and bodysuits trying to get "Physical" thanks to Olivia Newton-John, or wearing thirty bangle bracelets and lace, trying to be like the Material Girl?

Robert in Pennsylvania says, "The words don't need to always make sense to me; it's about how a song makes me feel. I like hearing 'Come On Eileen'—it makes me feel happy. I don't know what it means though." Whether it's '70s music, '80s music, or even country, it doesn't matter. Whatever resonates with you—and makes you feel good like Robert does—that's what really matters.

"The connection between the music and the fans who know every word, every note, and every personal feeling or memory attached to that particular piece of music is powerful," Amber in Oregon says. "I have songs that make me think of lost loved ones, former flames, when my children were born, when I was in Iraq, when I was little and a lost teenager growing up, when I worked in radio, when I lived with my dad, and songs that I danced to in my bedroom when no one was watching. Nearly every song I hear triggers a memory."

Whenever Jen and Karin reflect on their boom box, Delta 88, beach-cruising days and hear "Pour Some Sugar on Me," they still smile. Friends for almost forty-seven years, they laugh now about how cool they probably really *didn't* look while cruising the beach after all, and how smaller the boom box really is than they remembered. But the song still brings them a happy memory.

How much of your day do you spend listening to music? How does it make *you* feel? Does it give you some time to heal and reflect? Let music be your therapist, escape, or pick-me-up.

Create your own version of a *Live Aid* excursion and make music communal in your life—like we used to—the '80s way.

Chapter Rapture
Music is our therapy

Sixth Hour Bell

Music from the '80s is deeply tied to our emotions and memories. For some, it was an escape; for others, it was our map, with mixtapes serving as a true form of communication. The music of that decade moved us in ways we didn't even realize. Whether you're lonely, heartbroken, or lost in love, music has the power to guide you through every emotion. How much of your day is filled with music? How does it make you feel? Let it give you space to heal and reflect. Like David at *Live Aid* or Ken and Debbie at '80s in the Sand, be open to allowing music to be a communal part of your life

Extracurricular Activities

- Tune in to radio stations online from the town you grew up in or reminisce with *Casey Kasem's Top 40* on the Classic American Top 40 channel on the iHeart app—it's free!
- Dive into MTV's history with the original VJs book: *VJ: The Unplugged Adventures of MTV's First Wave*.
- Play your favorite '80s albums or soundtracks—especially the live versions. Alexa can handle it for you!
- Still have your mixtapes? Grab a cassette player on eBay and see what surprises they hold — yes, they even sell new ones!

After-School Specials

- The documentary *Sound City*, produced and directed by Dave Grohl, is a must-watch about music legends and what inspired them to record in California's Sound City studio.
- Whether you want to pull an all-nighter and experience the entire *Live Aid* concert or only watch certain artists perform, YouTube has a long list of live concerts.
- *We Are the World: The Story Behind the Song* and *The Greatest Night in Pop* documentaries are iconic to watch.
- Vintage episodes of our early music video experiences found on YouTube: MTV, *Friday Night Videos*, and VH1.

Passing Notes in Class

"Read *The Gospel According to Luke* by Steve Lukather, lead guitarist for Toto. It is one of the best books I've read about the 80s."

~Chandra in Georgia

"The Sunset Blvd area in L.A. has so much music history where many big music players started. Go see the Capitol Records building, The Roxy, The Whiskey a Go-Go, the Rainbow Bar and Grill, The Troubadour, The Viper Room. And Amoeba record store is one of the largest in the world."

~Bryan D in California

"My husband and I go on the 80s Cruises. Growing up I didn't have the chance to go to concerts. So I'm making up for lost time with the best music ever on the cruise!! I love meeting new people, dressing up, and decorating our cabin door. Everyone is so happy and the energy is fantastic."

~Carrie in Washington

Field Trips

- Explore and support a local record store, whether at home or while on vacation. Even if you don't have a record player, purchase a favorite album and frame it for wall art.
- Tour Prince's Paisley Park and First Avenue in Minneapolis for some epic '80s music history.
- Choose an iconic concert venue and plan a trip: Red Rocks, Hollywood Bowl, The Roxy, or The Rock & Roll Hall of Fame in Cleveland to name a few.

Chapter Mixtape

- "Turn Up the Radio" – Autograph
- "Juke Box Hero" – Foreigner
- "Radio Ga Ga" – Queen
- "I Wanna Rock" – Twisted Sister
- "We Got the Beat" – The Go-Go's
- "Pump Up the Volume" – M|A|R|R|S
- "I Love Rock 'n' Roll" – Joan Jett & the Blackhearts
- "For Those About to Rock (We Salute You)" – AC/DC
- "R.O.C.K. in the U.S.A." – John Cougar Mellencamp
- "(You Can Still) Rock in America" – Night Ranger

Shortcut to Spotify Playlist: beckykliss.com/CR05

section two

One Thing Leads to Another

Be Invincible with
Your Time and Choices

Chap. Six

Under Pressure

▬▬▬▬▬▬▬▬ 🖭 ▬▬▬▬▬▬▬▬

Time

> *"Life moves pretty fast. If you don't stop and look around once in a while, you could miss it."*
>
> ~ *Ferris Bueller*

My friend died last week. She was fifty-one. Pancreatic cancer—gone in seven months. It changed my perspective on this chapter. Time became something bigger than I had originally written about: It was more than our to-do lists, routines, structure, patience, and interruptions. Suddenly, those things didn't seem as important as the bigger picture of a life lost.

The chapter changed because my value of time changed.

How could someone so full of life like Chrissy—vibrant, healthy, and active—have her time cut to only fifty-one years? Shouldn't someone who lived a holistic, natural life and didn't abuse her body be living another thirty-plus years? It didn't make sense.

And sometimes it never will.

How many times do you look back at the end of your week and cringe because you didn't get to do all that you set out to accomplish? Do you find yourself saying, "There aren't enough hours in the day"? How often are you in a hurry and forget to actually enjoy the ride? *I plead guilty to all of the above.*

How many of us have had someone like Chrissy in our lives who is now gone? Maybe it's a parent, sibling, or friend? Did you wish you'd spent more time with them? I found myself thinking back to how many times she and her husband, Rob, invited me on their pontoon boat and I didn't go. What was I doing instead? Was it important?

Even more so, I wonder if we were in Chrissy's shoes, staring at our fate, what questions would we be pondering about our time?

We can't do everything. We can't be everywhere. We can't attend everything like we did in the '80s when we had only a handful of choices.

Kristen in Minnesota says, "Has our Gen X work ethic hurt us in our fifties?

Are we still trying to keep up when we shouldn't? How many of us have worked ourselves to death for 'more,' then ended up dead?" *Well, shit.*

"Don't wait until retirement to travel and do things you enjoy," Debbie O in Georgia recommends. "My dad was sixty-four when he died. He had only been retired for a few years. My mom and dad had all of these dreams their whole lives for when they retired. By the time my dad retired, he wasn't really able to do most of the things that they dreamed about."

So, where are we with our remaining days, CD-55ers? If we're lucky, we have maybe twenty-some summers left with hopefully decent mobility. Even the jelly bean video tells us there are only so many days left. What are we going to do with them?

Each of our days is made up of 86,400 seconds. It sounds like a lot, doesn't it? However, when you get up tomorrow morning, try to remember what you did with all of your 86,400 seconds the day before. Ask yourself, how many of them brought value to your life?

Norman Voss, bassist for Brett Michaels, wrote a song to his wife of twenty years titled, "Take Me Home." The lyrics read, in part:

> *I walked her home, said, 'Can I come inside?'*
>
> *and she said, 'Just for a second,' and I said, 'a second can last a lifetime.'*
>
> *So I went inside, and I sang her a song. Started getting the feeling it won't be long*
>
> *She says good things come to those who take their time, patience is a virtue*
>
> *to me, it's a crime*

Norman wrote these lyrics after reflecting on their first date and how "a second can last a lifetime."

And it's true; your life can change for the better in a second. But it can also end in that same amount of time.

So how do we get those 86,400 seconds to count each day?

For me, I'm learning that I have to pay attention to what consumes my seconds. Often, it's interruptions, because they break my flow, especially when I'm writing.

In fact, while working on this chapter originally, my phone went off repeatedly with texts. Here's what was coming at me in just a short time period:

- My BFF's dad is sick and headed to the hospital (*not good; stop, worry, and encourage her*)
- My brother is gloating that his CBD drink stock is up another 30 percent (*stop and kick yourself for not buying some when he told you about it*)
- My friend is looking for her water bottle and thinks she left it in my car (*okay, I'll get up in a minute and check*)
- Wayne is excited to tell me he's at Wrigley Field to see Lady Gaga in concert (*pause, call him names, and recover from FOMO*)
- Someone is sending me a video link to a new song titled, "Becky's So Hot" (*I'd like to ignore this one, but damn it, curiosity wins*)

The list above is an abbreviated version. It doesn't include texts confirming appointments, iPhone "like" and "love" text replies, Facebook messages, or actual phone calls—not to mention new email or social media notifications. They all have one thing in common: They are eating up my seconds.

Remember when we used to say to our parents, "I'm bored," as if we were dying? If only we could get all those seconds back.

As kids, many of our days were similar to the one I described in the prologue: wake up at 6:30 a.m. when the clock radio alarm goes off; attend school all day; arrive home around 3:45 p.m.; have a snack and watch *General Hospital* or the baseball game (go Cubs!); and do homework. We might ride our bikes, participate in neighborhood combat sports, or explore in the woods before family dinner at the kitchen table. Later that night, we'd talk on the phone, listen to the radio, play with Barbies or Pound Puppies, write in our diary, and go to bed.

"Imagination was key," Don in Raleigh says. "If we only had sticks, we'd dream something up. I remember spending an entire day with other kids having fun with those 99-cent inflated balls the grocery stores used to sell."

Robin adds, "When we were young, we spent our hours trying to fill our lives with discoveries. Everything was either an adventure or a chore; we had no (comparative) responsibility."

Here's a note I wrote to Robin in junior high:

> I think we should get together Wednesday and Thursday (and Friday so to speak) to study for exams, don't you think we should? Maybe I could come over Wednesday after school, then you come to my house Thursday after school (only 1/2 day). Then Friday, I'll get off the bus there (1/2 day again) and stay the night? Or, if our moms think it's too much, we'll forget about Wednesday and each of us study at home and then Thursday we'll study for science, and you can help me study for History and then - on second thought, I'm not studying for History. But I could help you study for Gym. Welp, write back and answer my questions and tell me what you think.
> Ok, Bye W/B   - Becky

We took an hour to plan how we would spend an hour! As kids, we had the time to calculate, think, process, and analyze.

Many of us now juggle five to ten conversations like this at a time. Are we choosing how to spend our time or are we on autopilot?

When I go on the '80s Cruise, I *love* the schedule packed full of events because I have options—but I also *hate* the schedule packed full of events. *Say what?* For seven days straight, there are umpteen choices of fun things to do every hour. At some point, you get tired and just want to go sit by the pool and do nothing or go to bed early and skip the late-night events. *And you can.* But this is a trip that comes only once a year, filled with people who look forward to it, invest their hard-earned money to go, and use their valuable vacation time. Being around CD-55ers with this level of energy, rallying like they were really back in the '80s, is mind-blowing. And just when you think you are going to poop out, someone says, "You can sleep when you're dead." That's when espresso martinis come into play *and you go*. It's about shenanigans, laughter, and time together with people you often see only once a year.

How would it feel like to drop everything, and just go?

When we look back, what are we going to wish we did more of? Going to bed early? Or staying out until 1 a.m. singing and dancing in the '80s disco with a room full of people who bring out the teenager in us again? Are we going to be glad we saved up all our vacation time like a pack rat or that we used every last day on traveling, fishing, going to the beach, or boating?

When we were teens, when someone asked us to do something, we most often went. Maybe it had something to do with the small number of choices we had—we were excited for the opportunity—*any* opportunity! Now, in the world we live in with fifty thousand things to choose from at any given time, it often feels like we are spread too thin. It's easy to be overwhelmed or even annoyed when someone presents us with yet another invitation or option.

My friends Shaun and Kris Robinson from Kalamazoo see their jelly beans differently. They say, "The most precious gift anyone can give you is their time. We love spending time with friends and family. We have a thing called 'Robinson Ready.' When someone calls us to do something, we adjust our day to Robinson Ready and we go. Moments with people are more valuable than almost anything we have to do at home."

There've been times when I haven't heard from Shaun and Kris in six months and they'll call up out of the blue and say, "Hey, let's go golfing today!" For those of us who like to live by an agenda, a typical response might be, "I'd love to, but sorry, I can't." But what if we view it as an opportunity rather than a hindrance? Isn't it really a blessing that someone wants to spend their precious time with us? Plans can be changed, adjusted, and rearranged. What if we just go?

Of course, there are only so many hours in the day and we have a long list of things to accomplish. But I don't remember feeling the pressure of not having enough hours in the day when I was younger. Was it a youth thing, or did our parents feel the same way we do now?

While my dad was working, my mom took care of the house by cooking, cleaning, sewing, mowing acres of lawn, and tending the garden. She sold decorated cakes, fruit, and veggies, canned what she grew, cleaned our church, and was the secretary on the Township Planning Commission. She looked after my brother and me and was always making home-cooked meals and desserts from scratch. If I wanted something in a can or a jar like Manwich or Mott's Applesauce, I'd have to go mooch them from my friends' houses.

My mom didn't have today's cutting-edge technology to keep her efficient, yet I don't remember her ever being frazzled about not getting things done. So, seriously, how did she do it?

"There was no reason to get stressed about work because if you didn't get it done in one day, it would always be waiting for you," my mom says.

When I was a junior in high school, my mom took a part-time job at the New Buffalo Public Library, and she *still* kept up with everything. How did our moms get more hours out of each day back then than we do now? Aren't we still pulling from the same 24 hours in a day? More importantly, are we capable of putting our heads on our pillows at night now with no timestamp stressors, like my mom did?

Here's the thing, though. My mom also says, "I was about fifty when I started thinking about time. Up 'til then, I did whatever I could accomplish in a day."

Is that where we CD-55ers are in life? That age where we start to shift and look at our time under a microscope versus running on autopilot? I suspect Chrissy's diagnosis forced her to look at life in a whole different way.

Sure, we all need downtime in this busy world to sit and read, build a puzzle, lay on our couch and veg out, unplug, check out, and relax. But are we thinking about it all wrong? When it's Memorial Day and you want to rest, but you have an opportunity to go sit at the American Legion with your 80-year-old dad and his old-timer friends, do you go? Or you're behind on lawn work and laundry, but have an opportunity to see your brother who you haven't seen in months, do you skip your chores and go? Or when your girlfriend, who you haven't seen in weeks, calls you up on a whim to go on her pontoon for a lake day, do you say "screw it" and dig out your bathing suit that doesn't fit anymore, *and go*?

You can always paint the fence, watch TV, or tend to your lawn. Are those the things you are going to be glad you spent more time on?

Choose those things that give you that true quality time with someone. For example, while I love going to the movies with my girlfriends, it doesn't necessarily give me the quality, heart-to-heart conversation and storytelling that sitting out on my deck drinking margaritas with them would. Go for those meaningful quality time moments.

And, yes, we all need downtime, but I say listen to your body, not necessarily your mind. Your mind talks you out of things that aren't in your comfort zone. Your mind wants you to take the easy route and stick with what you know and what's practical. Try getting out of your comfort zone. Listen to your body; it will tell you when it needs to rest. In the meantime, I say go.

During the COVID lockdowns in 2020, most of us had ample time on our hands, yet for many, it was a surreal setback in our lives. We emerged with bad habits, shitty routines, and mental roadblocks. Why is that? Were we simply left to our own devices, directionless, with too much time on our hands? Maybe. Or was it more that we weren't able to do the things that really mattered, like spend time with family, friends, and share love and laughter?

Kristen in Minnesota says, "The lockdown was a great reset for me. It was my first chance to slow down, take stock of my life, and pivot."

Many Gen Xers changed jobs during COVID, took an early retirement, or started to work from home. Some say they watch TV more now and go shopping in stores less. Sadly, many say that their health issues escalated, and their list of friends changed because of political differences.

Gen Xers were already in a challenging situation before COVID, though. We are a generation that has seen both sides: We know what life was like before the tech boom and now we're being forced to live in our technology-driven world and rely on screens to communicate and maneuver through our days. Technology that is designed to bring us efficiency—to save us from wasting seconds—also brings more interruptions. How do you think my mom's day would have differed if she juggled the technology and interruptions we do today? Maybe laying her head on her pillow would've been a whole different experience.

MY CHERRY PIE

The best analogy I heard regarding managing time is this: You're in charge of bringing a cherry pie to your parents' home for Thanksgiving. Your mom is counting on the *whole* cherry pie to serve the guests for dessert. On your drive there, you must stop for gas a few times. People see your delicious cherry pie and ask for a piece. You cave in and hand out a piece here and there because you're a nice, helpful, caring person who believes in sharing. But then, guess what? You show up with only a small portion of the pie left, and your mother is disappointed. Even more so, you are upset with yourself.

Why would you give up pieces of something already allocated?

That cherry pie *is* your day. The pieces of pie are your time. You have to know your nonnegotiables each morning. If someone asks for your time and there are no pieces available, you have your answer: "Sorry, my day is already spoken for," or, "No, I'm sorry. I can't." If you give away your pie pieces, you may later feel regret or anger. And, let's be clear, I'm not talking about the "Robinson Ready" things. Those are not cherry pie thieves; *those are opportunities.*

Time is the most precious thing we have. Yet Gen Xers say cell phones and social media accounts are their biggest time wasters. Resetting passwords and dealing with automated phone systems are huge, too. Scrolling—whether "doom scrolling" or paging through Netflix for an hour trying to figure out what to watch—eats up thousands of our precious seconds each day. Aren't these all things within our control—other than the damn automated phone systems and resetting passwords?

"Phones have become people's obsession. It's freaking crazy," Krysti in Colombus says.

Eddie in New Jersey agrees. "If I had no job and no friends, my phone could keep me busy all day. Games, eBay, Amazon, Google, TikTok, Netflix, chats, texts, Instagram, Facebook, fantasy football, sports news, etc."

Really, isn't our E.T. kind of like a cherry pie thief? We need to put our Inspector Gadget hat on and go to work to stop these invasive interruptions and time wasters. Turn off idiotic notifications, unsubscribe from unimportant or bogus emails, and avoid endless social media scrolling. Stop these "time crimes" and cherish those seconds!

We're already looking back and asking ourselves, "Where did our time go?" Don't let the answer be, "Toward stupid shit."

Before you say "yes" to putting anything on your schedule ask, "Would Becky's mom have put this on her schedule?" Okay, that may be corny, but stay with me. Mothers know there's a cost that comes with everything. Their job is to protect and keep their kids and family on track, so why shouldn't we? It's almost like reviewing what your return on investment (**ROI**) is if you are trading your time for something else.

"'No' is a complete sentence," Kim in New York says.

Can you tell people "no" if they need or want something from you without feeling the need to give them reasons or excuses?

Wait a minute. I know I told you to "just go" and now I'm telling you to "just say no." So which is it? It really comes down to what others want from you versus what you want for yourself.

The Facebook page *Sister, I Am with You* had a post that said, "Protect your peace. Boundaries are not selfish. You cannot be all things to all people or do it all. Don't let that inner voice make you feel guilty. This is not about them, it's about *you*."

Before agreeing to give your time to something, ask yourself:

- Will it add stress to me or my family?
- Does it bring value to my life or a loved one's life?
- Does it support the values you listed in Chapter 2?

Having clear boundaries (of what you allow into your time and space) with a mix of spontaneity is *número uno*.

The other day, my mom said, "I make my trips count now." I believe this needs to be our mentality, too—to make our trips count.

When we look at someone who's passed away well before their time—like Chrissy—it can be deflating. The minister at her funeral spoke of how many people told him that simply knowing Chrissy, and seeing how giving she was, made them a better person.

Don't we all want to leave a legacy like that? One where people remember us because we made them a better person? I believe we get that by giving our time to those who are important to us. Giving can be so rewarding.

Debbie in Ohio says, "My late husband taught me that no matter how angry or frustrated you are, never leave the house without saying 'have a good day' and 'I love you.' I didn't one day, and I've lived with that guilt for over seven years now."

Many people battling a health crisis like Chrissy use CaringBridge as a site to communicate and journal. Chrissy mentioned on her page while she was sick how excited she was to have her three kids and new grandbaby all together at one point. Two months before she passed, she wrote, "I am happy to say I feel pretty darn good!! With the weather today, I was able to go barefooted on a walk around the yard and get some sunshine!! I was also able to do six minutes on the stationary bike, I vacuumed, and I pulled weeds for a while!!!" Chrissy's valuable seconds were important to her and she spent them with family, visits from friends, and in nature.

Look for those opportunities to revert back to that "just go" attitude when we were analog kids. Try the Robinson Ready approach. Commit to spending as many of your 86,400 seconds a day being engrossed in things that make you feel alive, energetic, and full of love—especially time with others. And, yes, it could be as simple as walking barefoot in the grass or sitting outside and letting the rays of sunshine warm your face.

At Chrissy's luncheon after her celebration of life, we all ended up in a euchre tournament (for you non-northerners, it's a card game like spades). We were belly laughing and razzing each other's sarcastic remarks, misdeals, lack of skill (*or luck*), and *un*allowed table talk. An outsider looking in would've never guessed it was a funeral gathering if not for the flower arrangements. We were spending our seconds enjoying life.

At one point, Chrissy's sister laughed, and my friend Jan turned to me and said, "Chrissy would've loved this."

Years ago, Chrissy told her husband Rob that she planned to live to 100. Rob says now, "I wouldn't have guessed any different. She was the epitome of someone who *should* live to be 100." Her spontaneous nature was similar to Robinson Ready—she loved the outdoors, staying active, and being around people. She flourished when she was helping others and those qualities enriched Chrissy's life.

Your time is not infinite. Let the Chrissys of the world remind us of that.

> Rob,
> Hi-a I'm bored! Jamie's in the testing room so I have no one to talk to but you. This note will be messy I can tell already. I sure hope I can ride your bus home. If I can't then I will be very mad!!! Boy am I bored & And tired And on top of that I have a head Ache~~ oooooooooooooh What should I talk About? I'm going to try And talk those guys into playing Football Sat. or Sun. Who knows? It's now 11:05 on this April 14th 1981 I just did that for history I'm hungry! oooooooooh well I think I will stop writing I'll just sit here and day dream I'm writing with my eyes closed right now Not mad eh? Rocks

**Taking wasting time and boredom
to a whole new level in class
in Junior High in the '80s.**

Chapter Rapture 06
Find joy in the now
(aka protect your cherry pie)

Sixth Hour Bell

Remember when we had time as kids to discover, imagine, and create? We embraced spontaneity with a "just go" mindset, like the "Robinson Ready" approach. While we have 86,400 seconds each day, only about 21,000 are truly yours after life's essentials—make them count. You can't do it all, and that's okay. Don't let guilt hold you back. Listen to your body; it knows when to rest, while your mind often talks you out of things that aren't in your comfort zone.

Before committing your time, ask: Will it add stress? Does it bring value to my life? Does it align with my core values? Set clear boundaries but allow room for spontaneity to "just go" and spend time with the people who matter most.

Extracurricular Activities

- Practice meditation or mindfulness: Take a few minutes each day to focus on your breath and clear your mind, finding peace in the simplicity of the present moment.

- Buy a vintage Swatch Watch and embrace the nostalgia of the '80s by going analog occasionally—timekeeping with style and tranquility!

- Read *A Wrinkle in Time* and escape to a world where good triumphs over evil, revisiting a classic from our youth that reminds us of the power of love and courage.

After-School Specials

- *Steel Magnolias*: It will make you laugh and cry, celebrating the importance of friendship and cherishing time spent with loved ones.

- *Time Bandits*: A whimsical adventure through time, which shows how the moments we experience, no matter how fantastical, shape who we are and what we value.

- *Groundhog Day*: Let Bill Murray remind you to make the most of your time and to appreciate life's second chances.

- Listening to podcasts offers a great alternative to traditional media. Check out *Stuck in the '80s* (sit80s.com) for over seven hundred episodes spanning over twenty years of CD-55 favorites.

Passing Notes in Class

"We took a trip to Midway, Utah, to explore and found an amazing place to have a cheese lunch made from a local creamery in the freakin' mountains! Then we came up on a hot spring in a grotto; what the heck? My only regret in this life is the time I wasted doing nothing. Time is precious—live the dream and be seriously grateful." ~Bev in Michigan

"Money has never held great importance to me. Over the years, I've made and spent tons of it, and I can always earn more. The one thing I can't make more of is TIME. In the end, what will matter most are the people I've cherished, the stories I've lived, the love I've experienced, and how much I've given back in return." ~ Bob C in New York

"I love fishing or hunting. Even if the fish aren't biting or a shooter buck doesn't come into range, I'm still outside listening to nature and watching the animals taking in the sunrise and sunsets alone with no deadlines."
~Matt K in New Buffalo

Field Trips

- Attend your next class reunion or gathering, even if you're hesitant, just go! You might be surprised at how much you have in common with former classmates, even those you weren't close to, beyond just a shared hometown.
- Book a trip to experience a part of nature where time seems to stand still. Consider visiting Joshua Tree National Park (synonymous with U2's album *The Joshua Tree*), the redwood forests of California, or Grand Canyon National Park, and so many more.

Chapter Mixtape

- "Under Pressure" – Queen and David Bowie
- "Urgent" – Foreigner
- "Too Much Time on My Hands" – Styx
- "The Waiting" – Tom Petty and the Heartbreakers
- "Time After Time" – Cyndi Lauper
- "Heat of the Moment" – Asia
- "Time (Clock of the Heart)" – Culture Club
- "Patience" – Guns N' Roses
- "Lovin' Every Minute of It" – Loverboy
- "Right Now" – Van Halen

Shortcut to Spotify Playlist: beckykliss.com/CR06

Chap. Seven

Should I Stay or Should I Go

Choices

"This is the card I was dealt [a reference to Type 1 diabetes] and rather than become a victim to it and have self-pity, I chose to take the path of being spiritually and mentally positive."

~Bret Michaels

On most weekends, Robin and I were finagling sleepovers at one of our houses. If we stayed at her house on Bell Avenue, we'd have the full Atari setup, cable TV, and premium snacks, like Doritos and Dr. Pepper. If we stayed at my house on Maudlin Road, we'd play pool and air hockey in the basement and devour homemade popcorn and baked treats.

On this particular fall Friday night in 1983, we decided to stay at Robin's. While we were hanging out in my BFF's room ruminating over the older boys we were crazy about, a couple of them were out on the town making a choice that would almost cost them their lives.

The New Buffalo High School football game finished around 9 p.m. and a few teens headed to Buon Pronzo Pizza to start the night. Like in most small towns, there was a teenage hangout, and in NB it was the beach parking lot. After pizza, Tony, one of the players, split from his friends and headed to the beach; within minutes, Jim, an underclassman, showed up in his blue and white Chevy 4x4 truck with eight local friends on their way to go four-wheeling.

Eight turned to nine as Tony jumped in the back of Jim's truck and headed out with the others, including Perry and Bob D, who were also football players. After tearing up the hills, the crew headed back to the only gas station in town, ARCO. The local police officer on duty pulled in as well.

Since New Buffalo was a small town, almost everyone knew each other, including the officer and the boys. It was after midnight and past the curfew for minors. The nine local boys weren't causing trouble and didn't appear intoxicated—except for Todd, who remembers the officer ordering him out of the truck and instructing him to hoof it a few blocks home. The boys were told to call it a night as well, but they had no intention of doing so, especially since they hadn't finished all the beer hidden in the back of the truck. And with that, the Great Eight pulled out of ARCO in Jim's truck and headed out of town to a new spot to raise some hell in the fields.

Within five minutes, there would be a 911 dispatch call that we can only assume would haunt the officer and those involved for years.

The Great Eight turned on Maudlin Road. It was 12:25 a.m.

Jim had the gas pedal floored on the dark country road. There were three in the cab and five in the back. Tony and two others were standing up, holding on to the roll bar on top of the cab, while two sat in the bed of the truck.

All of them were familiar with the S-curve dip on Maudlin, but they were approaching it too quickly. The three standing in the back began pounding on the top of the cab and yelling at Jim to slow down; they knew the sharp curve was coming and could see the speedometer.

It was pegged at 80 mph.

Tony remembers looking at his friend helplessly and yelling, "It's been nice knowing you!"

As they came up from the dip around the sharp curve, Jim lost control of the truck. He tried to recover, but overcorrected. The truck went sideways, and two tires blew; the vehicle went airborne with a fury and pitched into a roll. Everyone in the back of the truck disappeared into the dark. Tony was launched into the air and braced for impact. He hit the road and slid down the asphalt, hearing a *whoosh whoosh* sound as the brake lights flew overhead. The truck landed in front of him, rolled three times, and came to a steaming stop in front of the Kliss home.

It was 12:30 a.m.

My parents were not strangers to tires screeching and metal crashing in front of their house—this S-curve dip was a common place for accidents. My mom would call 911 while my dad threw on his volunteer fireman coat and boots, grabbed the flashlight, and ran out to assist the accident victims.

This time was different, though. The three boys inside the truck cab, despite not wearing seat belts, were crawling out the passenger door pointed up in the air, bruised and cut up but not severely hurt. But when one of the older boys, Bubba, walked out of the dark holding his injured arm in shock and said, "Holy shit, we have to find the others!" that's when my dad knew it was bad.

The officer who just watched the teens pull out of ARCO was first on the scene. Witnesses say he appeared mortified by the dire state of the eight boys. It had only been ten minutes since he'd seen them.

Tony remembers him yelling, "Why didn't you guys just go home?" A few of the boys were frantic, trying to find the others as emergency crews began showing up.

Many of the eight were facing life-altering injuries.

Of the football players, Bob D was found unconscious with a severe head injury. He remained in a coma for three days with swelling on the brain. The paramedic who helped Perry knew him but didn't recognize him because his face was so marred. He needed three plastic surgeries to rebuild his face. Tony had a puncture wound seven inches long in his left side and severe road rash; his white painter's pants and Members Only jacket were bloody and ground into his skin along with gravel. His injuries would put him out for the remainder of the football season. The rest of the boys had severe bruises, lacerations, and cracked ribs that required stitches, neck braces, or crutches. All miraculously survived.

Tony remembers lying in the ER in shock when his dad walked in. "It's the first time I've ever seen fear on his face. I realized how I let my parents down. All I could say was, 'Dad, I'm so sorry.'"

Our choices in life shape us and make us who we are, especially the ones that come with the hard lessons. How many of us have made decisions we've regretted? Most of us have that story we look back on and say, "I can't believe I'm still here."

Let's face it, back then most of us didn't have twenty options on Friday nights, so we latched on to one of the few choices in front of us based on what our friends were doing. It was often about *who* was going far more than *what* you were going to do.

And we all know substances influence our decisions. It's better to avoid any decision-making when we are stuck in an emotion, or when we're under the influence and our judgment is clouded. There's a meme on the internet that says, "In alcohol's defense, I've done some pretty dumb shit while completely sober, too." *Guilty with a long, sad list.*

Today, our choices are amplified. Google is like the Yellow Pages on steroids. Want to buy a bean bag chair? You have six pages of options. Want to lose weight? Prepare to scroll until your index finger is numb. Want to search for the best places to vacation? You'll need to take a vacation to have enough time to sift through them all!

We have more options and solutions than we have needs and problems for. We receive suggestions for what we might like, event invitations, friend requests, and advertisements in our news feeds on social media. Email isn't much better—just the other day I started getting daily emails from both Bed Bath & Beyond and Victoria's Secret, and I can't think of one thing I clicked on or did to bring this on. *Stop invading my seconds!* Amazon alone gives us nearly endless shopping choices. Is there any category today where we *don't* have more choices than in the '80s? *I can't think of one.*

What are the ramifications of this change?

Today, I hear more Gen Xers saying how they don't want to be around people. Why is that? Aren't we used to interacting with people face-to-face, like we did when we were growing up? Is it because we interact with people constantly online and on our E.T., and we feel overwhelmed before even leaving the house? The other morning, I woke up and electronically conversed with more than fifteen people before I even hopped out of bed—talk about choices!

The days of being a child and making decisions based on "eeny, meeny, miny, moe" are long gone. We need like a thousand more *meenies* and a zillion more *moes* now.

More options require us to process more information. It takes far more brain power to choose what we want or need while trying to sift and sort through it all.

So how the hell do we maneuver through this process efficiently with minimal stress?

A lot of it goes back to the previous chapters on time and values. We have to look inward to find what's important. The days of our parents teaching us to make wise decisions by saying, "If Johnny jumped off a bridge, would you jump, too?" are long gone. Is the internet now our main source of peer pressure instead of the couple of bullies in your class in the '80s? If so, we know falling prey to it is not the answer—but it's there all the time. It never goes away.

Advertisers have more avenues to influence us with pop-up ads, email blasts, and telemarketing calls to our E.T.s. Everyone wants us to buy their product or service. They are pushing electronic ads using tailored algorithms. An article titled "Finding Brand Success in the Digital World" by Jon Simpson (*Forbes Magazine*) states that digital marketing experts estimate most Americans are exposed to between four to ten thousand ads each day—and that was in August of 2017!

When I was younger, my mom made cakes and Christmas tree ornaments to sell, but never once did she advertise. People flocked to buy from her in person because of the rave reviews they heard about her homemade goods. Word of mouth was her advertising. It wasn't about reading online reviews with critiques, thumbs-ups, or thumbs-downs. Now, people shop through apps such as Etsy, eBay, and Facebook Marketplace, only to experience *more* pop-up ads offering us similar items, continuously attempting to keep us sucked in. Yes, more options, better prices, and opportunities to find what we're looking for are good but think about the additional amount of information we have to process because of it.

"Never have we had so much information with so little wisdom," Dominic in California says.

The pressure to make the right decision can be overwhelming.

So, how do we get back to Friday nights in the '80s with fewer options?

Note to my BFF: Circle one. Do you want to spend the night Fri. to Sat. or Sat. to Sun.?

BFF circles "Sat. to Sun." and writes back: Because we can watch Saturday Night Live.

To BFF: Or we could watch Dracula movies on channel 32. P.S. I have a TV in my room.

Think of how simple that was compared to trying to decide what to watch on TV now!

"Fewer choices really end up giving us more freedom," Kristen in Minnesota says. "There's a reason why Aldi grocery stores are so popular—they offer fewer products to choose from and have a smaller footprint." Kind of like having only six TV channels again, *right?*

Kristen describes it as "decision fatigue." Could this be why so many people (like me) have attention-deficit/hyperactivity disorder (ADHD)? Do you have difficulty managing time, are easily distracted, and struggle with focusing more than you used to? Yeah, we are getting older—"man-o-pausal" and menopausal—but not *that* old and batty. I can almost guarantee you the '80s were *not* contributing to our ADHD symptoms like modern times. I think it's very likely it has to do with the number of choices and amount of information we process daily, available 24/7.

PROCRASTINATION AND FEAR-BASED DECISIONS

A therapist once told me that the definition of stress is *knowing* you have to do something *but not doing it*. I think that nails it. How often do you procrastinate when making a decision? Are you more stressed the longer you are in limbo?

"It took me a couple years to work up the confidence to get my CDL license to drive a school bus," Betsy in Massachusetts says. "I was worried if I could actually drive it and handle the kids, because I'm a quiet and shy person. The driving wasn't bad, but the kids were *very* challenging. At forty-three, I had to learn skills I never thought I could do! Now, I can't imagine doing anything else."

Many Gen Xers have shared in Facebook groups that they've made great choices, whether it was quitting smoking, getting married, having kids, moving to a quieter area, getting their first tattoo, or getting divorced.

But most of these decisions don't feel good at the time. Why? Because they may be out of your comfort zone. Maybe they disappoint someone else. Maybe you make a choice your friends don't approve of, or you're being lectured by your mother, who *still* doesn't think you should've gotten that tattoo. Maybe you're staying in a bad relationship for the wrong reasons, or you're disciplining your kids for something they don't agree with. Or you're bowing out from a night of four-wheeling. I'm sure the list goes on for you. The unhealthiest choices are the ones that disappoint *yourself*. Ones that you regret you didn't make sooner because you were worried about all the what-ifs.

Making a decision can be scary. No one ever *wants* to regret a decision. Holding onto regret festers and the next thing you know it steals your inner peace and consumes your thoughts. If your personal boundaries cave out of obligation—or as an attempt to avoid disappointing someone—you've made a decision for the wrong reasons.

In my late twenties, I was hired by a property manager, Mike, to clean two small offices in the evening after working a full-time job in accounting. As we became friends, Mike was always egging me on to quit my office job and start a cleaning business. I kicked it around but was too worried about all that could go wrong. Besides, I already had *two* other jobs.

One day, I ran into Mike and his friend (also named Mike) at a restaurant. They told me they were going to start their own cleaning business if I didn't. Adult peer pressure at its finest. To this day, I'm not sure if they were joking, but what I can tell you is that I went home and made the decision to get my ass in gear, leave my job, and pursue my cleaning business as a career.

I remember calling my mom at twenty-eight years old to tell her I was quitting my full-time job with health insurance and benefits to start my own business. My mom is a pretty practical person, and her concerns flew as she tried to make me reconsider. I remember panicking because of all the what-ifs she planted. Was she right? Of course she was! She is my mother! I could fall and break my leg while cleaning a toilet and have no health insurance; I'd have to pass up trips (with her) now that I'd have to work all the time with no paid vacation; and on and on.

The decision felt scary and wrong. *But it also felt exciting and right.* Sometimes it takes a nudge, a push, or encouragement, or even a well-meaning threat from a Mike and Mike—or scare tactics from your mother—to give someone enough confidence or fear to make a decision. Because most Gen Xers were left to their own devices and are clever self-starters, many of us pushed through adversity even when we lacked confidence.

Unless a teacher, coach, principal, or parent was in our Gen X face asking something or reprimanding us, we didn't need to make instant decisions often. We could process, concentrate, and decide by listening to our internal compass and intuition. We may have lacked wisdom and made some boneheaded moves, but in most cases, we had the time to think it through if we chose to.

Think about all the things in life that we have no say in now, such as changes in our health or loss of a loved one. As time goes by, we're going to be faced with some really tough decisions. Do we take that trip out of the country, knowing our parents are not in good health? Do we take the prescribed pills or embrace the holistic approach when we get sick? Do we retire early from a job we are tired of, knowing we have bills to pay? Do we go through the trouble of selling our homes and downsizing?

We all look through the lens of our experience to make good decisions, but the truth is, it's a crapshoot. Many of us have friends or relatives who didn't fare well because of a decision they made. Maybe they are like the Great Eight and got into a vehicle accident, but didn't survive. People not directly involved in an accident like that can be affected, too. If family or friends believe they could have prevented the tragedy, they might dwell on what they could have said or done to change the outcome. They might even feel guilt or regret for the rest of their lives.

Some words of advice: "Stop 'shoulding on' yourself." This is a concept introduced by psychologist Clayton Barbeau. After I heard about it from Mike Gathright of Storyline Church, I was blown away. I realized I'd subconsciously say, "I should have…" to myself many times a day. Remember, we want to be like my mom, Bonnie, and put our head on the pillow at night at peace with our choices, and we can't do that if we are "shoulding on" ourselves.

The internet exposes our character and leaves our reputation vulnerable. The ramifications of our words and choices can come back to bite us, far quicker than any decision we made in the '80s. If Jim's truck rollover accident happened now, news of it would have spread on social media a hundred-fold. Back then, it was just on the local news. Today, there would be judging in droves and heftier legal consequences, possibly with jail time or suspended licenses for alcohol use. Younger generations are shocked that people drove intoxicated as much as we did in the '80s. All they've ever known is Lyft or Uber. They have more choices now, and in this case, it's a good thing.

The eight teenagers never reunited to talk about the accident. Instead, they each looked inward and processed it differently.

"I never blamed Jim for the accident. We all made the decision to jump in the truck," Perry says.

"When we were banging on the hood of Jim's truck to get him to slow down, he probably thought we were hooting and hollering to go faster," Bubba says. "I learned not to hang out with people I don't know well or trust."

"Indeed, I felt I dodged a bullet," says Todd, who was sent home walking from ARCO that night. "The officer told us all to go home, and I know he felt awful because that's not what happened with everyone else."

As for me, I didn't hear about the rollover from my parents until I arrived home late the next afternoon after staying the night at Robin's. At fifteen years old, I felt regret because I wasn't there to help the boys I swooned over at the time of the accident. I avoided spending the night at my BFF's house for months after that. I worried something might happen again and I wouldn't be there to help.

Regret is a tough pill to swallow. I asked Bubba, "Do you regret your choice of getting in the truck that night with the others?"

He didn't hesitate. "Absolutely not! It was just a bunch of buddies going out to raise hell on a Friday night—very typical. That's how we rolled."

That wasn't the answer I was expecting.

Bubba was in a traumatic accident where he could've died, and he *did not* regret going through it. *Why?* Maybe he understands the negative power of regret more than most. Maybe he believes that living life to the fullest—incorporating an '80s footloose and fancy-free attitude—is the best way to go. Could that be the difference between making a choice as a teen compared to as an adult? We didn't overthink things and often went on impulse.

When we were teens, Robin gave me a button that I wore on my school softball jacket and still have today. It says, "Obey that Impulse." Now looking at it, I realize that was a *life lesson*. To try new things, enjoy life, and don't overanalyze and overprocess things. "Just do it," as Nike would say.

But have we gone to the other extreme since our youth? Are we second-guessing, overanalyzing, and worrying about our choices more than we should? Is it because the choices are out of our comfort zone or are there too many of them? It's important to know the difference.

"It seems nowadays more people would rather blame others than themselves for their choices, while in the '80s we had no one to blame but ourselves," Brooke in Tucson adds.

When Tony and I talked about the accident, we both realized how each of our choices, while unrelated, created a different experience for each of us. How bad Tony felt about letting his dad down. How his dad looked at Tony as the "Golden Child," but how grateful and thankful his dad was that he didn't lose his son that night. As for me, if I had been there, I would've probably been traumatized, because playing the role of an ER nurse that night just because I had a crush on someone wouldn't have been at all like the glamorous job I envisioned.

The universe works in mysterious ways, and I was not meant to be there for a reason. But I always thought I should have been. I didn't know how to stop "shoulding on" myself.

Hopefully, most of us have healed from our traumas and can talk about them openly. The choices we made back then can't be changed. We learn the lesson and life goes on. It's so important to let go of everything else.

The cool thing is that, at this stage of our lives, our days of pining after the cute quarterback have evolved into Tony, Robin, and I all hanging out as friends.

But when I met with Tony, I did have to ask the inevitable question: "Did you ever have a clue back then that Robin or I had a crush on you?"

He looked at me with a half-smile. "Somewhat," he said.

Let those choices we made long ago *go*. Acknowledge that they've shaped who we are and brought us to where we are today. Now, it's time to focus on what truly matters—narrow down our options, make thoughtful decisions with a touch of spontaneity, and stop "shoulding on" ourselves with regrets.

A random poll page in Sept. 1982.
We spared no filters in our teens!

Chapter Rapture 07
Fewer choices, more freedom

Sixth Hour Bell

We've all made decisions we regret, and many of us have stories where we look back and think, "I can't believe I'm still here." Back then, we didn't have countless options on Friday nights, and we often chose based on who was going rather than what we were doing.

Instead of dwelling on what you "should have" done, focus on what truly matters. Stress often comes from procrastination and indecision. The worst choices are those that disappoint you. Trust your instincts, try new things, and enjoy life without overanalyzing. Recognize when you're second-guessing because something is outside your comfort zone or when you're overwhelmed by too many options. Remember, everything happens for a reason.

Talk about your traumas, give yourself grace, and let go of regrets.

Extracurricular Activities

- Gather your kids and play the board game *LIFE*. Relive the days when we thought making big life choices was as simple as a roll of the dice.

- Read *Stolen Focus: Why You Can't Pay Attention-and How to Think Deeply Again* by Johann Hari.

- Call up an old friend you used to chase adventure with and swap stories about those "I can't believe I'm still alive" moments and have a good laugh.

- Play *Mad Libs* with someone from a different generation and see how a single word choice can completely change a story!

Field Trips

- Go camping (or "glamping" for those who aren't into roughing it) where choices are minimal, and enjoy simple pleasures like hiking, animal watching, swimming, camping, telling stories, and roasting marshmallows over a campfire.

Passing Notes in Class

"Never have we had so much information with little wisdom."

~Dominic in California

"There are days I'm dog tired when I get off work, and I want to do nothing, but I push myself to walk the trails on my property. It reminds me it's a whole other world out there."

~Rennie in New Buffalo

"Solo journeys are awesome; almost everything is on your terms. Need to pee? Stop when you want. Feel like eating all the snacks? Munch away! Want to listen to obscure or cheesy music? Blast it as loud as you can!"

~Shelly in North Wales, U.K.

After-School Specials

- Rewatch *Back to the Future* to remind yourself of how the smallest choices can change your destiny.
- Get a good belly laugh with Carol Burnett and Harvey Korman in the classic episode where she analyzes the items he's buying as she rings them up on the prehistoric cash register. Search YouTube for *The Carol Burnett Show - Supermarket Checker*.

Chapter Mixtape

- "Should I Stay or Should I Go" – The Clash
- "Pressure" – Billy Joel
- "One Way or Another" – Blondie
- "It Can Happen" – Yes
- "Delirious" – Prince
- "Twist of Fate" – Olivia Newton-John
- "The Gambler" – Kenny Rogers
- "Freedom of Choice" – Devo
- "While You See a Chance" – Steve Winwood
- "Go" – Asia

Shortcut to Spotify Playlist: beckykliss.com/CR07

Chap. Eight

Private Eyes

Social Media

"If your joy is derived from what society thinks of you, you're always going to be disappointed."

~ Madonna

On a Michigan winter weekend in 1982 when we were fourteen, my BFF and I bundled up in our snowmobile suits and headed out to go sledding on the small hill behind the neighbor's house. The toboggan glided down the hill as smooth as silk. But that wasn't good enough. It wasn't giving us the thrill we were looking for, so we decided to "Gen X it up" and build a ramp out of snow. The toboggan went up over the ramp and down, barely leaving the ground. That was certainly not the kick we had hoped for—we had to escalate the plan. We ran home, filled buckets of water, dragged them across the field, and poured them over the ramp with no other thought than to "see what happens."

By then, we were cold and wet and decided to run home for a break, knowing my mom's protocol was to make us hot chocolate while we thawed out before heading back. During this process, Michigan's frigid temperatures proudly turned our ramp into a solid block of ice. Indisputably, we transformed that bright-orange toboggan into a missile as it blasted straight up to the moon, along with us, too. The amount of airtime we had before crashing down allowed us to dangle long enough for a round of charades.

And the stunts began.

We were dying of laughter at each other's grand performances, but it was killing us that we couldn't see ourselves. So, we ran back home, grabbed a third friend—Tami—and our little Kodak camera, and snapped pictures of each other with freezing, wet hands, impersonating anyone and anything in midair we could think of. That evening, as we recovered from multiple bruises and probably some frostbite, we shared our adventure with our parents, brother, and, of course, our diaries. A whopping five or six people knew about our adventure, and that was it.

Back in school on Monday, Robin and I tried explaining our daredevil acts to our handful of friends, but no one really got it. We waited *impatiently* over the next week for the film to be developed at New Buffalo Drugs. When we finally got our hands on the blurry, matte photos, they revealed just how silly we looked. I appeared like a dork, with my scarf flying between my legs as I struck a cow pose in mid-air. Robin looked like a pint-sized disco dancer in her snowsuit impersonating John Travolta. We had no clue *what* we really looked like until the pictures came back, but they showed our performance was better than any *Cannonball Run* jump. It was *our* invention, *our* creation, and we nailed it the totally classic, innovative FAFO '80s way.

We have the memory etched in our brains forever, but no more than ten people ever saw those pictures. As Gen Xers, we all did crazy stunts growing up, *but the world never heard about it.*

Social media changed that.

With almost 60 percent of the world on social media, there's nothing private about it. What goes in must come out, *right?* We post on social media platforms, and we get likes and comments. The comments can range from encouraging to deflating, frustrating to funny. It's a crapshoot.

However, in our most heart-wrenching and wonderful moments, isn't our first instinct to want to share our news?

Let's put our sledding adventure into a DeLorean, add a lightning bolt, and send it into the future of social media to ponder the outcome.

Sadly—and most likely—we would've *never* been playing outside in the first place. We would've been warm inside on our phones and computers. Let's not choose this lame scenario, though. Let's assume we took our E.T.s with us and posted our death ramp jump pictures on social media before we ever left the hill for home.

We could have gone viral—especially if we had added AC/DC's "Thunderstruck" or Ozzy's "Bark at the Moon" songs to our post. The world could've seen exactly what we were doing *before* we even arrived back home to tell our parents.

Our parents might have been bashed by comments or critiques for poor parenting because they let little Robin and Becky conduct such dangerous acts unattended.

A high number of likes and encouraging comments might've escalated our confidence and self-esteem to the point of changing our future career goals from being secretaries to, say, stuntwomen.

A low number of likes and comments calling us amateurs or stupid could've sucked our self-esteem into a vacuum of disappointment and embarrassment. These bad feelings of not measuring up to what the other kids were doing might stifle our creativity and cause us not to do anything like that again.

We probably would've spent hours on social media responding and interacting, with our homework and chores falling to the wayside. We'd overanalyze who liked it and who didn't and be disappointed if someone we wanted to impress *wasn't* or someone we wanted to respond *didn't*.

Weeks later, if we ran into people who mention seeing our stunt but haven't commented on it, we'd think, *really?* How should we interpret the fact that they're watching what we do on social media but haven't interacted with our post?

SELF-ESTEEM ON SOCIAL MEDIA

The pressures of social media can really mess with our mindset, whether we realize it or not.

I had a Gen X friend tell me when she posts something on Facebook, her goal is to get ten percent of her friends to like it; otherwise, she feels it isn't worthy. She's fifty-seven years old! Another friend watches how many people like his posts to gauge whether his post was successful. He's almost sixty. How do you measure the success of your posts? More importantly, *why* are you measuring the success of your posts?

Kerrie in Minneapolis says, "It seems people are in need of validation constantly. Influencers are rated on how many followers they have. They make a living off of being relevant. Seems more are gauging their self-worth on it. Social media has exposed both the harshest of tongues and thinnest of skins."

The social bashing and keyboard wars on social media can be far more dangerous than the ice ramp itself. How many of these people are your close friends who care about you and who are important in your life? If not, why should their response matter?

Mike Tyson said, "Social media made y'all way too comfortable with disrespecting people and not getting punched in the face for it." He makes a valid point, even if it's a tad strong. *Wait, isn't that how we used to settle things in the '80s?*

An amazing therapist I knew said, "Never give your opinion unless someone asks for it." Isn't social media the perfect place for people to share their unsolicited opinions to try to influence others? It's great when their comments are helpful, but when they're degrading, it can become detrimental. How many times have you walked away from your keyboard, only to find someone's comments or posts still eating at you? Facebook was designed to *connect* people. Instead, it can tear people apart, especially if you've been unfriended because of a difference of opinion.

I've had my share of observations and interactions on '80s and Gen X social media groups with people overstating their opinions and disagreeing with others. At first, I'd stew about it and want to interject, while trying to come up with a cocky response to put them in their place. I didn't realize the amount of energy that it sucked out of me until I changed my habits—returning hate for hate is never good for the soul. We can't fix these people or send them to the Mike Tyson get-punched-in-the-face school like we want to.

Now, if I feel the need to respond to a negative comment, sometimes I post a reply in the form of a meme back with something humorous and off-topic, then simply block that person. Clearing the negativity out of my life is a far healthier approach. Famous author and inspirational speaker Dale Carnegie has a rule: don't criticize, condemn, or complain. *Try it, Mikey. You might like it.* Compassion and kindness move mountains.

SOCIAL MEDIA BUSINESS MODEL

Today's most popular social media sites are Facebook, YouTube, Instagram, TikTok, Snapchat, Pinterest, Reddit, X (Twitter), and LinkedIn. LinkedIn, Myspace, AOL, and Facebook were the first, created in the early 2000s. Facebook and YouTube lead the pack with 2.9 and 2.5 *billion* monthly active users respectively. In May of 2023, *Forbes Magazine* reported that the social media advertising market is predicted to be at $247 billion by 2027. Digital internet companies are some of the richest in the world.

Netflix's documentary *The Social Dilemma* is an eye-opener worth watching. The documentary, directed by Jeff Orlowski, describes the disturbing effects of social media, especially on kids. It was based on interviews from former employees of social media companies.

In the film, Tristan Harris says that billions of social media users are influenced by a mere fifty designers—25 to 30-year-old guys in California, hired to craft these platforms. These engineers have a single goal: to keep us scrolling like a gambler addicted to a slot machine. Not only do the apps continually refresh, but they also push notifications, track what we look at, record what we click on, and log how long we linger. They learn our personality type, analyze our behavioral patterns, and even predict what emotions trigger us.

The Social Dilemma implies that the apps hack users' psychology, so we have thoughts we didn't intend to have; the software attempts to change behavior, influence choices, and manipulate thoughts. Above all, the goal is to get us to share what we see with everyone else to get even more people engaged.

As with any business, cash is king, and social media companies need a way to generate income. By building models that predict our actions and emotions, they can tailor their advertising to a specific individual, increasing the probability of success. In the film, they say, "If you are not paying for the product, then you *are* the product."

The documentary goes on to say that if everyone Googles the words "climate change," we won't receive the same answers because the search engine decides what it shows us based on where we live. If the software chooses to show us only what *it* decides is relevant, how do we know what's really true?

While my dentist, Anjana Gupta, was working on me, she shared she'd taken her staff from Smiles on Niles to a conference. When one of the conference speakers challenged the audience to delete their social media accounts on their phones, her staff looked at her and said, "You can't do it."

In retaliation, she said, "Oh, yeah? Watch me." And she deleted the apps on the spot.

My dentist admitted, "My house was cleaner, I played with my child more, and I even exercised. I couldn't believe how much more time I had and didn't realize it until I tried it. And, when I came back to social media, it wasn't the same—it seemed a bit more *stupid*."

Maybe we should all try this experiment for a few days and see how it impacts our lives.

Here's something easy to start with. Take a good look at your social media feed with different eyes. Pull up your news feed and look at the first ten items. Here are mine on Facebook:

- A friend of a friend is in Puerto Rico.
- A distant friend who is ill posted her daily "Life is Good" challenge with her grandkids.
- Happy Birthday posts to my niece's friend (who I haven't seen in more than ten years).
- A friend of a friend's wife updated her cover photo.
- A friend of a friend is looking for a renter for one of their homes.
- Another distant acquaintance had a birthday.

The rest of the posts were advertisements: suggestions to friend people I may know, an ad in bold saying "THE TIME IS NOW" to become an "artpreneur," suggested reels to watch, and an ad for a plant-based diet.

Forty percent of what showed up in my own news feed was advertisements. Of all my friends' posts, only one was of interest to me. That means I'm scrolling through 90 percent of my posts to find the 10 percent that adds value. *And none of it improved my life.*

What were the first ten posts that showed up in your news feed? How many did you have to scroll through to find the ones that added value to your life? As we said in Chapter 6, time is the most valuable resource you have. How many seconds do you really want to give to inconsequential items on social media?

I used to razz my mom for only having twenty-eight friends on Facebook *(yes, you read that number correctly)*. Why wasn't she accepting all those friend requests from people who knew her? *Come on, Mom!*

Perhaps the Silent Generation understands how to keep it simple better than most of us. My mom uses *one* social media platform to stay connected with *only* the people she is closest to, and that works for her.

Isn't that the primary benefit of social media, connecting with people who share our common interests? Ultimately, we just want to feel like we belong—we want to be around "our people," "our tribe," or "our peeps." How often does it shift to a form of gossip, though? The kind where we're looking to see what everyone else is doing and what we might be missing out on?

In the '80s, what did we really know about what was going on in everyone else's lives? Maybe we knew the regular happenings of twenty to thirty of our close family and friends, *at best*. I friended an acquaintance who's a young mom the other day, and I almost fell over when I saw she had twelve hundred friends! I am probably twenty years older than she is and I have fewer than one thousand friends. But those are the times we live in now. Social media gives us the ability to connect with anyone worldwide at any given moment without ever having to meet that person face-to-face.

Mike Gathright of Storyline Church says, "One of the primary reasons our young people have been convinced to use social media by, admittedly, the smartest and richest people in the world, is that they believe they can have a meaningful life on screen. Here's the truth. Nothing wonderful is ever going to happen to you on a screen that's driven by an algorithm."

Mike is no doubt right, but let's face it: We don't have an infinite amount of energy or time, and social media is convenient and even somewhat efficient—if used *wisely*.

"I prefer socializing online because I can disconnect when I want, and they disappear," Eric in Canada says.

Fiona Hayward in Florida is an administrator of the Facebook group "Generation X: Our World (Built by latchkeys and powered by sarcasm)." The group had one hundred members when she started moderating it at the beginning of 2022. Twenty months later, it had one hundred sixty-nine *thousand* members! It continues to grow by thousands of people each month. *We might need our algebra teacher for this one.*

Fiona says, "Our group discusses topics, shares funny memes, and experiences a shared nostalgia. Everyone uses it differently. Some are looking for validation, some for a community, and some are lonely hearts looking for a connection, but most are there for nostalgic reasons."

Scott Braunfeld, moderator of the group, chimes in. "People feel less alone by having others within our generation to talk to or joke with and share ideas. Some can be very supportive, or some very rude. It all depends." He goes on to say, "What blows me away the most is what a horrible, cheesy sense of humor many people have and how some don't understand the difference between sarcasm and cruelty. Because people know they won't be meeting or talking in person, it gives them the bravery to be as rude, cruel, and judgmental as possible without fear of retribution."

A different Facebook group, "70's & 80's Memory Lane," has roughly one hundred twenty thousand members. Todd Newell, one of the group's administrators, explains, "Our group's purpose is to take people back to a memorable time in their lives and give good vibes." He says, "I think the majority of the people in our group are looking for acceptance with things they have in common with others. We all like to be accepted."

Some of the biggest controversies in Facebook groups comes from political posts—and spark fights and verbal attacks—or from spammers who create bogus fake accounts. I can't tell you how many times I almost fell for enticing messages from Rick Springfield and Brad Gillis (of Night Ranger) saying they wanted to connect. *Yeah, right. Just a bunch of idiot imposters.*

What advice do Scott, Fiona, and Todd give to those on social media?

Scott says, "The positives of social media are the sense of community and not feeling alone. Overall, I think social media has made people numb to the real problems of the world. Remember, there is a live human being behind the name and profile picture you're interacting with."

"Don't take it so seriously and make conscious choices about what to engage with," Fiona says. "Ignore content and block people that you don't like. Take control of your own experience."

"Use social media to connect you with things you have in common with others. The camaraderie with the members can be a sense of community," Todd adds.

Fiona, Scott, and Todd are all Gen Xers who fell into their social media roles and spend hours reading and watching endless posts and comments each day. Their observations summarize that we all long for a sense of belonging, connection, and relationships, which is pretty telling. You know when you think "me, too" when you meet someone because you share favorite things or experiences? And you find yourself actually saying, "Me, too!" out loud, over and over again while you're getting to know them? *Yeah, that's what I'm talking about.*

Elisa in New York says, "For me, situations like being at a Knicks playoff game or on the '80s Cruise where you look around at the cheering fans, knowing you all share a deep love and connection with something, outweighs any differences you may have."

Gen Xers were raised to believe that "belonging" is about doing things in person with others. We weren't wired for a computer program to replace in-person interaction. Today, Gen Xers say some things that give them a sense of belonging are music, the Armed Forces, book clubs, playing trivia at a local brewery, powerlifting, coworkers, dance classes, being in a band, and "the camaraderie of fellow weed smokers."

However, a large percentage of our generation *is* using social media to fill a void and find these "me, toos" and a sense of belonging. Whether it be groups on topics that interest you like Gen X or '80s nostalgia, a Cheech & Chong weed group, a Tommy Shaw (Styx) fan page, a group on fostering animals, or our very own *The Invincible '80s* Facebook group. Whatever your interest is, ten bucks says there is a group somewhere on social media where you can find "your tribe."

It bears repeating: in all of our wonderful and heart-wrenching moments in life, our first instinct is to share—and, whether we like it or not, social media *is* the primary source for that now for the majority of the population.

Remember, social media accounts are just one gadget in your E.T.'s toolbox that brings you community, belonging, business, or entertainment. Anything you give your precious jelly beans to should give you some satisfaction or benefit in return, and *not* be a crutch or an escape.

∞∞∞∞∞∞∞∞∞∞∞∞∞∞∞∞∞∞∞∞∞∞∞∞

One thing can't be disputed: that winter day when Robin and I rocketed to another galaxy in that toboggan wasn't shared with all the important people in our lives, but it also wasn't skewed by the world's input. *Always treasure those days, Gen Xers.*

Put your social media kickstand down. Always *choose* what things you want to see, *not* what automatically pops up. Follow specific groups or people that interest you and unfollow, unfriend, and uninstall what doesn't add value. And, as always, be mindful of what notifications you are getting.

How much time do you want to spend on social media? We all know habitual scrolling can turn into hours each day. Your social media apps suck you in, and next thing you know, you're in it for over nine months. Recognize it and *PULL OUT* (yes, I meant to say that).

Use social media as a tool in your toolbox for connecting with the groups, pages, and people that you share commonalities with. It can give you a sense of belonging and a ton of relatable "me, toos." While those groups can add value to your life—remember, they will never replace the warmth and love you can get from a face-to-face connection. Seeing a smile or feeling a hug is something only another human can give you.

MAGNIFICIENT * SEVEN

P1
MAY 18
19

Goings on--

Happy birthday Mary from the Magnificient Seven paper people

Last week Mr. Kissmans summer recreation groups first meeting was not really a success, only thirty people showed up. Saturday he had another one at 6:a.m.

Hope you were there,? He needs our support, when possible to go.

Hope you had fun in L.A.C. last Wednesday Tim and Jeff, because we sure didn't miss

you HA. HA.*** *

WHOS IN THE NEWS?

This girl has black hair hazelish eyes, is five foot two weighs ninety two pounds her favorite color is yellow, her favorite subject is math, her favorite clothes is jeans her favorite food is mushroom pizza, and her favorite flower is a rose.

WHO IS THIS?

PUZZLE TIME

Presidents in the dough. name the presidents on the money

- a penny   the newest silver whole dollar
- a nickle   one dollar bill
- a quarter   a two dollar bill
- a ten dollar bill   ANS IN NEXT WEEKS NEWS PAPER
- a fifty dollar bill

Cheese cake

Class of "86"

WHATS HAPPENING FISHERMAN

The Coho and Chinook are out on the lake but they are skattered.

The perch should be biting soon.

If you have any news or if you've caught a fish and want to brag about it, just contact Sylvia M. or Monique C.

COMICS   Crazy Pea Nuts

Is it 2:00 aclock yet? no Why? Because at 2:00 I have a — Date with Skippy — and at 4:00 I have a date ... oh

Social media: 1981-style, pioneered
by two NBHS Class of '86 grads.

Page. two   MAY 18 19
LUNCH WITH HARRIET
****

Mon.	Tues	Wed	Thurs	Fri.
ravioli	Ham and cheese	Pizza burger	breaded veal	burrito
vegetables	shoestring potato	chips	potatoes	vegetables
garlic bread	vegetables	vegetable sticks	veg	cheese sticks
fruit & milk	fruit & milk	fruit & milk	fruit & milk	juice bar (milk)

DEAR ZIGGY

Dear ziggy I sit by this girl and i know she talks about me some of the time, and I really feel like poping her in the mouth, what should I do.
                                        Frustration.

Dear frustration . school is all most out so pop her in the mouth after school s out   Ziggy

Dear ziggy I have these too friends that use to be my best friends until one of them started telling lies about me what should i do.
                                        Just wondering

Dear Just. Ask your ex friend what made her start telling lies about , you,
                                                Ziggy.

Dear Ziggy There is a guy I like in High school but im only in Junior high , And every time I see him my heart does flips. What should i do?
                                        Hopelessly in love.

Dear hopeless   Next time you see him say hi , he may like you also. You'll never know if you don't try. Ziggy

Dear Fans please write more often I can't ans letters if i don't recieve any.

Jokes with jingle   ZIGGY   Joke with jingle.
How many people does it take to   What happens when a elephant sits on a chair?
pop popcorn . ans 6 people.   ANS. time to get a new chair.
one to hold the pan and five
to shake the stove.   ETCH - A-SKETCH
                                      THESE FIRST TWO WERE   this one
What has two heads and six legs?   DRAWN BY Kathy Shelby   drawn by
ans / a man on a horse.   sylvia mullen

What's green and floats
in the sea. ans / Moby pickle.

Dear frustration, Dear just wondering,
Dear hopelessly in love...
what's changed since then?

Chapter Rapture 08
Pull out

Sixth Hour Bell

As Gen Xers, we pulled crazy stunts growing up, but the world never heard about them. Social media changed that. With almost 60 percent of the world online, nothing is private anymore.

Choose what you want to see, not just what pops up. Are you scrolling through 90 percent of content to find the 10 percent that matters? Social media should foster a sense of belonging, not detract from it.

Ask yourself: What part of social media makes you feel connected and adds value? Curate your feed by unfollowing or muting accounts that don't align with your values. Use social media as a tool for growth and connection, and follow pages that offer education, insights, or hobbies you enjoy. Turn your feed into a meaningful resource and know when to pull out when it's not.

Extracurricular Activities

- Take a break from social media and uninstall your apps from your phone for one week. You'll never know the freedom and clarity it can bring until you try it.

- Curate your news feed once a day. Take the first ten posts you see and unfollow the ones that don't add value or relevance to your life. By doing this consistently, you can train your feed to show content that truly matters to you.

- Find your tribe on social media. Choose one or two topics you're passionate about and join groups to engage in meaningful discussions with like-minded individuals.

After-School Specials

- Explore the impact of *The Social Dilemma* documentary to understand the profound effects of social media on human behavior.

- Consider watching the A&E series *Digital Addiction* with younger people in your life to help them understand the potential risks and impacts of excessive screen time.

- Let Mr. Furley remind us that not everything we hear is true in this hilarious *Three's Company* clip: "Furley overhears Jack and Chrissy."

Passing Notes in Class

"How ironic to hear the song 'Don't Talk to Strangers' when I'm talking to 100 strangers right now on social media."
~Mark in West Virginia

"Social media is a starting point, like back in the day when you were browsing newspapers. I feel like people fail to realize that social media is a platform for personal opinions and can take you down a rabbit hole. No matter what the topic, you will find someone who agrees with you. Does it mean you're right? No. Does it mean you're wrong? Also no. All of this info out there to help people open their minds, yet it feels like it has done the opposite."
~Yvette in Arizona

"The only reason I'm on social media is because I'm an admin for a nonprofit veterans organization, and that's important to me."
~Brian in Tennessee

Field Trips

- Host a nostalgic show-and-tell night with friends or former classmates. Share your memorabilia, old photos, and yearbooks, and reach out to any old friends who come to mind you miss.
- Attend a music event or '80s concert, and use social media groups to organize a meet-up with fellow fans who share your love for the era.

Chapter Mixtape

- "Private Eyes" – Daryl Hall & John Oates
- "Rumors" – Club Nouveau
- "What's on Your Mind (Pure Energy)" – Information Society
- "Nasty" – Janet Jackson
- "Breakout" – Swing Out Sister
- "Overkill" – Men At Work
- "Only You Know and I Know" – Phil Collins
- "Words" – Missing Persons
- "Borderline" – Madonna
- "The Reflex" – Duran Duran

Shortcut to Spotify Playlist: beckykliss.com/CR08

Chap. Nine

Video Killed the Radio Star

Screens

"Something happened to me when I turned 50... I found myself not settling for things that made me unhappy... I only have a number of days left... I find myself more and more stopping in the middle of something and saying 'I'm not happy here, what is this? I don't feel good about this,' and I try to do something about it."

~ *Alan Alda*

Were you one of the three hundred and fifty million people who camped out in the living room with your family on November 21, 1980, waiting to find out which culprit pulled the trigger and shot J.R. Ewing? Did you ditch school early November 16, 1981, to watch Luke and Laura get married in Port Charles on *General Hospital*? If you did, you weren't alone. Thirty million people were captivated by the hour-long show, the highest-rated soap opera episode in American daytime television history. In 1983, were you part of the largest percentage of viewers in history to watch a single TV show—the last episode of *M*A*S*H*? The '80s were certainly iconic for some of the biggest TV viewings in history and we Gen Xers were right there, front row.

Tink says, "I always watched *M*A*S*H*. I considered myself a pretty tough dude back then, but I can remember the last episode when Hawkeye and B.J. said 'goodbye.' I was pretty sad, but I'll never admit if I shed a tear or not."

In the '80s, "screen time" consisted primarily of watching TV shows, movies, and video games. There were three major television networks: ABC, CBS, and NBC. Most of us had only twelve to fifteen channels to choose from, making it much more likely we were all watching the same things. TV ***was*** limited and very predictable in the '80s—it didn't take us away from life unless we were addicted to the daytime drama soap operas.

"Screen time in the '80s was much more regulated," says Shaun in Kalamazoo. "It gave the whole world structure. Programming stopped at 2 a.m. You had an ending, a time for bed. We anticipated our favorite prime time shows that hinged on family traditions which we waited all week to see. TV offered an after-school release and felt like a reward."

Shaun's right. Screen time was all about the experience and anticipation for us. It gave us something to look forward to and often kept us on a schedule.

On Friday nights, our family gathered in the living room around "the boob tube" (as my dad liked to call the TV). My mom would bring us a big bowl of homemade popcorn doused in melted butter, and my brother and I would sprawl out on the floor to watch *The Incredible Hulk*, *Fantasy Island*, *The Dukes of Hazzard*, or *Dallas* on the 22-inch screen. That's correct, the average TV size back then was a whopping twenty-two inches. When it was time to change channels, one of us kids received the parental nod. That was our cue to get up and physically turn the channel knob, move the rabbit ears, or twist the rotary antenna dial. *Sometimes we did all three.* We *were the frickin' remote control.*

"Truthfully, some aspects of TV in the '80s stunk," June in Florida recalls. "Sometimes you had to decide between a favorite show and another activity. Sometimes your parents were watching the news when your favorite show was on. Sometimes the cable was out because a storm blew through. If you missed your show, you didn't get an opportunity to rewatch it until summer reruns—if you were lucky."

Fiona in Florida concurs. "I clearly remember fights with my siblings over what to watch because we only had one TV and my sister's favorite show was on at the same time as mine."

If the TV malfunctioned, families were down for the count, waiting for Mr. Frye, the TV repair man, to come fix it—which could take weeks. Even though our screen size was half of an average TV today, it weighed nearly two hundred pounds, and it took the neighborhood A-Team to move it. Our built-in TV furniture console was a tank.

God forbid we missed an episode of *General Hospital* before VHS and DVRs, because there were *no* options for watching it again. We'd then have to get on the horn to call someone who watched it to fill us in on the soap opera drama of the day.

TV Guide Magazine was a hot commodity. If our parents splurged for it, we then had the complete rundown of the week's shows so we could plan what we wanted to watch on all twelve of our channels.

- For our life lessons and family shows, we watched *The Brady Bunch, The Cosby Show, Diff'rent Strokes, Little House on the Prairie, Eight Is Enough, Family Ties, The Facts of Life,* and *The Waltons.*

- For romance and crushes, we watched *BJ and the Bear, Dynasty, Fantasy Island, Hart to Hart, Love Boat,* and *Moonlighting.*

- For belly laughs, we watched *Alf, The Carol Burnett Show, Cheers, The Golden Girls, Happy Days, Three's Company, Laverne & Shirley, Mork & Mindy,* and *Who's the Boss? The Simpsons* aired in 1989, closing out the decade with sarcastic, twisted humor.

- For our superhero/badass fix, it was *The A-Team, Charlie's Angels, CHIPs, The Greatest American Hero, Hill Street Blues, The Incredible Hulk,* and *Miami Vice.*

So many of us rallied to stay up late and watch *Saturday Night Live* or sneaked a segment of *The Johnny Carson Show* on a weekend until the 2 a.m. rainbow took our TV screen prisoner, cutting us off and sending us either relieved or reluctantly to bed.

Saturday morning cartoons were the highlight of our week as kids. We'd inhale our oversized bowl of sugar-infused cereal with half a gallon of vitamin D milk and watch hours of cartoons from *Tom & Jerry, The Bugs Bunny Show, Super Friends,* to *Scooby-Doo.* I'm embarrassed to say, it took me until my adult years to learn to stop gripping a spoon like a shovel because of those Saturday mornings.

Uplifting '80s commercials brought us cute, little old ladies demanding, "Where's the beef?" for Wendy's. And we all wanted Big Red gum so we could "kiss a little longer." Plus, Coca-Cola charmed us with music with the "You can't beat the feeling" ad campaign, inspiring us to dance in our living room whether we drank soda or not.

Now, we have commercials that often feel more fear-based. Advertisements evolved from "9 out of 10 doctors recommend" a medication to an endless list of warnings of how a prescription can harm us—*wait, wasn't it supposed to help?* Who would've thought there'd be commercials on public TV for erectile dysfunction, or ones prompting us to contact an attorney for a makeshift lawsuit *because we hurt ourselves dancing in our living room*?

The American Marketing Association (AMA) requires that advertisements invoking fear must be ethical. *The question is, whose definition of ethical are we using here?* Was seeing an egg getting fried in a pan while being told "This is your brain on drugs" an ethical or *educational* way to get their point across? Sure, we all want to be informed about new products, but not pressured into buying them out of fear.

"Advertisements are all related to having enough insurance, or medications for ailments and dysfunction with warnings like 'can cause death,'" Jackie in Illinois says. "Shut it off!"

Today, TV has transformed from being an "idiot box" to almost like a member of the family. You can talk to your Smart TV remote control, tell it what you want to watch, and it will change the channel for you. When my dad uses my remote control, I remind him, "Dad, you can talk to it," and I can never tell if he's relieved, pissed, or confused.

"Let's face it, anything that we enjoy doing outside can be simulated from our couch," Mike in Tulsa says. "The Fishing Channel, ESPN, reality TV, and more. Maybe we can place the blame on Richard Simmons, as he suggested staying at home rather than going to an aerobics class."

Nowadays, a TV weighs as little as twenty pounds, and most are considered disposable because it's often cheaper to buy a new one than repair a broken one. How many of us have more than one TV in our homes now? Does everyone disappear into a different room in the house to watch their *own* shows? Has binge-watching our programs become a hobby for us?

"The only thing we were binge-watching in the '80s was MTV," Grace in North Carolina says.

When Betamax, LaserDisc, and VHS machines were introduced, it brought a new level of home entertainment to our "idiot box." This was a major breakthrough! We then had options on what to watch and when to watch it. The briefcase-sized VHS machines were modern and magical; as their price decreased, they became the new technology everyone had to own. Suddenly, it was a dogfight to get to the local video rental store or Blockbuster on Friday nights to get the new releases before our friends did. Rental stores became a social hangout (*bonus!*) where we could run into anyone. And, of course, we were always reminded to *"please be kind and rewind."*

Being able to record new episodes of our favorite shows on blank VHS tapes was a game changer, although programming the machines was a "pain in the ass" according to many Gen Xers. We might find ourselves spewing some newly acquired curse words the next morning when we realized we screwed up the VCR program and didn't tape last night's episode of *Friday Night Videos*. Where were you, YouTube, when we needed you most?

Terry fondly remembers watching the movie *10* on his family's first VCR. "As a ten-year-old in heat, I learned how to stop Bo Derek on the machine in mid-jog with her braided hair, wearing her slinky one-piece yellow bathing suit on the beach. Oh, man, that made me…" *It's okay, Terry, we understand. We girls might have freeze-framed the volleyball scene in* Top Gun *to scope out the tan lines on the guys once or twice. Just maybe.*

Once Atari and Nintendo launched their video game consoles, nothing else was more important than playing video games after school. We'd transform that idiot box by running wires from a game box to the TV and turn it into our home version of an arcade game.

When paid cable TV hit the mainstream, options like HBO, Cinemax, and Showtime opened new doors, along with the iconic, era-blasting MTV in 1981. If our parents couldn't afford cable, we would surely try to finagle our way over to a friend's house whose parents *could* afford it.

Bonnie B in St. Paul says, "I took babysitting jobs based on if they had MTV or not. It was an extra bonus if they had HBO."

Now our TV is practically a computer. Smart TVs are the norm, running apps that make us jump through hoops by requiring passwords or codes to validate it's *really us* logging in. Netflix, Hulu, Tubi, Disney+, Peacock, Apple TV+, Amazon Prime, Max (formerly HBO), YouTube TV, and what, there's still dozens more? Exhausting! This *is* TV now—it goes 24/7 and has more channels every time we turn it on. Our *TV Guide Magazine* is now on the screen and feels like we are scrolling to Timbuktu just to see all the programs we can choose from. By then we're almost ready for bed and we haven't even figured out what the 'eff we want to watch. Ten bucks says we still have times when we want to watch something, but *we still can't find it in any of our current apps*. Then we chalk up another paid subscription or succumb to less-than-legal account sharing.

I do love that some networks (like Netflix) air retired shows like *Cheers, The Golden Girls, Roseanne,* and *Seinfeld* because it keeps the '80s culture alive and stirs interest from younger generations.

The other day, I was working on my laptop in my sunroom, focused on the screen, when for some reason I stopped and looked out the window. The most beautiful red cardinal was sitting on my birdfeeder curiously looking at me. I found myself wondering how long he'd been there. I'm pretty sure he was thinking that *I* was the one trapped in the cage—and he was right.

THE 24-HOUR NEWS NETWORK

We had minimal ways to access the media back in the day. The newspaper was our "24-hour news" because we could pick it up and read it whenever we wanted. Local news aired at 6:00 p.m. and 11:00 p.m. We had Andy Rooney on *60 Minutes* giving us various news stories and interesting topics *only* once a week on Sunday evenings. As kids, we'd pass through the living room on our way to beat up our little brothers and make mixtapes, when we might rubberneck at a random news event our parents were watching, such as the storming of the US Embassy in Iran, the attempted assassination of President Reagan, or the rescue of Baby Jessica. But was that more important than beating up our little brothers? *Of course not.*

In 1980, CNN made the push to deliver news around the clock and became the world's first 24-hour cable television news network. *If* we were lucky to have cable back then, we were probably going for anything but the 24-hour news—*maybe even the porn channels.*

Today, many people let their TV or devices run with news in the background, such as BBC News, CNN, Fox News, and MSNBC, and kids aren't just passing through anymore. They stay more aware of the happenings with news and politics at a younger age and even take sides on issues most of us would've never considered. We were out swinging in trees, cruising the main drag, or hanging posters on our walls in our room, not concerned with controversial issues.

"It used to be considered taboo to talk about politics and religion, but those guardrails no longer exist for today's kids. Being better informed has a price, and that price shows up in increased pressure and poor mental health, thanks to the 24-hour news cycle and social media," Terry says.

Bob C adds, "I spent most of my adult life as a journalist. We started to see the rapid decline of the news industry more when it was no longer a public service required of all broadcast stations by the FCC and became a for-profit business competing for viewership numbers and ad revenue."

"There is more truth in *Looney Tunes* than there is in the news," Andrew in Katy says.

I had a friend who conducted an experiment. He decided to watch every news channel, and the first negative story that came on, he'd flip to the next news channel. He repeated the process until the new channel did the same thing. He went through all of them in less than three minutes because of the consistent negative stories. How do we ever find peace and contentment if this is what we feed our brains?

"News went from informing to influencing," Matt from Washington says. "If they want to voice their opinions about what happens, fine, then start a podcast."

Bob C adds, "When I started in the news business, failure to verify your story with at least two independent sources could jeopardize your job, possibly even your career. Today, 24-hour media outlets often report on comments found on social media as if they were facts. The sad truth is that today, 'time to market' is emphasized over accuracy, and most media outlets spend too much time speculating, hyperbolizing, and mixing news with opinion over reporting and the furtherance of the truth."

What benefit comes from watching the 24-hour news channels every day? It divides us, stirs the pot, and can even drive an underlying anxiety. When I am at my parents' house and my dad has the 24-hour news on, they broadcast the same redundant, drab stories over and over. It causes worry about what *could* happen and most often it's something we have **no** control over.

I challenge you to ask yourself these questions about the programs you watch:

- Is it providing value to you?
- Is it educating you about something worthwhile?
- Is it providing entertainment, bringing you joy, or laughter?
- If it is news, have you checked it for accuracy?

If you answered "no" to any of these, then don't give up your precious jelly beans and finite mind space to ingest unbeneficial, potentially inaccurate, doom-and-gloom drama!

MOVIE THEATERS

Gen Xers went to theaters to watch exciting movies on the big screen in droves, and those films had a profound influence on us. Lory K became a nurse and married a soldier after watching *Red Dawn* and seeing the VHS version of *Silent Running;* Terry started doing one-handed pushups after being inspired by *Rocky;* John W became a Marine after watching *Heartbreak Ridge*; Shaun R enlisted in the Army after watching *Stripes;* and Mark K joined the Navy after watching *Top Gun.* For $3.55 (the average price of a movie ticket in the US in 1985), we might have been inspired to change the course of our lives.

"I was quick to purchase skis, a case of beer, and a season pass to Ski World after watching the party movie *Hot Dog,*" Mikey says.

Rennie was inspired by *Star Wars.* He says, "It taught me the little guys can win!"

Our early movie theater excursions started in the '70s with our parents taking us to movies like *Herbie Goes to Monte Carlo, Every Which Way but Loose, Grease, Saturday Night Fever, 1941,* or my ultimate favorite, *Smokey and the Bandit.* Cussing, romance, nudity, violence, and dangerous stunts filled our sponge-like brains and taught us a little more about our small world.

Our parents set different rules on what we could and couldn't watch.

Bryan in Chicago recalls, "We didn't have TV because my dad said it was bad for our eyes and would make us stupid and lazy. Why movies were okay, I have no idea. We'd watch old movies on the projector in the basement, old sci-fi films and such, but weren't allowed to watch *The Brady Bunch.*"

Mina in Houston remembers begging her mom to let her go see *The Rocky Horror Picture Show* when she was fourteen. "I loved that *Rocky Horror* was a dedicated place to dress up and act completely crazy, like rock stars you'd see in the magazines and videos. You could be anyone you wanted to be on a Saturday night at the movie theater, but then still put on your blue jeans and go to class on Monday morning." Mina's experience evolved into a passion for creating her own costume designs. She still follows the *Rocky Horror* community to this day and says, "What I thought was soooo cheesy then, turned out to be a huge influence in that aspect of my life."

In the '80s, popular films amused and captivated us, like *Bachelor Party, The Blues Brothers, The Breakfast Club, Sixteen Candles, Dirty Dancing, Footloose, Planes, Trains and Automobiles, Pretty in Pink, Purple Rain, Monty Python, 9 to 5, On Golden Pond, The Outsiders, Police Academy, Sudden Impact, Three Men and a Baby,* and the belly-busting Chevy Chase *Vacation* movies.

In 1984, I wrote in my diary, "I went and saw *Beverly Hills Cop* three times this month." Eddie Murphy's humor—you know, the banana in the tailpipe—was the best. Today, it's harder to see movies multiple times in the theater;

they play for a shorter time so they can go to streaming faster and generate a purchase.

"Movies left a permanent tattoo on us or a tasty, quenching swim in nirvana for a few hours," Shaun in Kalamazoo says. "And we kept going back for more."

Movies could do that for us, especially trilogies such as *Beverly Hills Cop*, *Rocky*, *Mad Max*, *Ghostbusters*, *Back to the Future*, *Superman*, and *Indiana Jones*. *Empire Strikes Back* and *Return of the Jedi* blew it out of the galaxy, exploding in the form of posters, dolls, action figures, toys, and collection cards. Unsurprisingly, they also earned billions of dollars at the box office.

Matt in California says, "The *Star Wars* trilogy helped me to discern right and wrong, morality, and truth about life in a family with no real role models."

Movies taught us so much thanks to some iconic producers.

We grew up in the "New Hollywood" era, where filmmakers like Spielberg, Lucas, Scorsese, and Coppola gave us famous movies such as *Back to the Future*, *The Goonies*, *Gremlins*, *Harry and the Hendersons*, *Indiana Jones*, *The Outsiders*, *Poltergeist*, *Raging Bull*, and *E.T.*, the highest money maker of the decade.

We also had record numbers of scary movies in the '80s—over one hundred horror movies. That averages to almost one movie released *per month* over the decade! Does anyone else find that a bit disturbing? Movies like *Alien*, *An American Werewolf in London*, *Beetlejuice*, *Children of the Corn*, *Scarface*, *The Shining*, *The Howling*, *Creepshow*, *Friday the 13th*, and *Halloween*, just to name a few. *A Nightmare on Elm Street*'s Freddy Krueger still causes nightmares for many of us to this day. And *The Lost Boys* were the hottest vampires in girls' dreams, even though they ripped people to shreds. Some of our '80s horror movies were pretty darn gory, and often young people were shown getting chased by an axe-wielding, freckled-face *Chucky*, or psychopaths armed with hooks, and machetes. What were we thinking, lining up to see these movies? Worse, what were our parents thinking, allowing us to watch people getting their body parts chain-sawed off and spread like grass seed?

Bryan in Chicago recalls, "I remember smelling popcorn at the movie theater with my dad and siblings, getting ready to watch *Halloween* in 1978, and my dad saying to us, 'Don't tell your mother.' There was a scene in the movie where Michael Myers had a sheet over his head. After that, I wanted to be a ghost for Halloween. It wasn't until after my dad passed away that my mom found out why."

Our curious, hormonal-addled minds loved movies like *Against All Odds, Endless Love, Fast Times at Ridgemont High, Porky's, Risky Business, So Fine*, and *Spring Break*. It was sex education at its finest—*and worst*. In 1984, *Red Dawn* received the first ever PG-13 rating, but it wasn't until 1990 that the first NC-17 movie rating was given to *Henry & June*. No adult rating was going to stop us, though. We'd long been circumventing theater ordinances by paying for a PG-13 film, then sneaking into the Rated R one.

In 2022, I took my mom to see *Elvis* at the theater, and she kept asking, "Where did the old fold-up seats go?" as I was comfortably reclined with an alcoholic beverage in the state-of-the-art motorized recliners. *Yes, I need to get her out more.*

When I asked random Gen Xers how much time they were spending in front of their screens, a handful of answers were: "I plead the fifth," "way more time than I should after work—it's terrible," and "probably a good 60 percent of my waking hours."

Why are we watching so much TV?

Ed in Virginia says, "I watch way too much most days. I started to set timers on my phone to remind me to back off forms of screen time to pass time. I doubt any of us want to admit the real hours."

We talked about smartphones in Chapter 4, and TV and movies in this chapter, but personal computers, laptops, and tablets also contribute to daily screen time. And how many of us watch "TV" *on* our phones now?

"Screen time is a concern—along with the loss of the simple structure we grew up with, where shows had a time and a place," Shaun in Kalamazoo says. "Now it can be anytime, anyplace. We're overfed. Everything happens in milliseconds. What we lost is our precious, simple compass called *anticipation*."

There are many articles on Google correlating brain health to screen time. Your eyes and brain have to funnel so much through screens each day. One article I found was literally titled "TV Really Does Rot Your Brain."

The National Library of Medicine investigated the impact of watching TV on the subsequent risk of dementia and longitudinal changes in brain structure. Their results suggest prolonged TV viewing is associated with a decline in language, communication, and memory, all of which are associated with dementia.

And shouldn't we all have that imaginary 2 a.m. rainbow screen come on for us, so we know when to *shut 'er down*? Our eyes need breaks, too!

What we choose to watch has an impact also. Doesn't watching the Coneheads or Gumby on *Saturday Night Live* sound more comforting than watching the world news? Ten bucks says we'd be in a better mood watching something lighthearted or with humor. Applying the principles of '80s planning—being intentional about what we're watching on TV—can make a huge difference in our lives today.

I consider myself a successful non-TV watcher. It's probably because I love listening to music and podcasts, which overrides my desire to watch TV. Here are some of my tricks for not falling into the TV abyss:

- I have a "What to Watch" list to avoid the aimless channel surfing tornado. Whenever I hear of a movie or show that perks my interest, I add it to my list app on my E.T. This acts as my personal *TV Guide Magazine*. When I'm ready to watch TV, I pick something from my list *before* turning it on. It's no different than going to the grocery store with a list.
- I'm selective about my TV habits. While I'd enjoy watching *The Today Show* or a morning program, I know it'd be a hard habit to break and would distract me from my priorities.
- I avoid watching the news unless there is a major event. My take on it is this: the news wasn't 24/7 back in the day, and we managed just fine. Today's constant stream of negativity isn't beneficial and will only fill us with anxiety. If I want daily updates, I let Alexa read me the headlines.

I had different versions of my polls from the '80s, where I'd have my classmates rate actors, actresses, TV shows, and movies from 0 to 5, with 5 being what they liked best. I'd list every person or show I could think of, get out my trusty ruler, and then draw a grid for mini score boxes. And my classmates would go at it. In one poll, Dave gave *That's Incredible* a 3, *M*A*S*H* and *Hill Street Blues* a 5+, *Fame* a 2, and the rest of the twenty-some shows a 0. *Say, what's with all those zeros?* Maybe Dave was on to something with his priorities.

What if you used that system for what you watch now?

Maybe a 5 is a show that inspires thought-provoking conversations, stimulates and expands your mind, or makes you laugh. Maybe you struggle to see the value in the ones you rate a 3, and they're just a way to kill time. Consider picking your cut-off number based on your jelly beans and quality of life. What if you eliminate shows that don't score above a 4? What would that feel like? Go for the things that feed your soul, bring you enjoyment, or add value to your life and say, "Hasta la vista, baby" to the rest!

1982 classmate poll. My bossy instructions read:
All ratings are from 0 to 5.
You may add + (plus) and − (minus) if you wish.
If you don't rate it, it will count as a zero (0).

Chapter Rapture 09
Disconnect to reconnect with nature

Sixth Hour Bell

TV in the '80s was limited and predictable, with just twelve to fifteen channels. It didn't pull us away from life but gave us structure, often leading us to watch the same things.

How much time do you spend staring at screens each day? Consider the negative impact of watching the 24-hour news channels daily. Be intentional about what you watch, applying '80s principles.

Does this add value? Is it educational, joyful, entertaining, or accurate? Does it make you laugh away your troubles? If not, don't waste your precious jelly beans and mental energy on it. Avoid unproductive or inaccurate doom-and-gloom drama, and instead, get outside and touch the grass!

Extracurricular Activities

- Set boundaries for your screen time, like imagining a 2 a.m. rainbow screen as a reminder to shut down.
- Rate the programs you watch from 0 to 5. Eliminate anything below a 4. Use an app to keep a "what to watch" list.
- Dive into the interesting '80s screen history by reading books on directors like James Cameron, John Hughes, or Steven Spielberg or even explore documentaries on them.

After-School Specials

- Hop on the Conjunction Junction train and watch Saturday morning cartoon clips like *My 80's Saturday Morning* hosted by Trey Trey on YouTube.
- Explore screen time's impact with documentaries like *Stare into the Lights My Pretties* or *Screened Out* on YouTube.
- Enjoy vintage humor with *Saturday Night Live* sketches; watch *SNL Classic Throwbacks – The '70s* compilation on YouTube.

Passing Notes in Class

"Check out the Ground News app if you want to compare how the same stories are being reported (or under-reported) by news outlets across the entire political spectrum. It helps everyone to be more informed by providing comparative coverage from all perspectives."

~Bob C in New York

"Get outside and see the world in person instead of on a television screen."

~Rich in Ireland

"When I was seven or so, my dad would bring me to the movies, give me popcorn money, and drop me off. I'd get to watch any movie. I was the first kid on my block to see *Jaws* and *The Shining*."

~Mike W in Alaska

Field Trips

- Grab a family member or friend and head to the movie theater—don't forget to splurge on a big bucket of buttery popcorn like we used to!
- Explore screen time history at a museum of film and television. Most large cities offer extensive archives of old media to view, like the Chicago Museum of Film and Cinematography.
- On your next vacation, look into options for signing up to be an extra in a movie or attending a live TV taping like *Saturday Night Live* or *The Tonight Show Starring Jimmy Fallon*.

Chapter Mixtape

- "Video Killed the Radio Star" – The Buggles
- "I Want to Break Free" – Queen
- "Freeze Frame" – The J. Geils Band
- "TV Dinners" – ZZ Top
- "Sleeping With the Television On" – Billy Joel
- "Electric Avenue" – Eddy Grant
- "The Message" – Grandmaster Flash and the Furious Five
- "Television Man" – Talking Heads
- "Wrap It Up" – The Fabulous Thunderbirds
- "Mad World" – Tears For Fears

Shortcut to Spotify Playlist: beckykliss.com/CR09

Chap. Ten

The Finer Things

Treasures

"In life, we chase what we want. We don't always chase what we need. And to reach a point where you understand what life is really about is freeing and liberating."

~Paul Stanley

Mikey had submitted his Christmas wish list early in '77. He was fairly confident he was going to land some of the items he wanted, like BMX bike parts, a stereo, the Farrah Fawcett poster, and a new KISS T-shirt. Mikey had just turned ten years old and was already a huge KISS fan. And why wouldn't he be? His dad was a rock and roller and KISS fan, too. His dad was also a prankster and loved surprising his kids with meaningful gifts that he knew they would love. All the gifts under their Christmas tree would be numbered. His dad would reference his cheat sheet, drawing out the process of opening presents, tormenting Mikey and his sister with which number they'd get to open next.

Mikey opened his first gift (number 2)—*and, score!*—the Farrah Fawcett poster. His younger sister, Paula, opened gift number 4 and was tickled to have the game Perfection. Then it was Mikey's turn again. His dad picked gift number 6. Mikey was less than excited. Number 6 was the smallest of all the presents and the package size matched nothing on his list. He was dying to open number 8, the biggest one. His dad was enjoying Mikey's anguish too much to waver from the plan, though. So Mikey did what any kid would do in this situation, and ripped off the wrapping paper in a hurry, and dismissed the gift to get to number 8 quicker.

"I remember looking at this 4-inch button of KISS thinking 'big whoop' and tossed it aside," Mikey says. "But when my dad said, 'Son, you might want to look at that again.' I picked it back up and turned it over. There was a Ticketmaster envelope attached to the back of the button. I tore it open and almost fell over—there was a printed ticket to see the band I loved more than anything in the world: KISS at the Chicago Amphitheatre. At that point, *none* of my other gifts mattered anymore. My dad knew that KISS ticket to my first concert would be more important to me than anything else, *and he was right.*"

What were those things that mattered to us when we were kids?

Allison in Texas says, "I still have a battery-powered metal train engine that would light up and blow smoke when it rolled across the floor and made a train sound. It's inoperable now, but it was like magic, and I can't seem to give it away because it's the only childhood toy I still have."

"My real treasures from the '80s were all the love notes my wife wrote me in high school," Steve in Minnesota says. "I sure hope our kids never find them."

"I have a comic book collection and vinyl record collection going back to childhood. My kids collect these, too, and I'm saving them because I know they'll enjoy mine someday," Michael in Massachusetts says.

MJ in Virginia says, "I have a couple toys and a few football cards—oh, and some scars. I'm thankful for what I still have, even though it's not much."

Our bedrooms were our sanctuary. They were filled with our collections of bottle caps, coins, rocks, key chains, stamps, Matchbox cars, football memorabilia, baseball cards, beer cans, models, Charlie's Angels cards, Star Wars figures, magnets, cereal box prizes, stuffed animals, and even unicorn-themed trinkets.

We covered our bedroom's four walls—*and, yes, the ceiling, too*—with our favorite posters. Posters of sports stars, actors, bands, singers, and even those cute posters of kittens and puppies ordered from Scholastic. The walls displayed who or what we were obsessed with: Duran Duran, Huey Lewis, Rick Springfield, Shawn Cassidy, Metallica, and Van Halen. Heartthrobs like Erik Estrada, David Hasselhoff, Heather Locklear, Daisy Duke, and Cheryl Ladd. Sports posters of The Bears, Dwight Clark, Joe Montana, and Magic Johnson, or of cars, motorcycles, and BMX bikes. Posters and music pulled everything in our room together and brought it to life—including our stereos, tape recorders, stacks of cassettes, and records.

Of course, for any boy, receiving Farrah Fawcett's poster with her wearing that infamous red bathing suit would make their Christmas dreams sweeter.

Steve in Minnesota says, "I had an orange bean bag chair and orange phone, *Star Wars* and *Close Encounters* posters. I had one trophy from playing basketball. You could never see my floor because I had a pretty good collection of dirty dishes and my clothes were thrown all over the place, but it was easier to hide my *Playboy* magazines in the mess."

When we weren't in our rooms, we were usually outside with our boom boxes, water toys, jump ropes, hula hoops, bikes, skateboards, softball mitts, and basketballs. It seemed like we had so much to keep us busy, yet most of us really *had* so little.

I looked back at the polls I took to school. In 1984, I asked my fellow eleventh graders, "Your Most Prized Possession?" Some of the answers were: my stereo, my car, my truck, my camera, my gold, my bike, and—adorably—many listed their boyfriend or girlfriend. Three classmates surprisingly answered, "my life." *Really? At seventeen, your life is your most prized possession?* As adolescents with so little knowledge and insight, is it possible we actually did know more than we thought we did?

Kristen in Minnesota says, "I couldn't care less about 'stuff' now with what everyone has going on with their health—and I used to be pretty materialistic and selfish. It's shifted. I've moved from valuing things to valuing love. Your truck won't be next to you on your deathbed."

Can you relate? Are your most prized possessions now good health and great experiences? I know mine are.

But we still have all this "stuff."

Is this the point in our lives where we need to purge the shit shoved under our beds, in our closets, and buried on garage shelves for good, and stop bringing new things through the door? Everything is so abundant. Things come fast, easy, and drop on our doorstep in the blink of an eye. The average size of a home in 1980 was 1,595 square feet and in 2018 it was around 2,400 square feet. That's a fifty percent increase in space! Most of the closets we grew up with were narrow (2' x 6'). Compare that to today's walk-in closets with high ceilings. We can store so much more, and many of us who own homes or have apartments have consequently accumulated ***a lot*** of shit. It can be overwhelming.

"Our kitchen is an electric gadget shrine. Air fryer—yep. Rice cooker—we got that. Pressure cooker—check. KitchenAid mixer—a little dusty, but there it is. Slow cooker—of course. A sous vide machine? Yes, we have that, too," Kerrie in Minneapolis jokes. "But there are never enough scissors, ever."

"With the kids grown and gone, I was finally able to spend money to upgrade my house," Julie in Madison reveals. "My husband built me a dream craft room with a gift-wrapping island. I love it, but the only problem is the more you craft, the more craft supplies you buy. There will be no downsizing for us!"

When I look around my house at my age, I ask myself, What do I really need? What am I actually using? And, when—and how—do we part with the stuff we don't need?

One Sunday morning, while peacefully paddleboarding on the beautiful St. Joseph River with my two yoga besties, Vicki and Adrienne, the conversation of when to part with something came up. In 2021, I moved *three* times (*yes, a modern-day horror story*). Until you go through the H-E-double-L of moving, you don't realize how much you have. But moving gave me the opportunity to downsize, donate, and sell a significant portion of my belongings. I decided to sell my one and only authentic, mint-condition Madonna *Like A Virgin* concert program on eBay. I only paid $25 for it. I sold it for $275. I was in awe—that is eleven times return on my investment for those crunching the numbers.

Looking back, I realized I was so focused on purging that I let go of something I wished I would've kept. I found myself analyzing what that $275 had brought me…maybe a few times eating out and a couple of margaritas? Yes, I still had the incredible memory of seeing the Madonna concert in 1985, but my vintage treasure from the experience was gone.

Ultimately, I think it's important to know what our "finer things" are—ones that bring us joy or joyful memories.

While paddling, Adrienne said, "When I have to make a decision like that, I close my eyes and visualize my life without the item. I look to my inner voice to find what's in my heart."

We've all fallen prey to the ease of online shopping, indulging in impulse buys, hauling home finds from resale shops and garage sales, and even taking in items someone else was giving away. But how do those habits align with our future plans of downsizing?

"The older I get, the more stuff I accumulate," Bonnie B in St. Paul says. "I've got stuff from my elderly parents, my deceased grandparents, from friends who've passed. I need a bigger house!"

Aren't we all at that age where we are (or soon will be) sorting our parents' belongings? And—not to be even more morbid here—when do we start thinking about who is going to sort through all *our* possessions when our ashes are sitting in a jar somewhere or being infused into a piece of jewelry or guitar?

There is a process called Swedish Death Cleaning, which is basically cleaning like there is *no* tomorrow. It's a permanent form of organization that makes our lives run more smoothly, where we spare those we will leave behind the hassle of getting rid of our junk.

Darcy in Michigan says, "My hope is not to tie too much emotion up in 'things.' I remember having to clean out my parents' stuff. I found it painful because I didn't want most of it, but there was also guilt in getting rid of it."

How do we work around guilt? It's such a heavy word for many of us when it comes to letting things go.

"Other than family heirlooms, I've decided it's gone," Debra in Ohio admits. "The kids and grandkids aren't going to care about 90 percent of the stuff I have."

Minimalism, a 2016 film directed by Matt D'Avella, is a profound documentary to watch on Netflix or YouTube. It explores how people are living simpler, more meaningful lives and their motivations for doing so.

"What changes our perception of what it means to live a good life?" Sam Harris, a neuroscientist and author, asks in the documentary. "We have things we are obsessed about, but then a new version comes out, which is new and improved. And now you no longer care about the one you have. The one you have is a source of dissatisfaction. I think we're confused about what's going to make us happy. Many people think that material possessions are the center of the bullseye and that gratifying each desire will somehow summate into a satisfying life."

Neuropsychologist Rick Hanson, Ph.D., adds, "We want what the item will *bring* us. We want to feel whole and content."

Isn't this the same thing Adrienne was trying to tell me while we were paddleboarding? Are some of us at crossroads where we are deciphering and shifting our definition of what our items actually mean to us?

One Gen Xer says, "After I moved out when I was twenty-two, my folks put our house up for sale. I never thought they'd be able to scale down to a two-bedroom condo so fast, but they did. They got rid of dated furniture, gave their life a new makeover, and began traveling more. There was space for us to visit, but *not* move back home."

I believe decluttering and downsizing to the items that really matter to you is key to contentment.

When my company, GLC, cleaned for Stryker Medical, the large hospital bed manufacturer in Kalamazoo, Michigan, we did walk-throughs of their office areas. We documented misplaced items and noted things that didn't belong or weren't necessary. The more things sitting around, the harder it was to keep the building clean. These types of things collect dust, and we all know what dust and dirt do to our allergies. Indoor air quality was important to Stryker, so it was essential to minimize clutter.

It's the same for us at home. The more things we have, the more challenging it becomes to stay organized and keep things clean. It's a fact—clutter negates cleanliness. The saying "The easiest way to organize your stuff is to get rid of it" is painfully true—*but not easy.* Do we choose the minimalist style, the saver/pack rat style, or some other variation?

After selling my cleaning business, I opened a store called Re-Imagine, selling repurposed and vintage items. (Yes, sadly, our '80s treasures are now considered "vintage.") I have long had great aspirations of transforming my existing items into something new, like turning concert T-shirts into pillows or blankets, or framing my grandma's vintage jewelry into a rhinestone heart to hang on the wall. At Re-Imagine, I was amazed by how many people I met who crafted with repurposed materials and put thought into minimizing waste through a hobby that transformed discarded items into art. One consignor took old bed sheets, ripped them into pieces, and weaved them into durable rugs. Your grandma's colorful vintage sheets that are buried in a closet are now off of the shelf and put to practical use as a bathroom rug.

Jackie from Chicago says, "I needed furniture for my first apartment in 1987, but I had no money. So, I painted most of my grandpa's old furniture to use—out of necessity came creativity. I have carried that craft on to reinvent old furniture by painting colorful patterns that people love. There's something nostalgic about our generation that brought repurposing to the mainstream."

Similar to Jackie, our passions, hobbies, and collections can actually be sentimental and rewarding, *and* allow us to make a few bucks on the side. In the meantime, we have to keep our possessions organized so we know what we need or don't need anymore.

My autistic friend Parker has a method for this that works. His process of sorting is to pull everything out of every bin or cabinet, find joy or humor in the items that resonate with him, pocket the items he finds useful or fun, then forget the rest and go do something else. Putting it back was *not* the fun part;

the piles were overwhelming. I encouraged him to categorize the items. He loved doing it because then it made sense—it broke everything down into parts and a system. He would make piles via category type and purge the duplicates or items no longer needed. He was unstoppable. When Parker was done, he was bursting to show me how he had busted through the mess. He came out with a big grin, buoyantly proud of his accomplishment.

Just like Parker can sort through the mess, so can we. We can categorize, sort, purge and break through the mess and be unstoppable too.

Pick a room or an item category and get it organized. Don't forget, though, that stopping what goes *in* that room at the doorway is a big part of the process.

Laura in Georgia says, "Our parents trained us well. *Wants* were not *needs*. Our needs were met. I had clothing and a school budget. Anything past that was my responsibility."

Could our childhood training of "Needs versus Wants 101" be a guide for us now as CD-55ers?

Do a walk-through of your living space to identify which of your possessions are tied to a treasured experience. Is that lovely nature scene framed on your wall a picture you bought at Target or something breathtaking you've seen personally? Did you purchase the vase full of seashells at a craft store, or collect them while enjoying a walk on the beach?

Ask yourself these questions about the items you see:

- Do I enjoy it? Is there a memory attached to it?
- Is this something I'm going to ever create a memory with?
- Will I miss it when it's gone or regret parting with it?

GLC would walk through and identify clutter, and then Stryker would address and declutter those areas. That's similar to what you would do in your home. Clear the space, and then let your creative mind open up to what meaningful items buried in closets or attics can be put to use. Remove the items that don't hold weight in your heart and replace them with ones that do.

If this is hard for you, try looking at it like Debbie in Myakka City does. She says if you are going to move across the country and have to pay to pack and move the contents of your home, go for the easy road and let most of it go. Only take your treasures, heirlooms, and favorites. It's just stuff—start over when you get there.

What are those items you'd be packing versus donating or selling?

As an example, I counted the number of vases I have: eight. Two hold repurposed flowers that bring joy to my creative side, one holds button flowers I made with my mom one day sitting at a card table in her living room, and the other five are just wasting space and collecting dust. Why not frame my concert tickets sitting in a drawer or a funny card my BFF got me and sit them in place of those five meaningless vases? Wouldn't that be a better way to fill my space with joy?

When I asked Gen Xers what material items bring them joy, I loved their answers: manual transmission cars, pottery collections, bird feeders, books, dance shoes, and tools; others said a 1970 Chevelle, a VR headset, a garden, a basketball, a pool, a guitar, a grill and smoker collection, a camper van, a pontoon boat, music (and anything that plays it), *and bacon*. Most of these are related to being active with friends or family, or peaceful moments. Rarely is it ever about the meaningless vase collecting dust—*even bacon is more important than that.*

Making gifts is a good way to create meaningful treasures for others, and also giving is good for the soul.

Sherri in Fresno says, "I love making gifts for people with my multitude of 'in progress' art projects."

I'm like Sherri. I create to give and repurpose, and collect vintage items that bring me joy. I have a framed poster of Jon Bon Jovi hanging in my retro-themed basement. He has crazy '80s hair, and is wearing wild, purple-print spandex pants. Every time I look at it, I smile. It's because it's the original poster from my bedroom in the '80s—*well, and the tight spandex helps.*

Ren in Massachusetts may have the perfect answer for what brings her joy: "my passport."

And isn't a passport really a thing that opens a door to an experience? It's no different than a plane ticket to the Grand Canyon, or a concert ticket to see KISS.

"My land and my animals bring me the most joy," David in Kentucky adds. "I live on a 700-acre farm with nine cats, sixty-six cows, and eleven horses. I love looking out my bedroom window and knowing this is my little slice of heaven."

Are those the *finer things* that are important in life now—ones that offer an experience and the memories that come with it? The ones that may cost a little more, but are going to add more meaning to your life than something from T.J. Maxx, HomeGoods, or Amazon?

Before that day in the sunroom when I had my meltdown, I planned to order a new soap dispenser for my bathroom because the one I had didn't match the rest of the decor. *Sounds petty, right?* The weirdest thing happened after that day when my values shifted, though. Suddenly, I didn't care if the soap dispenser matched or not. I realized I'd much rather be out shopping with my girlfriends or my mom and randomly come across a soap dispenser that's cute and make a spontaneous purchase instead. Then, whenever I used it to "washy-washy" (*as they say on the 80s Cruise*), there'd be a memory tied to it. That may be a minuscule example, but this principle can be applied to almost everything.

And finer things can be multi-generational in many ways.

When my two nieces were in their early twenties, we took a trip to Washington D.C. with my mom, who just turned seventy. My mom inadvertently packed some clothes that, let's just say, her daughter (Gen X) and her granddaughters (Millennials) viewed as not exactly flattering. I say "inadvertently" to be gentle here, but the truth is my mom had functional clothing, but not necessarily modern clothing. She often went for neutral or bland colors, prints that made us cringe, and pants that were far from flattering. While we may have silently thought of them as 'old lady clothes,' my nieces weren't shy about voicing their opinions, saying, "Grandma, you need to get up with the times and be more hip."

And so it began. Suddenly, the museum tours weren't as important that day as getting Grandma to the Lucky Brand store for some upscale—*and updated*—clothing. We shoved her in a dressing room, ignoring her detailed excuses of how much she wanted "to be comfortable," or the history of how long she had her outfit, and started handing her items to put on. It was a rough go at first, but then she finally walked out of the dressing room wearing Lucky Brand jeans that perfectly fit her slim figure, and made her look twenty years younger. It was a score, *just like Mikey pulling the KISS ticket out of the Ticketmaster envelope.*

<><><><><><><><><><><><><><><><><><><>

So, in 1978, at ten years old, Mikey went to his first concert: KISS' *Alive II*, escorted by his parents, along with a couple of his dad's friends. Mikey still talks about the memory to this day. Then, in 1980, his parents took him and his nine-year-old sister to another KISS concert (*Dynasty Tour*) with Judas Priest opening. This time, they let him bring three friends. These kids had the thrill of a lifetime and still tell Mikey how cool his parents were for letting them all go to the concert.

Mikey's sister Paula says, "I still wonder what my parents were thinking by taking me to see KISS that young with my brother and his friends. My dad borrowed a friend's utility van to get all of us kids there. I remember we all sat in the back on the floor because there were no seats. My parents sure knew how to give us interesting experiences!"

Mikey adds, "I kept all my concert ticket stubs in a book. I'd write who opened for the band and who I went with on the back of the stubs. The ticket stub book carried so many memories for me, including seeing my dad take a puff off his friend's joint at the concert. Looking back, my dad was just as happy to see KISS as I was, but now I believe it's because he was able to give *me* the experience with *him*."

Mikey's dad passed away a few years ago at seventy-three. "I think of all the things he taught me, including my love of music," Mikey says. "When I look at my KISS albums, I remember the concerts with my dad, so much that when my son, Kyle, was eleven, I took him to see a KISS concert with me. At least I didn't take him when he was ten, right?"

Kyle, now thirty, says, "I was a huge KISS fan like my dad. I even carried my dad's original KISS Army card in my KISS wallet. When he took me to see KISS with Aerosmith in 2003, it was his idea to have my face painted like Gene Simmons. We stopped at Hooters before the show, and I remember eating messy wings and my make-up had to be redone. It was quite the experience!"

Kyle, Mikey, and Mikey's dad bonded over a shared love for a band. Anything KISS related will forever remind Kyle and Mikey of their adventures together. And, what a cool tradition they created across the generations in their family.

Look around. What things do you see that make you smile or lift your spirits? Maybe it's your first record album framed hanging on the wall, a homemade card your grandchild made you on the front of your fridge, a concert program on display in your office, or refrigerator magnets from all your vacations.

Christina in Reno agrees. "I save stuff that helps me remember the timeline of my life like some rocks from when I hiked the Appalachian Trail."

Whenever my mom wore those Lucky Brand jeans over the years and my nieces and I were around, we'd always look at each other, give the nod, and smile. Watching "Grandma" almost faint spending $125—the most she'd ever spent on a pair of jeans in her life—was not the pretty part. The bonding and humor the four of us experienced over something as silly as a new pair of jeans was one of my favorite parts of the trip. That pair of pants became a "finer thing," no different than Mikey's KISS concert ticket stubs were to him.

The things you have that are tied to an experience—ones that remind you of people you love or add meaning to your life—*those are the ones to keep*.

Paula says, "I remember it felt cool to hang out with my brother and his friends. My dad knew how to create amazing vacations and adventures for us kids. I got my love of travel, planning, and organizing vacations from him."

Are we doing what Mikey's dad did, and giving our friends, family, or kids more *experiences* than *things*? If not, why not start the process now—pick something simple and just *go*!

Chapter Rapture 10
Collect experiences, not things

Sixth Hour Bell

Reflect on what mattered most to you as a child and compare it to your current values. What items around you bring joy, make you smile, or lift your spirits? Consider purging what lacks meaning and avoid accumulating stuff that doesn't add value to your life or surroundings.

Remember, less is more! The more we own, the harder it is to stay organized and maintain cleanliness. Ask yourself: What do I really need? What am I actually using?

Identify your "finer things"—those that bring joy or hold precious memories. Keep only what is necessary or meaningful. Prioritize experiences over possessions to nurture your soul and focus on what true luxury means.

Extracurricular Activities

- Read *Enough: Finding More by Living with Less* by Will Davis Jr. for insights on simplifying your life.

- Walk through your home and identify items that lack meaning or don't create calm. Choose a room or category to organize by asking: Does this have a memory? Will I create a memory with it? Will I miss it or regret letting it go?

- Get creative with gift-giving by crafting something or supporting local artisans. Creating a personalized photo gift on platforms like Shutterfly or Walgreens can be both easy and affordable.

After-School Specials

- Watch *Minimalism*, the documentary directed by Matt D'Avella, to learn more about the benefits of living with less. Consider following it up with *The Minimalists: Less Is Now* for additional insights.

- Enjoy George Carlin's comedic skit "A Place for My Stuff," which humorously critiques our obsession with accumulating things we don't need.

- *Detroit Rock City* is a must-watch that captures the passion of a treasured experience, like attending a KISS concert. The movie rekindles the excitement and energy of being a true fan.

Passing Notes in Class

"Weird. The older I get, the more it all just feels like stuff to me."

~Glinda in California

"We're doing what is called a Swedish Death Clean. It's been great getting rid of stuff. Watch *The Minimalists* on Netflix. It has been great for downsizing your lifestyle. It even gave my semi-hoarder husband good ideas."

~LB in Paris, France

"Do not look for luxury in watches…luxury is laughter, friends, rain on your face, hugs and kisses. Don't look for luxury in shops…luxury is being loved by people, being respected, having parents alive, being able to play with your grandchildren."

~Clint Eastwood

Field Trips

- Take a field trip *in* your home! Find items to repurpose or upcycle, and give new life to things like old furniture, clothes, or unused gadgets. At the same time, declutter and let go of what no longer serves you.
- Dust off your passport and start planning a trip that excites you! Whether it's a country you've always dreamed of visiting or revisiting a favorite place, immerse yourself in researching the culture, food, and must-see landmarks.
- Spend a day wandering through a flea market or antique mall, searching for vintage treasures from the '80s. Memorabilia like vinyl records, classic video games, action figures, or retro concert T-shirts.

Chapter Mixtape

- "The Finer Things" – Steve Winwood
- "I Want It All" – Queen
- "What You Need" – INXS
- "Detroit Rock City" – KISS
- "Your Love" – The Outfield
- "In My House" – Mary Jane Girls
- "You Got It" – Roy Orbison
- "Living in a Fantasy" – Leo Sayer
- "Everything She Wants" – Wham!
- "Don't Dream It's Over" – Crowded House

Shortcut to Spotify Playlist: beckykliss.com/CR10

section three

The Secret of My Success

Be Invincible with Your Work and Money

Chap. Eleven

Another Brick in the Wall

— 📼 —

School

"When I was five years old, my mother always told me that happiness was the key to life. When I went to school, they asked me what I wanted to be when I grew up. I wrote down 'happy.' They told me I didn't understand the assignment, and I told them they didn't understand life."

~John Lennon

When my brother Jeff was in eleventh grade, he went to our mom and said, "Mom, I'm quitting school."

My mom cried and said, "You *have* to go to school!"

But Jeff wasn't backing down. "I want to work on equipment. I like working with my hands. I know what I want to do, Ma." Jeff's report cards were primarily filled with 'Ds' and 'Fs,' with one shining, stand-alone 'A' in machine shop. He loved learning how to rebuild things, like the air fan on the rooftop of the local ice cream shop, Oinks.

My mom went to the next parent-teacher conference and met with his English lit teacher, Mr. T, who told her Jeff was failing his class. She expressed how worried she was that her son wouldn't do well in life if he didn't stay in school and further his education.

Mr. T's tone changed, and he looked her straight in the eye. "I'm going to tell you something, Mrs. Kliss," he said. "Jeff *will* succeed in life. I can't give him a good grade, but I can't be angry with him either. He doesn't want to be here. He's lit up with excitement before class when he brings in his machinery magazines to show me what he wants to do. Then, during class, I look over, and there's your son with his head down on his desk checked out. College is *not* for everyone."

Perhaps Mr. T is right. Back then, the expectation was that we *should* go to college or a trade school because we'd get a better job, but it usually wasn't a deal breaker if we didn't. Many of our parents didn't have the financial wherewithal to pay our way through four or more years of education.

Pew Research says roughly 29 percent of Gen Xers have a bachelor's degree or higher, compared to 39 percent of Millennials. Roughly 24.5 percent of Baby Boomers hold a bachelor's degree. Unless we were awarded a scholarship, it was more than likely we incurred debt to make college happen. For many of us, earning money was more important than earning a degree. Then there were kids like my brother Jeff, who had no interest in school, even if it was handed to them on a silver platter. Out of my NBHS class of '86 alone, almost 7 percent quit school before graduating to join the workforce.

Looking back, how did Gen Xers view our time at school?

"Our high school experience was about friends and the school groups we belonged to," Kelly in Tallahassee says. "It wasn't about learning. *It was about passing.*"

Steve in Minnesota agrees. "The caption under my senior yearbook photo said, 'The only thing I want out of school *is myself.*' By the skin of my teeth, I graduated, but I had many friends quit school and start working."

"We learned more in the hallways and on the bus than we did in the classroom," Mike in Tulsa says. "I cared more about *Casey Kasem's American Top 40* than GDP or $E = mc^2$."

For many of us, it's true: School was a huge part of our social life, and our agenda in the classroom often had nothing to do with what we could get out of a textbook. We had other priorities—we were transforming from a kid into a proto-adult, concerned with landing a boyfriend or girlfriend, contemplating whose side we were going to take during the fight after school, counting down the days until we could drive, and hoping to make the sports team. Often, our brains weren't in the classroom with our bodies—they were at the arcade, the mall, the beach; they were plotting and planning when and where we'd meet our friends, and *who* could get the alcohol. We were overthinking our days and under thinking our future. We were writing notes and analyzing who we liked or hated each day, complaining about what our parents were making us do, or whining about how bored we were. We couldn't see past the weekend, let alone the rest of our lives. This note proves how skewed our priorities could be.

Note to my BFF:

> I spent 31 minutes writing a note to Shorty and Tami. Now I have 26 minutes for you. It's 6th hour and very boring. I just know I'm going to fail this class.

Sometimes, a deal could be cut if a teacher felt you were putting in effort. My fifth-grade teacher, Mr. Stella, offered up an 'A' in social studies to anyone who memorized the Gettysburg Address and recited it in front of the class. "Four score and seven years ago our fathers brought forth …" *Yep, I did it.*

"Our first-hour teacher liked chocolate chip cookies and coffee," Carl from Detroit divulges. "When we learned he was willing to give ten extra credit points for the delivery of these items, we'd drop him off a steaming hot cup of coffee and two warm chocolate chip cookies every morning before skipping his class. I got an 'A+' and never sat through the class once."

Even NBHS assistant principal Mr. Hart cut deals.

"Every year on March 1st in NB, when the infamous hamburger joint Redamak's ("Come On Bite Into A Legend!!!"™) opened back up for the season, there'd be an attendance slip a mile long full of absences. It drove Mrs. Grant's blood pressure through the roof," Mr. Hart says of his secretary. "Finally, one year on opening day, I went to Redamak's and just sat there, waiting. Sure enough, the kids skipping school all came to get their first cheeseburger of the season. I had kids offering to buy me a burger so they wouldn't get in trouble. I ended up making March 1st a Teacher In-Service Day." Adjusting for a win-win is what Hart knew best.

But every school had that one teacher who did *not* cut deals. At NBHS, it was Mr. T. When you walked into his English class, you felt like Luke Skywalker boarding the Death Star. He had his own set of rules that he delivered clearly and directly. He lived by structure, and anyone who crossed his classroom's threshold was expected to live that way as well. When someone made him mad, his face would turn tomato-red; some even reported seeing steam shooting out of his ears. Mr. T expected nothing but the best at all times. Here are some of his requirements:

- Handwritten papers were to be one inch from each edge and could not have one letter written past that measurement. If your name, class period, and date were not in that order and legible in the upper right corner, your paper would not be accepted. And never, ever were you allowed to use the word "got."

- Term papers had to be typed with a perfect 1-inch margin around each side, including footnotes. Each time you used White Out on your paper, your grade dropped by one point. As a painful reminder, these manual typewriters had no button to configure margin settings. Getting them perfect required a wooden ruler, beads of sweat, and many curse words.

- When Mr. T felt students weren't properly paying attention, he'd nonchalantly stroll over to the windows, open them to allow in the subzero winter temperatures, and freeze us to full, pissed-off alertness.

- Above all, the legs of every desk chair had to be *perfectly* inside the four circles he had drawn on the tiled floor before you left his classroom.

Mr. T addressed every student as "Mr." or "Miss" with their last name. If he caught Jesse looking at the clock in class, he would say, "Mr. Wilson, time will pass. Will *you* pass?" If Selwyn leaned back in his chair and stretched his arms out to yawn, Mr. T would say, "Mr. Jones, I don't appreciate seeing the bottom of your abdomen." There was no goofing off in his class, not even for the bold. He expected perfection, and we all knew, especially Jeff, that cutting corners was a game not to play with Mr. T.

Terry recalls working on a paper for Mr. T's class with Robin at the library. The subject? Prison reform. *How's that for irony?* They had run out of time and were rushing to finish when Robin blurted out, "I need a word that means 'to get rid of.'"

Terry grabbed a thesaurus, quickly looked through the list of words, and spieled, "Defecate!" Neither of them had a clue that the definition of defecate was, in so many words, *"to take a shit."* Because nothing slid by Mr. T, he critiqued her report openly in class, specifically in regard to the use of the word defecate. Let's just say Robin and Terry are still the best of friends to this day—*just not on that day.*

At the time, we described teachers like Mr. T as relentless, cruel, pedantic, procedural, demanding, and stern. Today, however, many of us look back and realize they taught us the importance of presentation and self-respect. Mr. T was fair and despite the hard exterior, he was a truly caring teacher who was just trying to get us ready for the big, cruel world.

"Mr. T's process felt ridiculous in the college preparatory course. The three-by-five cards, excessive notations, Chicago-style (and hand-measured) footnoting, and the ban on White Out. It was brutal," Bob C says. "Now, I have nothing but mad respect for him. He made every paper I wrote in college (and after) a breeze."

Terry reflects, "If you asked me today what I learned from that prison reform term paper, I couldn't tell you a thing. What I did learn was how to manage deadlines and work within parameters. It wasn't about the content in the paper, it was about finishing what we started." *I'd guess Terry also learned the importance of fully checking the common usage of synonyms, too.*

When it came down to it, if the teacher inspired us or we liked and respected them, we were open to learning from them. "My second-grade teacher told me I'd invent something someday. It always helped when a teacher encouraged my creativity. I went on to publish two novels later in life," Caren in New Jersey says.

Mark in Florida adds, "Mr. Lauricella, my history teacher, told me in junior high, 'Even if you dig ditches for a living, dig them better than anyone else.' I've thought about this often throughout life. It drove me to be at the top of my profession as a master tech."

Mike Rowe, star of *America's Dirtiest Jobs* said, "Not every child will become a lawyer or a doctor. Teach your kids that it is okay to work with your hands and build cool stuff."

On the flip side, we had role models who could take us backward. If we didn't like a teacher, we often became rebellious, slacked off, and were, unfortunately, discouraged.

If you ever heard, "Why are you wasting my time?" or "Write with your right hand" (when you were left-handed), or "You're not working to your potential," you understand what I'm talking about. I still have a note I wrote to Robin in junior high, when I was agitated because I felt my guidance counselor wasn't readily supporting my career dreams.

Note to my BFF:

> In so many words, they told me not to look forward to being a Trucker. They also tried telling me that if I wanted to write, I should take college, but that's not the real reason. They told me I should go because I have high enough scores. I don't want to go to college. I want to write, do secretarial work, maybe even be a Trucker. The trucking business isn't doing so well. My dad gets laid off a lot in the winter. And, oh, I'm confused. I want to have a career with you. Mrs. Lamport kept telling me, "Leave the doors open." I mean, like I'm really gonna close 'em.

Our career choices seemed limited, based on what we heard from our teachers, parents, coaches, and counselors, what we learned in our community, or what we saw on our twelve TV channels. On top of that, we didn't have the internet to research data or make truly informed decisions.

"Exposure happens at the click of a button now," Mrs. Ripley, NBHS principal says. "Gen Z can simply click to see new opportunities and jobs being offered."

While Gen Z and Gen Alpha definitely have some things easier, other things have become harder.

Wayne, former principal at NBHS, states, "Kids are under a lot of pressure now compared to in our day. Money is involved. There is a more aggressive effort to tie achievement and test scores to scholarships. We take bus trips to tour colleges and campuses that look more like high-end resorts. The big universities like Michigan State want the kids with the high ACT/SAT test scores." He continues, "School was a safe place to fail back then, unlike today."

"No one ever talked to me about college, other than my dad. I did zero prep for the SAT," Natasha in California says. "I remember the word 'plethora' on the test. Good thing I learned that word from watching *The Three Amigos* movie when El Guapo says, 'Would you say I have a *plethora* of piñatas?'"

Some schools now have counselor positions whose roles are to ensure students achieve academic success.

"Maybe schools today push kids to 'dream big' without a reality check?" Cori in Oklahoma wonders. "We aimed for ownership and families, not a lifetime of student debt. Most of us didn't get to live in our parents' basements until we were thirty. Adulthood came faster, better preparing us for the future based on reality, sacrifice, and practicality."

How has the approach to preparing for the future evolved with the changes in high school courses from then to now?

Classes such as typing, home economics, welding, horticulture, and shorthand have disappeared into curriculum heaven at most public schools. Less time is spent on civics. Metal/wood shop and auto shop have transformed into 3D printing labs and science, technology, engineering, and mathematics (STEM) classes. For the younger readers who've never heard of shorthand, do *not* go by Urban Dictionary's obscene definition—shorthand was penning squiggly marks and symbols that represent words in order to write faster. It was kind of like Morse code, only not nearly as fun.

Now, high schools offer courses that include college and SAT prep classes. Some classes, such as personal finance, environmental science, engineering, robotics, street law, and leadership development sound more like seminars for adults. You can even find fun classes like dance, 3D design, guitar, Shakespeare in the Real World, resistance training, film appreciation, radio and audio production, and vocal ensemble.

Mrs. Brooks, former Spanish teacher at NBHS, adds, "There are so many resources available to us teachers now, such as online curriculum development, idea blogs, and teacher project groups."

However, many believe that children are no longer being taught basic math and English skills.

Kindra in Michigan says, "If a kid isn't doing well, the teachers get blamed. If kids don't prepare for a test and don't get a good grade on it, they complain and often are allowed to retake the test. I've seen instances where the parent calls the teacher to complain, and the teacher will just change the grade. I've never seen anything like it."

"They didn't pass students back then just to keep rankings up so schools could get funded. If you didn't do the work, you failed!" Brooke in Tucson exclaims.

Michelle, a schoolteacher in Indianapolis, says, "Parents let teachers do their jobs back then, and kids were held accountable, not handheld, like today."

Are teachers taking the hits and more deflated by failure now, as compared to the '80s?

Mrs. Ditto (aka Mrs. Piersma), a former English teacher at NBHS, says, "Our culture was different from bigger schools. We knew each student individually and their family dynamics. Parents were always part of their kid's education. Respect for teachers and the administration was the norm."

But not everything was better back then.

Mrs. Brooks recalls, "In the '80s, it was a challenge to meet the needs of students with different learning styles and backgrounds. Materials and resources were limited and often outdated, especially at a small school. As teachers, though, we had more autonomy with decision-making abilities with the curriculum relating to student behavior."

We will never stop learning no matter how old we are, but the type of learning will change. We are truly students for life, always evolving and expanding our minds and hearts. It's not what's in the textbook anymore—as much as it is about who believes in us now.

"My mom and dad inspire me to work harder and excel," says Madi, a Gen Z college student about her Gen X parents. "They push me to step out of my comfort zone, and know that I will fail at times, but they remain proud and supportive. They help me find and develop my strengths. Their belief in me makes all the difference in the world."

So, what happened with my brother?

In the end, Jeff did exactly what he set out to do. He quit school his junior year and went to work. Today, he can excavate, remove trees, and operate more pieces of equipment than I can count, including handling a one-hundred-foot crane. Our dad and grandpa put my brother on a tractor before his leg was even long enough to reach the pedal.

"They made a believer out of him," my mom says.

Mr. T saw Jeff's potential outside a classroom.

Now fifty-three, Jeff looks back and says, "Mr. T was the hardest teacher I've ever had. He'd tell me, 'Jeff, you can't pass with an 'F,'" but he understood me and never talked down to me. It was all I could do to pass with a 'D+' but I wanted to show Mr. T I could do it because I knew he respected the person I was. *He believed in me.*"

Jeff decided to quit school because he recognized what he wanted and what he *didn't* want based on his skillset.

How many Gen Xers have similar stories? Ones where you or someone you knew weren't going to recite Shakespeare anytime soon, but instead might have the knowledge to fix vital infrastructure? Could their success story have something to do with someone believing in them?

Our level of education and grades did not dictate what we became. Our motivation and work ethic did—supported by those who inspired us and taught us to believe in ourselves.

In 2010, NBHS was partially torn down and the remainder was turned into condos. Mr. Hart was shocked when NB graduates started calling him to ask for an original floor tile from Mr. T's classroom to keep as a souvenir, specifically those with circles drawn on them for the desk legs.

Think about how our lives might have evolved *without* those positive influencers. Where would we be today without them? What would've happened if Mr. T had ignored the signs and turned his back on my brother when he put his head down on his desk? Certainly, Jeff's life wouldn't be the same.

Who are those people who believe in *you* right now?

Who prompts you to get out of your comfort zone and live life just a little fuller? *Who* gives you hope to try new things and creates a safe place for you to fail? *Who* helps you grow to be a better person?

Those are the people you want in your life.

And that's the person many of us are becoming, too. It's not about yourself as much as it is about the bigger picture of giving back and making a difference in someone *else's* life.

It's easy to forget that today's youth still need positive influences just like we did. The inspiration doesn't have to come from a teacher like Mr. Hart or a Mr. T—it can come from a boss, coworker, family member, or friend—*or us*.

It only takes one person to make a difference.

Consider guiding adolescents in your life like Madi to discover their strengths and potential, and empower them to work for what they want. You don't (and shouldn't) have to do it for them, you just have to believe in them. Believing in someone opens a powerful door to learning.

Being firm and unyielding—like the way Mr. T drove accountability with his students—ultimately earned him respect in return. Who knows, maybe someone you inspire will want a piece of your "floor tile" someday to hold fast to the memory of the difference you made for them!

Chapter Rapture 11
Pursue your passions

Sixth Hour Bell

Our education and grades didn't determine our future; it was our motivation and work ethic, shaped by those who inspired us and taught us to believe in ourselves. We continue to evolve as lifelong learners, with the nature of our learning shifting over time. We remain students of life, evolving and expanding our minds and hearts. It's not what's in the textbook anymore, but who believes in us.

Who are the people who support and encourage you now? Who challenges you to step out of your comfort zone and live a fuller life? Who gives you the confidence to try new things and creates a safe space for failure? These positive influencers help us grow into better versions of ourselves.

Extracurricular Activities

- Learn a new skill: Step out of your comfort zone by signing up for a class like computer programming, cooking, Pilates, or playing guitar.

- Mentor an adolescent in your life to help them discover their strengths and potential. Offer support and belief in their abilities rather than doing everything for them.

- Reflect on how reading the classics like Shel Silverstein's *The Giving Tree* or Judy Blume's *Tales of a Fourth Grade Nothing* and *Otherwise Known as Sheila the Great* shaped your perspective.

- Browse LykaStore on Etsy for notebooks made from record album covers and VHS boxes handcrafted by a former band member of the Verve Pipe. These notebooks also make a great gift!

Field Trips

- Send a thank-you note to a teacher who impacted your life, or arrange to meet for coffee or a phone call.

- Take a trip down memory lane by visiting your old school to see how it has changed.

- Explore mentoring opportunities in your community, such as at your local Boys and Girls Club.

Passing Notes in Class

"It doesn't matter whether you can help many or just one. I volunteer and have seen how helping one person can effect major change and send a ripple effect to others. That's why I do it. Knowing that something good was done, even for that one person, is one more person that is happier or feels more thankful in this world. Love really does make the world go round."

~Bryan D in Los Angeles

"My 24-year-old son is now listening to Duran Duran on his own. My job here is done."

~Khrystyne in Connecticut

"In the Book of Life, the answers aren't in the back."

~Charlie Brown

After-School Specials

- Watch movies like *Dead Poets Society*, *Good Will Hunting*, and *Stand and Deliver*. These movies highlight the impact of life choices, self-discovery, and therapy and how they can change your path.
- Enjoy some laughs with Rodney Dangerfield and watch *Back to School* for his witty one-liners and classic humor.
- Let Linus, Lucy, and Charlie Brown take you back to your youth by watching *Peanuts* "School Anxiety."

Chapter Mixtape

- "Another Brick in the Wall, Pt.2" – Pink Floyd
- "Adult Education" – Daryl Hall & John Oates
- "Teacher, Teacher" – 38 Special
- "School's Out" – Alice Cooper
- "Holding Out for a Hero" – Bonnie Tyler
- "Break My Stride" – Matthew Wilder
- "Believe It or Not" – Joey Scarbury (Greatest American Hero theme)
- "The Logical Song" – Supertramp
- "Subdivisions" – Rush
- "Drive" – The Cars

Shortcut to Spotify Playlist: beckykliss.com/CR11

Chap. Twelve

Working for the Weekend

Work

> *"Do something you really like, and hopefully it pays the rent. As far as I'm concerned, that's success."*
>
> ~ *Tom Petty*

Remember the angry teacher in Twisted Sister's music video "I Wanna Rock"? It's the same actor who plays the angry dad in their "We're Not Gonna Take It" video and yells out at the beginning, "Whatta you wanna do with your life?" Each of the kids in the videos looks up and confidently replies, "***I wanna rock!***" How many of us were always dreaming and drumming up fun ideas, but didn't realize that probably a third of our lives would actually be spent *at* work?

In our teens, we were hit with a more serious question: "What do you want to be when you grow up?" A small handful of us already knew, or *thought* we knew. However, most of us preferred to continue dreaming about possibilities. Whenever I polled my classmates in grades seven to twelve, I always asked the question, "Future occupation?"

Here are some answers solidifying how volatile our career goals were during our teens:

Tink: At fourteen, he wanted to be a stud, then a drifter. At fifteen, a professional football player. Then, 'don't-know-yet,' to a Marine next, then a welder. Ultimately, school wasn't his thing. Today, Tink is a successful manager at an environmental company. He didn't become anything he said he would (*well, except for a stud*).

Shorty: At fourteen, Shorty wanted to be a veterinarian and work with horses. At fifteen, a keyboard player in a band, then 'I'm-still-debating,' to a call girl by her Sweet Sixteenth. Today, Shorty is in her thirty-third year of bartending and says the money is great and she loves what she does. She laughs now and says, "I thought being a call girl meant you just got to dress up, go on dates, and have nice dinners—I didn't know it meant I'd have to sleep with a bunch of dudes!"

Whit: At thirteen, Whit wanted to be a baseball player, and at fourteen, a porn star. Then he aimed high for years in the polls, saying he wanted to be a "millionaire, millionaire, millionaire." After graduating, he enlisted for a six-year term in the Marines. He didn't want his parents to have to pay for college, and the Marines offered him a full ride. Whit now works in construction. He laughed, saying he doesn't even remember wanting to be a millionaire.

Lisa, "Miss Pretty in Pink": Lisa knew exactly what she wanted to do and had the same answer in the polls every time, year after year. She wanted to be a beautician. I'm not sure how ammo and hairdos correlate, but today Lisa works in customer service for a company selling ammo. Besides cutting her Barbie doll's hair, she never touched a hair on anyone's head for money. I asked her why she didn't pursue becoming a beautician, and she said, "Did I ever want to do that?" Our memories may fade as we age, but the polls live on!

Mikey: At fourteen, Mikey wanted to be a pilot; he still did at sixteen. At seventeen, he wanted to be a lawyer. Today, he is a senior operating technician at a steel plant. He was married at twenty-two and had his first child at twenty-four. I asked if he uses his business degree for his job now. "Hell, no," he said. "I turned down management twice because it would be a pay cut."

Terry: When Terry was fourteen, he wanted to be a lawyer, then a dentist. But at age fifteen, he upped his game, saying he wanted to be a cameraman for *Playboy*. By the time he was sixteen, he aspired to be a pitcher for the Chicago Cubs. After college, Terry became a regional sales rep for a vodka company before becoming a full-time father to four boys.

Other poll answers from the class rebels were: hooker, gigolo, drug addict, drifter, and male prostitute. Our late class clown, "Fatty," wanted to be a gynecologist in *tenth* grade. Some of us had more practical career goals, like relief clerk, order entry clerk, secretary, or travel agent, and then some had ones like auto mechanic, doctor, dentist, state trooper, and electrician. Most classmates changed their minds as often as quarterly (when a new poll came out).

Only a small handful actually made a career out of what they said they would.

Pam, in LaPorte, says, "Ever since I was in 7th grade, I knew I wanted to become a nurse because of my mom. She was a nurse, and I saw the positive impact she made, and I wanted to do that as well. I've been an RN now for thirty-four years."

So how did we end up in the career we're in now if we didn't know what we wanted to be?

Most schools had "career day," which introduced us to businesspeople and tradesmen to help us decide what we should do. Of course, college could change our path, too. But most of us were out beating the pavement and looking for odd jobs before we were of legal age to work.

We wanted to work because we *wanted* out of the house. Getting a job provided a much-needed avenue to social connections beyond school; earning money was just the bonus. Suddenly, washing grimy dishes at TK's Corral, where the cute cook from a couple of grades ahead worked, was considered enjoyable. Scooping ice cream with friends at Oink's was hip, because, *duh, it was ice cream*. We perceived it as lucky or cool to be slinging burgers over a greasy restaurant grill.

Bob C says, "I loved it when I started working at Redamak's at thirteen. I started there as a busboy working non-stop, picking up people's food garbage and emptying the trash—it was gross, and I was glad when I was promoted to a host the following year. I made a lot of good friends there and have a million stories from that place that I'll never forget."

When I went to work at fifteen at the New Buffalo Public Library, it was *not* because I loved being in quiet places or was an avid bookworm; it was because I admired the librarian, Merry, who *wasn't* quiet. She made the job fun, and I always looked forward to walking there every day after school to be with her and my coworkers, even though it was *work*.

We weren't thinking about aligning our career goals with our first jobs; we were focused on where our friends worked. Plus, jobs weren't plentiful in many towns, so we took what was available. Our parents usually gave us the ultimatum: go to college, get a job, *or* get our ass kicked. They had no intention of letting us sit home, lounge around, and have a relaxing, lazy life at their expense. We were programmed that in order to *get*, we had to *give*.

That's why so many Gen Xers are driven, despite our generation's reputation for being slackers. We've been dubbed the "work hard, play hard" generation, who thrived without handouts. I'd even go so far as to say that we *were* the "give-to-get" generation.

If you wanted a TV in your bedroom, you opened a credit card and made payments. If you wanted gas money or trendy new clothes, you picked up extra shifts babysitting or delivering newspapers. If you wanted a car to drive, you were told to "get an 'eff-ing job and buy yourself one."

That pretty much meant after high school graduation, one of four things was likely to happen: you would start working full time, attend a college or university, serve in the military, or get married and start a family.

"College was my escape from small-town living, and a chance to discover who I was," says Bob C. "I would've never had the balls to move to New York alone had it not been for moving out of the small town to experience more cultures and opportunities—more than what getting a degree taught me."

Shaun in Kalamazoo says, "Life wasn't so magical and cute anymore after the summer of graduation. Some left for college, others began to work full time, and some got married. Others, like me, were lost and unsure, and responsibility didn't come naturally. After a year and a half of college, money, and jobs, options ran out. Eerily similar to the movie *Stripes*, my friend Rod and I joined the Army. It seemed to be a better option than *Salem's Lot*, ending up in jail or six feet under."

Most of us learned responsibility by fending for ourselves after school while both our parents worked outside the home facing the demands of their bills. Many of us latchkey kids raised our younger siblings, taught ourselves how to cook, and had a hands-on approach to problem-solving; this fostered our independence.

Gen Xers are self-sufficient, results-oriented, and hardworking. Our initiative and drive also built the bridge from analog to digital, and we became tech savvy. Some of the big corporate gurus are Gen Xers, like Sara Blakely, creator of Spanx , Satya Nadella of Microsoft, Michael Dell of Dell Computer, and Sergey Brin and Larry Page of Google. Our generation is known for being independent thinkers, resourceful, adaptable, ambitious, and eager to learn new skills; we don't like to be supervised and strive to accomplish things on our own terms. We value diversity, challenges, and responsibility.

That brings me to another point. Were we in training to become future workaholics, though?

One Saturday while I was working at the library, I had alcohol-induced flu-like symptoms prompted by poor choices from the night before. In between waiting on library patrons, I'd run to the bathroom and heave my Cap'n Crunch into the porcelain bowl. I was completely miserable for hours, but still worked my shift with a green face because missing work wasn't considered an option. That's how we rolled in the '80s.

Kristen in Minnesota says, "I was a server in my teens. We'd get drunk, dance all night, and show up to sling hash in the morning, reeking of booze. But we never missed work."

That mentality carried onward through our adult lives. After graduation, I worked forty hours a week in accounting for a company *and* at JCPenney on weekends to support my retail shopping habit *(you know, the job where you spend your check before earning it)*. I was breakdancing every which way trying to make ends meet, but still carrying credit card debt and struggling to pay my bills.

My boyfriend, who I lived with at the time (*Mr. I Kept Your Stereo*), suggested I take a third job cleaning a local truck rental and repair office with my only two free nights per week. (I think he wanted to raise my rent plus have me learn how to clean his house better.) I wrestled with my bill pile, jonesing for more cash flow, and I surrendered to the third job. How hard could it be to buy a mop and a bucket, and clean some greasy floors, right? And, I learned how to clean properly by getting chastised for *not* cleaning properly.

I became efficient and word spread. Gaining new customers encouraged me to quit my other two jobs. And, in 1996, over a case of beer, my dear, late friend Jerry Fasbender designed my Great Lakes Cleaning, Inc. logo. It wasn't about having a career goal or a plan; I just knew I was responsible for my shoddy spending habits and stack of bills. *I had to give, in order to get.*

In all my library, office, or burger-serving days, did I ever say, "I want to start a janitorial business?" Nope. No more than Tink thought he'd be in waste management instead of playing for the Steelers, or Miss Pretty in Pink imagined she'd be selling bullets instead of rolling perms, or Terry dreamed of distributing vodka instead of being a photographer for Hugh Hefner. We didn't have a set plan, we just pushed through the obstacles in front of us and made it work— the Gen X way—and now here we all are, some forty years later.

And that was the downside of the '80s work ethic instilled in many of us: trading a normal family life for our career. We sacrificed vital time in our thirties and even forties in exchange for long hours and unhealthy habits. Every vacation I took, I had a phone stuck to my ear dealing with stressful work and employee issues. We might have had a "work hard, play hard" mentality, but how many of us considered work to be our biggest priority?

Last fall, I met Bailey, 22, when she came to my house as part of a company I hired to clean my windows. So, of course, I had to talk her up since she's a Gen Z *and* in the cleaning business. Turns out her parents named her after the character Bailey Quarters in *WKRP in Cincinnati*, the '80s TV show.

This is Bailey's story: she's cleaning windows while trying to figure out what she wants to do. She doesn't want to be running up big bills in college while guessing her career path. Her work ethic came from her parents; at eighteen, she was told to get a job and pay for her own car. She was taught no job was beneath her as long as she was earning a paycheck. Her dad is a late Baby Boomer and her mom is Gen X. Her last comment is what hit home for me. She said, "How you are raised determines your work ethic."

Isn't that the truth? Our parents taught us responsibility and a solid work ethic. Bubba's taught him to never come up the ladder empty-handed, Selwyn's taught him not to shortchange anything or cut corners, Mary's taught her to do her best at whatever she did, and Vicki's taught her not to do anything half-assed. When we reflect on those lessons, it makes sense why we've often done things the way we have.

When we find ourselves looking at the younger generations critically and pointing fingers, we may want to ask ourselves what we've taught our own kids about responsibility and work ethic.

Robin, who works in HR for a large, reputable, janitorial company, says, "Even getting people to come in for an interview is hard. In a three-day period, I had sixteen interviews scheduled, and only one of them showed, so I hired her, and then she didn't show up for her first day of work! None of them called to say they couldn't make it. They were just no-call, no-shows." Granted, janitorial work has a reputation for not being high-end, but many entry-level janitor positions now have a starting hourly rate well above minimum wage.

Guy, an owner of a security company in Florida, tells his interviewees, "If you want to work with me, I have three requirements: 1) you can't live with your mommy; 2) you must have a cell phone that works; and 3) you must have your own car. If they have those three things covered, they are usually good with everything else."

"It's unbelievable the youngsters who are hired into the mill where I work because their dads or brothers work there," Mikey says. "But they constantly call off, don't want to do anything, and feel entitled to the same treatment as their relatives who've worked there for decades and have seniority. Some of these young employees are calling off 30-plus days a year. They don't understand the concept of 'you have to pay your dues.' How do they even live that way?" Many working CD-55ers feel Mikey's frustration. Even Wayne, former NBHS principal, says schools deal with more attendance issues with students now than in the past.

"We made it more important for our kids to have good grades than to earn items," Kelly, a Gen X parent in Elkhart, says. "The best we hoped for as parents back then was for a scholarship. Now parents want professional sports, swim programs, and more. If kids aren't in school sports, they should have a job. Kids should know how to mow a lawn, do laundry, and complete various chores. There's a big difference now in responsibility, tolerance, and discipline."

James in Chattanooga says, "My kids' work ethic is a lot like mine, but their 'REST ETHIC' is 'effing epic! I've been taking notes."

"I love my kids, but they are crazy entitled. Going to Starbucks every day after school to get a Refresher and a treat, because it's 'what everyone does' is *not* how I grew up," Julie in Chicago says. "My kids think I'm so strict. If they want Starbucks, have at it, but I'm not funding it. I've suggested they make their own money, deliver flyers in the neighborhood looking for work for babysitting, washing cars, mowing lawns, pulling weeds, whatever. Don't ask me for Apple Pay to pay for your Starbucks."

Are the younger generations holding out for entry-level, feel-good jobs that pay upwards of $20 per hour now when we took on *three* whatever-we-could-get jobs to earn our $20 per hour? Hell, we'd even run ads in the newspaper *offering* our services for hire. I've seen signs on windows and doors of businesses, especially since COVID, that said, "Closed, no staff," "Now hiring non-stupid people," and "Hiring people that show up." In the '80s, if there was a Help Wanted sign in the window, there was usually a dogfight over getting our application in first and making sure it outshined all the others in the stack so we would get hired. How many of us wrote on our first applications, "I'm a hard worker"? *How times have changed.*

Today, it's more common for kids to look for a job that aligns with their values, and they'll go without a job, and forfeit the money and anything they planned on buying with it, if they don't find one. For those who passed math class, we ask, is this how the new Common Core math shit works? *Because it doesn't add up.* Gen Xers weren't choosy, nor were we wired to use phrases in our vocabulary like, "It's not my job," or "Pay me first, then I'll do it." Hell, we were even taught to work for free, quite often out of respect for our elders and to stay in our family's good graces.

In the '80s, responsibility came first, *then* play. Is that reversed for most young adults today and they have to like what they do first, or they won't do it?

Mrs. Ripley, NBHS principal and mother of two kids, says, "COVID completely altered the priorities of Gen Z. They work to live, not live to work. They are able to explore opportunities that previous generations didn't have access to. The priority has shifted to enjoying life and working enough to enjoy your time. I am not so sure that they are wrong!"

Within every generation, we know there are people who lack motivation to work. But it seems the twenty-something Gen Zs are getting the bad rap.

"When I looked for a job when I was young, I'd apply for one as soon as I saw it," Amy in Dayton, says. "My daughter in her twenties wants to think about it and wait until she feels like applying. She works at a used bookstore instead of using her $60,000 degree for a better paying job. Their ambition, or lack of, is so much different than ours."

Meanwhile, back in the '80s, we were beating our heads against the wall working whether we loved what we did or not.

We've all heard the saying, "Work smarter, not harder," but it seems the "work smarter" part may have been left off in the '80s—maybe because we were programmed by default to *"work harder"?* And we put up with a lot of shit, like long hours, doing whatever it took, and prioritizing work over family and fun more than we probably should have. However, there were benefits—most of us gained hands-on experience, ramped up our value of responsibility, and learned real-world lessons from being on the job at a young age.

"Our generation has always done what had to be done. I was often in survival mode, and it never occurred to me that I should plan *fun*," Laura in Georgia says. "My kid understands that work doesn't define us. He works to pay for his life, but he prioritizes small things that bring him joy, like going fishing once a week and training for a marathon."

We know the Baby Boomers are over halfway into retirement and that the oldest Gen Xers will be retiring within the next five to ten years. If this is the path younger generations are taking, who will replace us?

At the NB Class of 2023 graduation ceremony, each student's anticipated career path was announced as they were handed their diploma. They ranged from architecture, elementary education, finance, pre-law, psychology, engineering, marketing, aviation transportation, forensic science, aviation, dental hygiene, cosmetology, culinary arts, and marine biology.

These are all outstanding, impressive careers. What's missing? Only a small percentage of the graduates were going into the trades, like construction, welding, and machining.

In an interview with Dave Ramsey at EntreLeadership, Mike Rowe, host of the Discovery Channel's *Dirty Jobs,* discussed the multi-generational workforce and the lack of incoming workers. "Every year for the last twenty years, for every five skilled tradespeople who retire, two replace them. The math is unsustainable. It's going to run out. The problem is not unique to one industry, to a state, or to a zip code. For the last sixteen years, we've been pushing this rock up the hill. We've made progress because more people are aware of the problem of recruitment."

Rowe is a Gen Xer who has a foundation that has awarded over nine million dollars in work ethic scholarships. He is known for pushing the vocational trades. Kudos to Mike's foundation, because many of us wonder where the future plumbers, electricians, HVAC techs, and such will come from.

Where does AI fit into the future of replacing the soon-to-be missing workforce? McDonald's recently reported the company is pushing for its entire process, including the cooking, to be robotic. Should we be more concerned about *Short Circuit's* "Prototype Number 5" cooking our burger, or what happens when "Number five is alive!" and takes over humanity?

I circled back to my NB peeps above and asked them what they learned along their four-decade career journey.

"Tink has been working thirty-five years and living the dream," his wife, Connie, says. "He pulls rank more than ever now and uses vacation time not to miss school or sporting events for his six grandkids."

Wayne retired as NBHS principal after sixteen years. "After thirty-two years of public service, I needed a break. If I can't be at my absolute best, I need to be done," he says.

Mikey is eligible for retirement after twenty-five years of working at the steel plant. He has three to go and says, "Money isn't everything, as long as we can be somewhat comfortable. I don't even mind if I have to get a part-time job. I've been working since I was thirteen. It's time to relax." Mikey's parents recently passed away in their early seventies. This reminds us that how we spend our time is more important than ever.

Money can't buy back time with someone.

Being financially secure is still a priority for many of us but working sixty hours per week instead of spending time with our elderly parents, kids, grandkids, or friends isn't worth the trade-off anymore. We've all heard the sad stories about how people retire, ready to live the good life, and then keel over. We realize now that could be *us*. *F%#k that*.

So, what were *my* answers in the polls asking what I wanted to be when I grew up? I wanted to be a writer at thirteen, a truck driver at fourteen, computer programmer at fifteen, and a Floridian at sixteen *(like that was a paying job!)*. Then I set my goals on becoming a secretary—*you know, the high-end job that was inspired by Dolly Parton in* 9 to 5.

Fifteen years after the start of my business, Great Lakes Cleaning, I sold the company to get back stress-free time in my life. GLC had grown to almost two hundred employees and one hundred sixty customers spread over five counties. It was a fast-paced, fun, rewarding, hard, crazy business, but when it lost that enjoyment factor, I knew I had to make a change no matter how nice the paycheck was.

Let's pose this question again to our wise CD-55 selves: "What do you want to be when you grow up?" And let's add: Do you like what you're doing now? Can you see yourself doing what you do now for the next five to ten years?

Of all the jobs you've had in your life, which ones:
- Gave you the most joy?
- Were the most rewarding?
- Did you like and why?

We've worked our asses off for decades, putting in long hours and sacrificing family time for career goals. And, the funny thing is, many of us found satisfaction in staying busy and achieving a sense of accomplishment through our work. But now being CD-55ers, it's essential to shift our focus and consider doing things based on what brings us joy.

Mike P in Ohio says, "I've been a pharmacy tech for nineteen years. The last few of them, the lack of support in management has been horrible, but I loved the people I worked with, and I had accumulated so much vacation time, so I stayed. Three added years of stress went by. I finally bit the bullet recently, took a few benefit cuts, and changed jobs. I don't get anxiety about going to work anymore and wish I would've changed sooner."

Mike is just one of oodles of Gen Xers who are making changes to now love what they do—*because they're doing what they love.*

Bryan relishes working from home because he can wear whatever he wants and spend the day with his dogs. Mina loves to sew and sells her creations proudly. Daniel bartends because he enjoys being around people and staying active; plus, it's never boring. Angie fancies freelancing because she gets to work in different environments where really good food is provided. John W is in social work because he finds it rewarding to help recovering addicts who are scared and frustrated turn their lives around. Vernon is in the building trades because that's what his dad taught him, and working reminds him of his dad.

David in Kentucky says, "I walked away from twenty-two years of a good, steady paycheck with the full benefits package fifteen years ago. I can't work for small-minded people whose own sense of importance exceeds their abilities. I now have five hundred sixty-four bosses on my cattle ranch. Life doesn't have a rewind button, and this tape ends too soon. I've never regretted my decision, even for a millisecond."

I'm with David—it just took until my early fifties for me to pull the trigger. I've come full circle to pursuing my childhood dream of becoming an author. What was your childhood dream job? *Who* did you want to be when you grew up? Do you want to be content, happy, and live with less stress? Maybe those are the real answers instead—and, it's never too late to pursue some version of that now.

Remember, **work to live, not live to work.** As tough as this is to swallow for Gen Xers, this Gen Z concept, in a way, may be a life lesson to adopt. Make sure to include the "work smarter" part in there, too—especially the enjoyment factor.

Now, go drink a couple of Bartles & Jaymes wine coolers, play Loverboy's *Get Lucky* album or Rick Springfield's *Working Class Dog* album, and ponder the future job options that could bring you the most joy.

Dear Sexy, (Bert),

~~■■■■■■■~~ I have a dream, my friend and I want to be like you and Jerry Reed. We may be both girls but we have already figured it out. I'm going to be the trucker and my friends going to be the car driver. We're thinking of some handles. Anyway were not sure if we should film it (if possible) or make it happen in real life (we doubt it) First of all for a rig like that (yours) did you have it specially made? or where can you get a rig like that? Was that a transam that you drove? This time instead of men picking up the women were going to pick up the men. We are very serious about this. Please write →

A fan letter I wrote to Burt Reynolds after watching "Smokey and the Bandit" and before I knew how to spell his name correctly!

> back and give us hints and answer ~~us~~ our questions. Believe me we need all the help we can get. Thanks a million for your time.
>
> Love,
> 2 of your best fans!
> Becky ~~Kliss~~
> and
> Robin ~~Hamann~~

If there's one thing we nailed back then was to: Dream Big!

Chapter Rapture 12
Work to live, don't live to work

Sixth Hour Bell

Gen X is known for being independent, resourceful, and ambitious. We were the "give-to-get" generation. We tackled challenges on our own terms, often without supervision. But did that set us up to become workaholics? Many of us sacrificed family life for career success and responsibilities, driven by the "work harder" mindset, putting in long hours and prioritizing work over family and fun. Now, it's time to "work smarter."

As the "work hard, play hard" generation, we've realized that working sixty hours a week at the expense of time with loved ones isn't worth it. We've seen retirees keel over soon after leaving the workforce and realize that could be us.

As CD-55ers, it's time to adopt the "work to live, not live to work" mindset. Embracing this Gen Z concept might be a tough adjustment, but it's a valuable life lesson.

Extracurricular Activities

- Grab a notepad and list everything you enjoy about your current work. What do you see yourself doing in the next five to ten years? Reflect on the jobs you've had—which brought you the most joy, were the most rewarding, and why?

- Next, make a list of hobbies that have the potential to earn money. Look for intersections between your passions and potential income sources; this could lead to a new venture! As the saying goes, "If you do what you love, you'll never work a day in your life."

Field Trips

- Think about volunteering to speak at a career day at a local school.

- Take a break from work and plan a long weekend getaway. Explore '80s-themed festivals (or events) like "Retromania LIVE" in Branson, Missouri, "Bringin' Back the 80s Fest" in Frankenmuth, Michigan, or go big with a vacation to the "Rewind Festival" in Berkshire, U.K.

- Plan your vacations and take field trips! Work will always be there, so don't postpone your vacation time. Use it intentionally to recharge and enjoy life.

Passing Notes in Class

"I will be retired before I decide what to do when I grow up because lots of things are interesting! I just really want to travel to historic sites around the world."

~Elaine in Texas

"I quit high school to raise my son. Had two more kids and was a stay-at-home mom for 22 years, and then my husband passed away. I had to figure out how to do everything. Went back and got my GED and now I run a successful party business."

~Colleen in Kentucky

After-School Specials

- Check out classic MTV videos like Twisted Sisters "I Wanna Rock" and "We're Not Gonna Take It." The options for watching our beloved MTV videos are endless on YouTube.
- Explore Mike Rowe's insights on *America's Dirtiest Jobs* or at mikerowe.com. Watch "Best Moments from the New Season Dirty Jobs" on YouTube, and check out his interview, "Could Gen Z Revolutionize the Trades," for a fresh take on the future of work.
- Watch classic movies like *9 to 5, Gung Ho, The Secret of My Success, Take This Job and Shove It, Wall Street,* and *Working Girl.*

Chapter Mixtape

- "Working for the Weekend" – Loverboy
- "Allentown" – Billy Joel
- "9 to 5" – Dolly Parton
- "Workin' for a Livin'" – Huey Lewis & The News
- "She Works Hard for the Money" – Donna Summer
- "I Wanna Be a Cowboy" – Boys Don't Cry
- "Just a Job to Do" – Genesis
- "Morning Train (Nine to Five)" – Sheena Easton
- "Working on the Highway" – Bruce Springsteen
- "Manic Monday" – The Bangles

Shortcut to Spotify Playlist: beckykliss.com/CR12

Chap. Thirteen

Money for Nothing

--- 🎞️ ---

Money

"When I was growing up, if we wanted a Jacuzzi, we had to fart in the tub."

~Billy Ray Valentine (Eddie Murphy)

On October 7, 1975, the first instant lottery game ticket was sold in Michigan. My dad took full advantage of this to try his luck from the start. The third day after the lottery launch, my dad and his cousin Ronnie stopped in Saugatuck, Michigan, after work with the semi to see "if the fish were biting." They bought a six-pack and four scratch-off tickets at the local party store by the lake, drank the beer, pocketed the tickets, and headed home.

That night, my brother Jeff and I picked which ticket we wanted to scratch off and asked, "But, dad, what do we get if we win something?"

My dad said, "Well, what do ya want?"

We both piped up with, "New bikes!"

He responded, "If you win enough moolah, you two can have your new bikes."

We were told we needed three matching numbers, and we eagerly began scratching off the squares with our quarters. I scratched off a block that read "$10,000," followed by another that read "$10,000." When the last block I scratched off also read "$10,000," I held up the ticket and asked, "Is this good, Dad?"

My mom snatched that winning lottery ticket from me faster than Speedy Gonzales could say "Arriba!" News spread like wildfire. Willy Wonka and his Golden Ticket was nothing compared to this very real $10,000 winning ticket in little New Buffalo, Michigan. A week later, my mom, with her horn-rimmed glasses and beehive hairdo, and my dad, with a big grin, stood outside of the New Buffalo Savings and Loan and had their picture taken by a newspaper reporter while they held the unfathomable check. That picture was featured on the front page of the *New Buffalo Times*. It was epic for our family.

We learned about money at a young age: give the Tooth Fairy your tooth, get a dollar. Wait three hundred sixty-five days and become another year older, get cash in your birthday cards. Give up your entire Saturday night babysitting, get ten bucks *if you're lucky*. Put in sweat equity to earn a good report card, receive a pat on the back, and hopefully some "toad hides" (my dad's slang for dollar bills). Give sixty dollars of Monopoly money, get Baltic Avenue. Ninety-nine percent of the time, it was about giving in order to get.

Could our attachment to the almighty dollar have been shaped by the fact that we knew if we wanted something, we had to earn it?

As children, we took whatever cash gigs we could get: washing cars, mowing lawns, raking leaves, detasseling corn, picking berries, baling hay, chopping wood, delivering newspapers, shoveling snow, cleaning houses, collecting cans to recycle, and yes, even listening for the song of the day on WLS radio, "Raspberry Beret," to win $100 (*another rotary phone notch on my belt*).

In addition, how many of us found questionable entrepreneurial endeavors to try when we were young?

Levi in Oregon would buy a pack of Starburst candies at the store, then sell the pieces individually at school for a hefty markup. Mac in Texas would illegally pick blueberries and sell them to neighbors to put gasoline in his motorcycle. Mina in Houston would get $20 to mow the lawn, and then pay the neighbor boy—who had a crush on her—$15 to mow it instead. *Brilliant!*

Mina says today, "I wouldn't say I had great work ethic, but I was motivated and worked to get out of the house at eighteen, which is what I wanted."

I earned the nickname "Weasel" from my Uncle Quennie when I was five because I'd swindle my cousins and the neighborhood kids trying to trade up or make 25 cents. I'd carry a brown, crinkled lunch sack with my treasures and trinkets in it, ready to reel in my next victim. I ended up being the sucker more often than not because everyone I hit up was older than me and knew the value of my junk better than I did. *Suuuumbitch.*

Carl from Detroit would buy weed, roll one hundred joints a day on a stolen McDonald's tray, and sell them in high school for a buck a piece or the Gordon Gekko special–six for $5 dollars. Carl and his buddies also scalped concert tickets. They'd go to the Hudson's CDC ticket outlet the night before concert tickets went on sale and party all night long in order to be the first people in line. The next morning, when the ticket window opened, they'd buy the maximum number of tickets allowed, walk to the end of the one hundred fifty people waiting in line, and solicit them. They'd sell half of the tickets they bought with a markup high enough to cover the cost of their own tickets. *Gen X entrepreneurship at its finest.*

In a 1983 poll, I asked my classmates, "If you were granted three wishes, what would they be?" Most wished "to be rich" or "have lots of money." And we already know Whit's goal was "to be a millionaire."

Why did it seem we were so focused on money at such a young age when most of us were raised with just the basics by frugal parents?

Most parents addressed our clothing needs a few times a year, usually during Back-to-School shopping, Christmas, and birthdays. If we wanted Calvin Klein or Jordache jeans, we better knock on more doors that week to drum up the extra cash. Otherwise, we were getting Brittania, Levi's, or Lee jeans.

Kristi in California says, "I grew up seventy miles from the closest mall, so Sears and JCPenney catalogs were the only options locally. I started working at fourteen so I could buy my favorites: Gunne Sax, Benetton, Esprit, Guess, Reebok, Charlotte Russe, and Jellies. And people wonder why Gen Xers are badasses!"

"We had to look good when we left the house," Miss Pretty in Pink adds. "Cute clothes, makeup, accessories. I spent a lot of the money I earned at Claire's and Fashion Bug because my mom wasn't buying that stuff for me."

Some of us looked at the kids who were given everything they wanted as spoiled, while others viewed them as desirable friends to hang out with and enjoy the perks we lacked at home.

"I always wanted a pool and a basketball court like Bruce and Tink had, and they wanted my Tonka trucks," Vernon from New Buffalo says. "We learned how to work the system by pairing up with friends who had things like cable TV, video game systems, swimming pools, and Doritos at their house."

As kids, our spending habits were pretty simple. We'd slap down our cash for toys like video games, the Bionic Woman (or Man) doll, Care Bears, Glo Worms, Transformers, Hot Wheels, marbles, Star Wars cards, Scratch 'n Sniff stickers, or outdoor toys—like a new frisbee, squirt gun, or jump rope. And, we were all about the candy and pop. Heppler's was NB's small downtown grocery store with old, scuffed wood floors and a bountiful penny candy aisle. We'd raid the place for candy cigarettes, Now and Laters (that would dislocate our teeth), three-foot licorice ropes, and Hubba Bubba gum.

When we went shopping, often our top two hot items were posters and music. We'd peruse Spencer's and flip through the posters while sneaking our way to the wondrous naughty aisle. We'd thumb through *Tiger Beat, Teen Beat, Circus*, and *Sports Illustrated* at the Hallmark store looking for the pin-ups who were most worthy of spending our allowance on. It didn't matter if it was Billy Joel's *Glass Houses* or Van Halen's *Women and Children First* from the record store or a poster of Erik Estrada or Cheryl Tiegs—there was always a wish list. And we certainly kept the manufacturers of TRACS or BASF blank cassettes in business.

When Sweet Sixteen hit, many of us upped our shopping game because we could drive ourselves to the mall. Gen Xers are known for being "Mall Chicks" or "Mall Rats." We'd cruise Casual Corner, County Seat, and Contempo Casuals for the latest and greatest. We'd check out the makeup at Merle Norman, load up on rubber bracelets and earrings at Claire's, try on the Members Only jacket or parachute pants at Chess King, buy nylons at JCPenney, and obsess over the 45s, LPs, and cassettes at Record Town, Camelot Music, or Sam Goody. We'd go to Fox Jewelers and size up the shiny, thick gold chains and concoct a plan to purchase them, often by making payments. We strolled the pet stores, tapping on the glass, *oohing* and *ahhing* over the cute puppies and kittens. We spent more time strutting the mall trying to look cool, and scoping out who was there, than actually shopping. Ultimately, the sound of the arcade, the *pew-pews, beeps, boops,* and *wobble-wobbles* lured us in. The games sucked up every last one of our quarters or tokens until we landed high score *or ran out of coins*.

Once our hard-earned checks started rolling in during our teens, Gen Xers say their money went for gas, fishing gear, BMX bike parts, car accessories, music, posters, Atari or Nintendo cartridge games, fireworks, kegs, Kessler whiskey, and maybe even cigarettes and a dash of weed when no one was watching.

Our big purchases were cars, waterbeds, stereos, TVs, and for some, a college education.

Tink remembers working seventy-seven hours at $3.35 per hour at Little Bohemia Restaurant during the town's busy Ship & Shore festival weekend. "When I opened my check of $257.95 (minus taxes), I was like, 'Oh my God, what am I gonna do with *all* this money?' I was pumped because I knew it was going to put a lot of gas in my truck."

How fast do we all blow $250 these days?

Back then, most every household wished Ed McMahon would stroll up to their door and present them with a giant check for two million dollars for buying a couple of six-dollar magazine subscriptions.

Many CD-55ers concur that their parents lived within their means way more than we do now. Mine did for sure—although my parents had two different styles of saving money: one saved, and the other *didn't*. When my dad purchased his first bag phone in his work semi, he called everyone he knew to tell them he was having a ball. He'd call 'ol Uncle Bill in the Upper Peninsula (UP) and rave about how cool it was to be talking to him at the same time while going down the highway at 60 mph. When the $1,200 phone bill came in the mail and my mom opened it, my dad *wasn't* having a ball anymore. My mom would be home balancing her checkbook, trying to figure out why she was off by three cents, while my grandma L was sitting back collecting 18 percent interest on her accounts. Meanwhile, I was loading up on the candy aisle, buying as much as I could with the three dollars to my name.

What our parents taught us often determined if we grew our savings account or spent every dime.

In sixth grade, I created a club called "Pre-Teen Sensations," inspired by the secret club in Judy Blume's *Are You There God? It's Me, Margaret*. As club president, I requisitioned each member to write a letter to Shawn Cassidy. I then wrote a note to members saying, "If you want the letter mailed to him, you are either going to have to bring a stamp from home or pay me an extra 15 cents. I cannot afford to pay another 15 cents. I hope you understand." *I definitely took after my mom that day.*

Every set of parents were different in what they taught us. Selwyn learned to work hard by watching his mom sell Avon on the side while working two full-time jobs. Mina saved her lunch money to put jeans on layaway in high school. Trish made payments with her boyfriend on a trailer in a park they wanted to live in once she was out of school, and Terry's dad taught him his house payment should never be more than one week of pay.

Every generation has to deal with money and the struggles that come with it.

Mike in Tulsa says, "The difference nowadays is our generation often thinks we are living within our means as long as we don't breach the credit limit on our credit cards. My parents didn't look at it that way."

"Our parents didn't pay cell phone bills, laptops, Wi-Fi, security cameras, or all the streaming services now because our family had free network TV," Kristin in Maryland explains. "I feel like our parents had less to pay for and their costs were lower. For us, college costs went up, but the value of a diploma went down. Car insurance went up. Ads are in our face all the time and with the ease of buying Amazon, I'm struggling to make it."

But on the flip side, some things are so much cheaper these days. Leslie in Three Oaks remembers, "My mom purchased a microwave on credit in the '80s and had to make payments because it was so expensive." A microwave sells on Amazon today for a third of what Leslie's mom paid back then.

Nancy, also from Three Oaks, was excited when her mom bought her a car at seventeen. That was until her mom said, "Oh, by the way, *here's the payment book*."

Back in the day, the Sears and JCPenney catalogs *were* our Amazon, especially the Christmas catalogs. To make a purchase, we either used cold, hard cash, wrote a check and snail mailed it in with a handwritten paper order form, used a parent's credit card, or signed up for layaway, which was ninety days and cost the same as cash. We'd have to wait for the UPS driver to eventually deliver our item, unless someone could take us to the mall to pick it up. *Yes, there were times when riding in a station wagon with your mom to the mall could actually be exciting.*

Today, we can buy anything we want online. Even groceries can be dropped on our doorstep, packed in reusable ice blocks. Stores are not stocking as much inventory as they once did because demand for in-person purchases has decreased. Not long ago, I needed a new scanner, Jello, and one-ounce Jello shot cups *(for an 80's party, you know)*. I could either spend time and gas to run to the office supply store to see if they had a scanner in stock, drive to the grocery store for Jello, then go to Gordon's for the plastic cups, **or** I could take less than five minutes and order my three items on Amazon and have them in two days or less. *Am I part of the problem?* Or is it even a problem? Are people more willing to go the electronic route and trade a couple bucks to save their precious minutes? Remember the obsessive little shit paperboy in *Better Off Dead*, who screamed, "I want my two dollars!" as he chased John Cusack? Maybe today it's more about wanting our *two hours*.

When we hear Amazon has robots that whiz around their massive warehouses at 45 mph filling orders, it certainly suggests online shopping is the way of the world now. Where does this leave brick-and-mortar stores? And what's left of our '80s trailblazing malls? They are sadly diminishing.

Remember, we were the ones meticulously trained to balance our checkbooks in school and now that has virtually been replaced by online banking and payment methods like Apple Pay, PayPal, Venmo, Zelle, debit cards, or online payments (EFTs).

In 2022, I went to see the Loverboy, REO Speedwagon, and Styx concert (*Live and Unzoomed Tour*) in Tinley Park, Illinois, and the sign on the venue read, "You are entering a cashless facility." You could have all the cash in the world in your pocket (*since you can't carry your purse in either*), but if you didn't have a credit or debit card, you weren't buying jack shit. Even the Daytona 500, with three hundred thousand people in attendance, doesn't take cash. And the list of venues that don't take cash is growing.

Many kids today have a debit card or credit card linked to their parents' account to pay for their Amazon purchases, gas, food, and streaming or music services. Most of us Gen Xers were cut off by the time we were twenty, if not sooner.

We perceive that Millennials and Gen Z generations are not motivated by money like we were. Could that be because they simply don't have the need for it? *Or is it back to how we were parented?*

Courtney, a Millennial in Ann Arbor, says, "I feel like my generation is less willing to sacrifice our health and mental well-being to support someone else's dream and corporate profiteering. We already feel it's impossible to get ahead with the cost of living now. We'll work hard for something we believe in, and for me, I appreciate what I have, but I also want to enjoy my life now, while I'm healthy and able to do so. Millennials care about balance; most of us aren't interested in working ourselves into an early grave."

"The biggest shift of wealth is happening in the USA right now," Mrs. Ripley, the **NBHS** principal, says. "Baby Boomers are retiring or dying, which is shifting significant wealth to the next generation. The younger generations are living off of their wealth, which is allowing them not to have to work as much."

Today, we can all buy whatever we want right from our phones. Nearly every store has a website to purchase from, and with little effort, even the smallest one-person businesses can sell online. We have so many shopping sites, like craigslist, eBay, Etsy, Target, and Amazon. We have bigger houses to fill, and we have the pressures to keep up with the latest gizmos and gadgets. We have bigger incomes, and we want bigger toys. Some of us even have two homes.

Minimalism, the documentary mentioned in Chapter 10, while exploring ways to make our lives simpler, further looks into our motivations for doing so in a world where we need to rent 2.2 *billion* square feet of personal storage units just for our extra belongings.

"We're living our life depending on the space we've got rather than creating our space to fit our lives," Frank Mascia, an architect, says in the documentary. "It's so easy to go wrong."

Jacqueline, a middle-aged woman interviewed in *Minimalism*, shared how she was commuting a couple of hours to work in a cubicle all day, was gaining weight, and was unhappy. She asked herself, "What's wrong with me? I have all this stuff, a nice home, and a great husband." Jacqueline realized she could quit her job if she and her husband simplified. They purged 90 percent of their items and opted for living in a tiny house. She says, "It was an incredible experience going to a smaller space. I had never felt calmer in my life. There was less stuff to think about and our overhead was lower."

Dave, a CD-55er, has been a certified public accountant since 1984. He's had clients from every walk of life, from Florida to California, including very wealthy ones. No matter what net worth his clients had, large or small, he'd sit down with every one of them at the end of the year and have the "quality of life" talk.

"The saying that the love of money is the root of all evil is true," he says. "I have some of the richest clients who are the most miserable because they have too much." Dave helps his clients realize that they don't have to spend or make a lot of money to be happy if they live within their means. I know, because I was one of his clients and his quality of life talks with me make more sense than ever now.

Many of us were raised with the mentality that having wealth equaled security. If we had financial security, that equaled a good life. So many of us worked our way up the ladder to buy bigger houses, cars with more features, boats or motorized toys, gadgets, and gizmos.

But now it's time to start thinking about retiring. So, I asked Dave, "What if you want to retire but don't have the money for the things you want to enjoy?"

His answer was on point. "Then you live within your means." He went on to explain, "I've had the same group of friends from my hometown, and for thirty-five years, every Friday night is poker night. They pick one of their houses; everyone shows up with their 6-pack of Busch Light and snacks and they play nickel and dime poker. When the night is all done, it might cost each of them three bucks. They don't need a fancy boat. They just want to be around each other." *Who wants to sign up for a fun night like that with our friends?*

What brings you happiness? Is it owning a boat and spending your time on the water or fishing? Is it watching TV at home, playing video games, enjoying a round of golf, or going camping twenty-six weeks out of the year? The answer is different for everybody. When it comes down to it, don't we just want to be around people who care about us, doing something that fills our time with joy?

Some of Dave's clients are CD-55ers who've been programmed to work obsessively all their lives. He also sees many of his clients' kids—the twenty-something Gen Zers. Dave's observed they don't live the way the CD-55ers did—they have boundaries. Once they're off work or the weekend comes, it's family time. Many rent apartments or homes instead of owning and choose to live within their means. They know financial status doesn't bring happiness.

Mark in Florida says, "For me, it comes down to two things. When I was younger, I asked myself if I wanted it. Now I ask if I *need* it. With retirement looming, this is how I process every non-essential purchase. A lifetime of saving means nothing if you're still living like it's 1984."

"In my youth, if I had the money in my account, I would spend it. Future be damned," Eric in Canada admits. "Now it's a whole process. How will it affect my budget for the rest of the year? Will I use it more than once? Then again, sometimes you have to spoil yourself a little bit."

Drew in Ohio says, "My ultimate concerns when I die are two-fold: 1) Don't let my wife sell my shit for what I told her I paid for it; and 2) If it didn't take three auctions and two experts to catalog and price all my stuff for the estate sale, you didn't do it right."

I believe all generations have one thing in common: None of us want the pressure that comes with debt, but we still want what's important to us. So what material items do we really *need* now?

I have friends in Michigan who are contractors. They built a 720-square-foot home out of two repurposed train boxcars, aka shipping containers, and rented it out as an Airbnb. It's continuously occupied. People love the cozy, uncluttered feel. So, imagine walking into the Airbnb container home rental, all serene and cozy, with no clutter or stacks of bills on the counter. Look around your home. How does this visual compare to your space?

"I have gotten rid of anything not usable in a motorhome," Christina in Reno says.

Shelly in Utah goes even further. "In many cases, you have to choose time or money. Our family has learned the hard way to live beneath our means so we can afford other things that are more important to us instead of a new house or car." She continues, "We prefer to have the freedom to have family time and experiences with our two boys over buying the latest and greatest. We've always made it clear that just because you can pay for something doesn't mean you can afford it. Cost of ownership is a big deal sometimes."

So, what happened on that day in 1975 after my parents deposited their lottery windfall from the State of Michigan?

The winnings were my parents' saving grace as they'd fallen behind on house payments since my dad had been laid off that winter. They used the money to pay down their second mortgage. My dad declared that each of us would get a gift from the winnings, despite my mom's disagreement, insisting that the practical approach would be to deposit the extra money left into their savings account.

My dad has never been one to listen to reason when it comes to money *(or rarely to my mother for that matter either—haha)*, and one day he and Ronnie backed the truck up to the door and unloaded a used organ for my mom to play at holidays as her gift. She still has that organ almost fifty years later, and every Christmas, will play songs on it for sing-alongs at family gatherings. Ronnie landed a new watch, and, of course, my brother and I each snagged a shiny new bike. When I asked my dad what his gift was from the winnings, he replied, "I restored Grandpa's first Allis-Chalmers tractor, *oh and I celebrated!*" as he held up his beer, grinning.

It's about what's in your heart long before what's in your bank account or paycheck.

Let's consider these three questions Dave asked his clients about quality of life:

- What made you happy in the '70s and '80s?
- What makes you happy now?
- What do you think will make you happy five to ten years from now?

Before spending money, incorporate your values into the decision-making process. Consider the sacrifice of your time in exchange for what you want or need. Above all, understand what you must *give up* to get what you want.

At seventy-nine, my dad lives on his Social Security and pension checks. He recently bought a used truck and said to me, "It's the first vehicle I've *ever* owned without a payment book. It feels good."

Not having a payment does feel good. That's living within your means. It's not too late to change—my dad can vouch for that.

My grandma L used to say to us grandkids, "If I had a million bucks..." Then she'd elbow us, give us a wink, and go back to clipping her coupons or hitting the blue light special at Kmart.

When Grandma passed away at ninety-two, we held her funeral in her front yard. Her open casket sat under her favorite tree, where she'd rest on a gardening break in her wicker chair with an ice-cold Miller Lite. She had a tremendous work ethic, saved her money, and lived a frugal, happy life, content with what she had. The setting was perfect except for two things. My cousins and I wanted to send our grandma to heaven dancing up a storm, so in her casket we laid a bottle of wine and a handwritten check for a million bucks with one caveat: "Can only be cashed in heaven."

We sent her off chuckling and dancing through the pearly gates, waving her bottle of wine and a million bucks so that she could elbow all her friends and show them. Knowing Grandma L, *she probably elbowed God, too.*

Ironically, I think if my grandma *had* been given a million dollars, she would've still lived the same way: simple and frugal.

Don't make life about money. Make it about your happiness. Make it about *who* you spend your time with and the experiences you have, not about your bank account balances. Know the answers to the three questions above.

Live within your means and always weigh out the value of your time.

The goal is to die happy and content like Grandma L.

Chapter Rapture 13
Live within your means

Sixth Hour Bell

In your younger years, you might have asked if you wanted something; now, we should be asking if we truly need it. With retirement on the horizon, let this mindset guide your non-essential purchases.

Life is about spending time with those who care about you and doing what brings you joy. Reflect on what defined your happiness back then, what brings you joy now, and what you believe will make you happy in the years ahead.

Understand the trade-offs needed to achieve contentment and live within your means. Focus on experiences and the people you spend time with rather than financial gain—make it more about your two *hours* than your two *dollars*. Enjoy activities that bring fulfillment without breaking the bank. It's about what's in your heart, not what's in your bank account.

Extracurricular Activities

- Surround yourself with professionals who can help secure your future: a financial advisor, an accountant, and an attorney. Determine how much you need to live comfortably now and in retirement (and draft the dreaded will!).

- Start a side hustle. Find a freelance gig or side business that utilizes your skills to generate extra income.

- Start a new tradition that costs very little, like a monthly card game night with friends or an '80s-themed potluck.

- Search for a Sears or JCPenney catalog from your childhood to reminisce and share with your kids. They can be found on eBay or possibly in your parents' or grandparents' attic!

Field Trips

- Visit an indoor mall and go shopping! For a larger experience, consider Mall of America in Minnesota and search for stores familiar from your '80s mall days.

- Organize a board game night with your kids or grandkids to teach them about money. Play a dueling game of *Monopoly*, *Pay Day*, or *LIFE*. Add excitement with an instant lottery ticket as the grand prize.

Passing Notes in Class

"Who got an allowance? I was allowed to live there. I was allowed to do chores. I was allowed to go to school and church. That was my allowance."
~Staci in Texas

"Anything over $20 is business."
~Dave M in Michigan

"I didn't grow up with money and even paid for my own college. I have zero debt and have always known the difference between needs and wants—needs first. I have never wanted to be rich, just make enough to where I'm comfortable for me and the things that make me happy."
~Kelly in West Virginia

After-School Specials

- Watch *The Money Pit* for cringe-worthy humor, *Arthur* for a taste of luxury, and *Trading Places* to revisit the theme of swindling. Richard Pryor (and John Candy) in *Brewster's Million*s will give you a taste of "the wimp clause" as it relates to greed and wealth.

- Check out *ALF's* "Keepin' the Faith" episode for a humorous take on managing expenses and how ALF goes to work selling makeup to pay for his splurges.

Chapter Mixtape

- "Money for Nothing" – Dire Straits
- "Material Girl" – Madonna
- "Don't Pay the Ferryman" – Chris de Burgh
- "Money Changes Everything" – Cyndi Lauper
- "Rich Girl" – Daryl Hall & John Oates
- "Opportunities (Let's Make Lots of Money)" – Pet Shop Boys
- "Poor Man's Son" – Survivor
- "The Glamorous Life" – Sheila E.
- "Smuggler's Blues" – Glenn Frey
- "Moneytalks" – AC/DC

Shortcut to Spotify Playlist: beckykliss.com/CR13

section four

Eye of the Tiger

Fight Your Way to Invincible

Chap. Fourteen

We're Not Gonna Take It

Rules

> *"I wasn't kidding when I wrote, 'We're Not Gonna Take It.'
> I wasn't kidding. I'm that guy and I will always be that guy."*
> ~Dee Snider

While you might hear a Gen Xer say sarcastically, "We had rules?" they really mean we had only one: be home when the streetlights come on.

Mike R in Florida reflects, "We respected our elders and teachers, but were afraid of them because there was discipline and consequences back then."

Even our music choices had consequences.

Our parents *somewhat* screened the music we listened to, if for no other reason than they inadvertently heard our music playing from our bedrooms. Our song choices were fair game for parental commentary unless we listened to them at micro-volume, *which wasn't the point.*

Kim in Oklahoma remembers KISS with their dicey lyrics. She says, "My mother threw my friend's KISS album out the front door for 'bringing Satan into her house.'"

"Unbelievably, I couldn't listen to Mötley Crüe because of the pentagram on the front of their album *Shout at the Devil*," Mikey says. "I got in trouble for sneaking it onto my Walkman, even though my dad listened to Black Sabbath! I'd come home, and sometimes my frickin' posters were gone. It was probably my mom who put the hammer down."

Mikey's mom may have been on to something. If you haven't seen the movie on Netflix about Mötley Crüe called *The Dirt*, it is a jaw-dropping display of how severely the band broke the rules in the '80s. *Legendary!*

John in Missouri shares his frustrations, too. "My mom threw out my AC/DC album *Back in Black* about three times and *Appetite for Destruction* by Guns N' Roses a couple of times. She read a book about backmasking and thought everything I listened to was 'devil music.'"

Backmasking, also called backward masking, is a recording technique that embeds a hidden message in a recording that can be heard only when playing a track backward. In 1983, Arkansas and California attempted to ban backmasking over the song "Stairway to Heaven" by Led Zeppelin and albums from Pink Floyd, Queen, and Styx. What did we want to do then? *Right. Listen to them more.*

"My parents hated 'Relax' by Frankie Goes to Hollywood, as well as Prince and George Michael," Chandra in Georgia recalls. "My mom told me it was the music of the devil. So, I blasted it in my car. I wasn't allowed to listen to Mötley Crüe, Poison, or Ratt. I remember when the churches burned records—she got caught up in that. I tried backmasking on my stereo with my friend's KISS album, and we heard all kinds of things in it."

Stacey in St. Joseph cringes and says, "My mom took my Prince album away from me when I was in high school. It was the first *and last time* I yelled at her that I hated her! It was a devastating moment, and it just slipped out, but I went right out and bought another one."

When Prince released "Darling Nikki" in 1985, our '80s music came under intense scrutiny. A group of politicians' wives started the Parents Music Resource Center (PMRC) with the goal of blacklisting or censoring certain music to "protect children." Tipper Gore spearheaded the committee after she bought Prince's album *Purple Rain* for her daughter and heard the lyrics of "Darling Nikki," which referred to masturbation. (*My hands are tied legally so I can't include the lyrics here. Feel free to Google them if you don't remember those grinding words.*) PMRC released the "Filthy Fifteen," a list of top songs they felt should be banned. They attacked songs like "Sugar Walls" recorded by Sheena Easton and written by—*no surprise*—Prince because it referenced a *vagina*. Others on the banned list included "Dress You Up" by Madonna, "She Bop" by Cyndi Lauper, "We're Not Gonna Take It" by Twisted Sister (for violence), and of course, "Darling Nikki," *who was just trying to take care of herself.*

Dee Snider of Twisted Sister, John Denver, and Frank Zappa united forces to defend '80s music and testified at a Senate hearing about the topic. Yes, that's right, John Denver rallied for our '80s music! In 1985, Frank Zappa spoke on CBS Nightwatch saying, "Hogwash, I say. Censorship is bad for you, and sex is good for you." The debate continued with Zappa asking, "What's wrong with masturbation?" Zappa's point was that it's a parent's job to teach kids right from wrong and not the PMRC's responsibility.

Sheena Easton agrees. On the '80s Cruise in 2024, I sat in on a Q&A session with Easton, facilitated by Downtown Julie Brown. I was able to ask Sheena how she felt about her song, "Sugar Walls," being on the banned list. "I feel strongly about this, especially being a parent," she answered. "Look, if there is a parent out there who listens to the lyrics of my song, or any song, that doesn't feel it's appropriate for your kids, then don't let your kids hear it. I don't think it's a healthy society to ban art. If it's offensive to you, don't partake in it." Sheena's answer received full-on applause.

In late 1985, record companies began putting Parental Advisory labels on selected releases at their discretion. Some stores, including Walmart, refused to sell albums with the label. Meanwhile, our cassettes kept rolling with songs like "Pearl Necklace" by ZZ Top, "Turning Japanese" by The Vapors, and "Erotic City" by Prince. *No sticker was stopping us.*

◇◇◇◇◇◇◇◇◇◇◇◇◇◇◇◇◇◇◇◇◇◇◇◇◇◇◇◇◇◇◇◇

When we were kids, rules, laws, and bans affected our lives far beyond our music.

In kindergarten, we may have been cute and innocent, but we quickly upped our game. By first grade, I was part of a pack of girls with one primary mission: to chase and catch boys. That mission was temporarily aborted after latching onto one of them and ripping his shirt as he bit the dust. Of course, he ran and tattled. *So much for taking it like a tough Gen X six-year-old.* Mrs. McIntyre, our first-grade teacher, lined all of us girls up, and, one by one, we went to the front of the classroom, bent over her lap, and were gifted with the 'ol one-and-done butt swat. Mrs. McIntyre looked to be eighty years old back then, so, *fortunately,* there was no fear of pain. Instead, it was more about embarrassment because your classmates watched your sorry ass bent over in shame. By the next recess, we were back at it again.

In fourth grade, Wayne remembers putting rubber snakes in Miss Dion's desk. He wanted to scare the holy hell out of his favorite teacher, *and it worked.* Mr. Heit, the principal of NB Elementary School, demanded that Wayne write an apology letter for his stunt. Some thirty years later, as the principal of NBHS, *Wayne* would be the one asking kids to write apology letters.

As the president of the Pre-Teen Sensations club, I loved making rules—for everyone *but* myself. Here's a note I wrote to the club members at age twelve:

> Here are the rules you must follow to be a good club member. If you break #2 or #4 more than three times, the judges will decide if you should get kicked out. The boys are going to chase us on recess today, so when you get outside, run!

The rules I assigned to them were:

1. No fighting
2. Must bring 25 cents a week for dues
3. Keep all secrets
4. Come to meetings
5. If you have a job, do it!

Man, we Aries girls sure were bossy at a young age!

By sixth grade, food fights in the cafeteria were a troublesome trend. We can blame that one on John Belushi bellowing, "FOOD FIGHT!" in the 1978 movie *Animal House*. As participation grew to the size of a small platoon, our parents were mailed a letter from the principal—yes, that means an *actual* mailbox was involved. The "snail mail" method with a three-day delay (compared to the three-second delay you'd have now) stated that he was sure we weren't allowed to use orange peels as projectiles at home, so we shouldn't behave like that in the school cafeteria. *Seriously, though, what else do you do with orange peels in elementary school?*

Paddling was still legal and allowed as punishment in many schools in the early '80s. At NBHS, Mr. Lauricella was feared most because his paddle had aerodynamic holes drilled through it in order to achieve maximum speed when he whacked your ass with it. Afterward, you *earned* the dubious honor of signing the paddle—*lucky you*.

In class, Jesse and Brent would disassemble their ink pens, hollow out the insides, and transform the pen tube into a spitball torpedo gun barrel. Mr. Handley, a substitute teacher and coincidentally a NB police officer, would witness this and say, "Mr. Wilson and Mr. Gallaro, you might want to put those away before you choke on them." As soon as Mr. Handley wasn't looking, the torpedo spitballs would start firing again. *Ironically, Jesse and Brent both went into law enforcement.*

It was tough when we got busted because we knew the school *and* our parents stood united; we knew double punishment was coming. We had no choice but to own the consequences.

When Mr. Hart's door slammed, it echoed throughout the building, and everyone knew someone had just about *"bought the farm"* as he'd say when they were in trouble. He believed in making students work instead of suspending them when they ended up in his office for breaking the rules. If he suspended you, he knew you'd probably be out having a good time. So instead, he made you listen to '60s music while you sat in detention, or you'd be sent to help senior citizens in the community.

"One time, the band director got provoked because the kids in percussion were acting up, so he kicked them out of his class and sent them to my office, all eleven of them," Mr. Hart recalls. "I'd never had that many kids in my office at once. I looked at them and said, 'Well, what do you think we oughta do?' Before they could answer, I said, 'I have a great idea. Let's file music!'" Instead of assigning detention or calling parents, he divided them into teams of two and made them file music sheets for three hours straight. Mr. Hart smirked proudly. "I never saw any of them in my office again."

Times have changed for kids when it comes to rules and forms of punishment, though.

Doug, a former high school security officer and father, believes kids today think the world owes them something. "They don't have as much responsibility or rules to follow when it comes to work or chores, and they back talk more. Parents don't say 'no' to many things. When they do, they are super cautious. It seems the roles are reversed, and parents are afraid of their kids."

He went on to explain, "Confusion comes into play on what *is* parental discipline versus child abuse. Many adolescents have the differences skewed in their minds. It's not unheard of for a kid to threaten to call 911 on their parents for abuse if they don't like the consequences handed to them." He says, "In addition, many kids don't even have to sneak to do things anymore because they know their parents won't follow through and hold them accountable."

NBHS graduate Bob James is now a middle-school teacher, football coach, and father living in Indiana. He says, "Kids aren't different now; they're the same. The parents are different. Parents let their kids get away with more. Today, if a kid is sent to the principal's office, the parents will call up bitching because they were. Kids can still be respectful and will do what you tell them to do, but as teachers, we often have to fight through the barrier of their parents. Our parents taught us respect, and that doesn't happen now." Bob believes parents are busier now. If the child pleads, begs, and pushes back after being told "no," parents often take the easier route, caving in to avoid a battle or having to deal with the hassle.

Wayne, former NBHS principal, adds, "Parents will ask their *kid's* opinions, but not *teachers'* opinions. If you tell a parent their kid screwed up, the parents want an extensive investigation. And, sadly, kids lie. I have to do more hand-holding with parents to get the same result as Mr. Hart did with us in the '80s. It's a much longer, more exhausting process now."

Mr. Hart claims we now live in a "What have you done for me lately?" society.

This shift from what Gen Xers experienced—simply breaking rules, getting paddled, and suffering the consequences–is significant.

"The rules I had to live by were simple. If a teacher said, 'Do it,' you did it. If I put it on my plate, I ate it. We respected our elders," Mark in Florida says. "Now, parents don't want their children to suffer, so the rules are more lax. We didn't worry much about hurting someone's feelings in the '80s. It made us stronger as adults, or we became serial killers."

What's driving this change? Is it the education system, parenting, society, or a lack of cohesion between these systems? While rules are more documented than ever, it seems the burden of proof has shifted from the rule breakers to the enforcers. Are we coddling and protecting our youngsters too much? If so, what are the ramifications? Do kids have more or less accountability? Do they experience fewer consequences than we did?

"As a Gen X mom, I never tolerated bratty behavior or entitlement. I've turned the car around more times than I can count for my kid's bad behavior at the zoo or Chuck E. Cheese. I even walked out of grocery stores and left groceries behind if my kid was whining and crying for 'more'," Kristin in Maryland says. "I love my child and it's my job to raise a human with the ability to care for people other than herself. She's nineteen now and capable, self-sufficient, and very caring."

In 2023, NBHS students were given the school handbook before they started the year. Each one must agree to all seventy-seven pages of it. Back in the day, our parents *may* have had to sign a couple of forms and read a short handbook before we started school. So why the significant shift? Is it because we live in a much more litigious society? Or is it more that we weren't held accountable by a rule book, but instead kept in check by the guaranteed consequences from our parents and teachers? *Fear of getting our asses beat.*

"I swear, if something happened six doors down at the bus stop, my mom knew about it before I hit the door, and she was at work!" Tracy in Alabama exclaims. "We were disciplined by the entire neighborhood, which doesn't seem to be the norm anymore."

At home, your punishment could be devastating. Nothing was worse than being told, "No going outside" or "No Atari."

"Along with a heaping cup of guilt from your mom," Bob C adds.

"Back then we had freedom, *lots* of freedom," Matt in Washington says. "If we were eight miles from home, it didn't matter as long as we were back at a certain time or called. On the other hand, if we violated specific rules, we lost that freedom for a while."

Is that the ultimate difference between Gen Xers and the younger generations? That we had the freedom to break the rules, make mistakes, and learn from them and they don't?

Many feel society expects perfection from Gen Z and they don't have the luxury to get away with trying things like we did. With social media, home security systems, and tracking devices (such as the Life360 app), they have little freedom or room to learn on their own through their mistakes. Correction is more instant now.

The days of Bart Simpson's famous line, "I didn't do it! Nobody saw me do it! There's no way you can prove anything!" are long over for younger generations.

At sixteen, Shay, a Gen Zer, is a well-behaved kid with good grades in school. He's active in sports and works after school. On his cross-country team, there is a tradition where the boys pick a day and prank the girls. TP-ing each other's houses is "expected," he says. Shay and his buddy decided they would one-up the tradition, and on a Saturday night, they found a construction site with a porta-potty and hoisted it into Shay's truck. "We made sure it wasn't loaded up with, *you know, stuff.* We drove it to one of the girl's houses and placed it strategically on her front lawn."

The girls had a good laugh on Sunday morning, then called Shay, saying, "Okay, my parents want this thing outta here now." So, Shay and his friend went back, loaded up the porta potty, and put it right back from where they took it. By Monday, however, the police were at Shay's home, threatening him with a felony for larceny over $2,000. *First of all, who would have thought a porta-*

potty costs over $2,000?

The neighbor across from the construction site had exterior house cameras and reported the video of Shay's truck to the police. Since the porta-potty blew over that night from the wind, Shay was also accused of vandalism. Luckily, the construction contractor opted not to press charges. Shay expressed his overall frustration by saying, "I know what I did was wrong. My mom let me have it for being so stupid. The world is kinda crazy now. Trying to please your parents, work, school, sports, and still be a kid without getting in trouble stresses us out one thousand percent. I got suspended from school three times for not wearing my mask properly during COVID, and since then, everything is stricter than ever."

Yes, we Gen Xers may not participate in stunts like these now, but *come on*, moving a porta-potty in the '80s was considered a harmless prank that happened weekly.

Does this instant hammer coming down on kids push them into being more reserved and apprehensive…or more defiant? Do kids even have time to process their actions and feel remorse before the guillotine drops? When I asked Shay how he felt about getting caught, he laughed and said, "It made me realize how lucky I was that I didn't get into worse trouble. But next time, I'm using someone else's truck!" *Thata boy. Shay's thinking like a true Gen Xer!*

When she was eighteen years old, Madi experienced similar instances with the inundation of rules. In Southwest Michigan, the Queen Contest is a tradition where the community crowns a queen in their town to compete for the title of Miss Blossomtime. Madi was ecstatic to be crowned the first runner-up to Miss Blossomtime. She had to sign a 12-month contract with a list of rules she must follow to avoid losing her crown. She couldn't be seen on social media holding a red Solo cup, even if there was water in it. She couldn't be photographed and tagged on social media with someone drinking alcohol, even at a family dinner with her parents. She wasn't allowed to wear a bikini or reveal too much skin in any pictures posted. She wasn't allowed to date any male pageant winners.

So, at eighteen, Madi had to walk on eggshells for an entire year. "It created more stress," she says. "I was always worried that I'd get in trouble for something. I work at my dad's restaurant where alcohol is served—what if someone took a picture of me serving beer to a patron? Would that count and I be criticized?"

Now, Madi is twenty and a sophomore at Michigan State. "My generation feels like we're being watched constantly," she says. "In some ways, it's good because it makes me think more about what I'm doing before I do it. But for most of us, it's not good. We either turn the location off on our phones so our parents can't track where we are, or worse, when we were in high school, we'd leave our phone at home and sneak out to be with friends. It would've been bad if something ever happened because we couldn't call for help."

◊◊◊◊◊◊◊◊◊◊◊◊◊◊◊◊◊◊◊◊◊◊◊◊◊◊◊◊◊◊

Laws and bans are generally implemented because something isn't right or safe. Some make sense, others don't. We had some good laws in place in the '80s that made sense: desegregation, endangered species protection, and child labor restrictions; we could no longer smoke on an airplane or in some public spaces. Some states had increased the legal drinking age and passed seatbelt laws.

Then there are laws that don't make sense. In 2020, Good Housekeeping released an article recapping some ridiculous modern-day laws. For example, in Indiana, riding a horse over 10 mph is illegal. In Kansas, tire screeching is banned. In Kentucky, a woman cannot marry the same man four times. In Michigan, vehicles cannot be sold on Sundays. In New Jersey, bulletproof vests are illegal to wear while committing a crime. In South Carolina, you can't play pinball if you're a minor. In Tennessee, it's illegal to share your Netflix password.

Those are some pretty idiotic laws. *For crying out loud, what kid shouldn't be allowed to play pinball?* All it takes, however, is someone to disagree and rally others to their side on social media, and *boom!* you have an uproar. Next thing you know, a legal ban is in place.

Controversy has existed since the beginning of time. Some radio stations in the '60s even refused to play The Beatles because John Lennon's remarks were perceived to be anti-Christian. Elvis faced conflict over his provocative pelvis-swiveling dance moves, which left his fanbase rabid. And we know how popular they both were despite this. Now all these dissensions are amplified through social media.

In *Footloose*, we just wanted to see Kevin Bacon's cute peppy dance moves—including popping up on his tiptoes—but truly, the $80 million movie with the soundtrack we loved was about *breaking rules*. In the movie, the town's preacher tried to ban alcohol and public dancing because he believed these acts were detrimental to youth. When school officials started burning books, the preacher realized things had gone too far. He stopped them, shouting, "Who elected all of you to save everybody's souls? Satan isn't in these books; he's inside of you. Now, go home." It's a perfect example that an overabundance of rules can have an adverse effect.

Interestingly, in 2024, students at Payson High School in Utah, where *Footloose* was filmed, rallied for Kevin Bacon to return to their school's prom after forty years, and he did. Speaking to the students, Bacon shared, "I think it's amazing the power this movie had to bring people together and connect to the basic ideas behind this movie, you know, standing up to authority sometimes, and to being forgiving of people who are not exactly the same as you, and for standing up for your own freedoms, and your right to express yourself and for having compassion for other people."

Mariana in South Carolina says, "I taught at a school that had two hundred separate rules that students were supposed to remember. Two hundred! I thought they were being over-policed, which does not lend itself well to learning. So, now, in the great wisdom of many state legislators and school boards, we have decided to over-police teachers and librarians as well."

Oh, boy, libraries are near and dear to my heart, and my local library was an excellent resource for old newspapers and town history when writing this book. I'm going to have to get on my soapbox for this one for a minute because, in my family, we had three generations of Kliss women who worked at the New Buffalo Public Library.

I love taking my four-year-old niece with me and letting her explore the wonders inside the library. In the '80s, before the internet, libraries were our primary source of information. Without being able to research papers at the library, we would've never passed science or received an 'A' on our book report. Now, in some communities in America, legislation is being proposed that says if the library carries certain books or doesn't follow new protocols, it could lose funding, *and* a library employee could face legal action. Who'd have ever frickin' thought working at a library could put someone in jeopardy for legal action?

In the '80s, if we came home with books written by Jackie Collins filled with steamy sex scenes or V.C. Andrews' *Flowers in the Attic*—which was a *far* cry from being about *flowers*—or a Stephen King book with people being slowly dismembered, our parents probably would've had a few questions. But they would've never thought to blame the library. Historically, libraries have been considered neutral ground where you can acquire an uncensored education for free. It wasn't left to politicians to decide what we could read.

How many of us have read a Judy Blume book? Do you know she has a number of books that have been banned? Some say she is one of the most banned authors in America. Why? Because she writes about adolescents trying to figure out religion, bras, boys, menstruation, masturbation, and teenage sexuality. As the bossy former president of my ad-hoc Pre-Teen Sensations group—named after a club in the banned book *Are You There God? It's Me, Margaret*—I'd strike back with: isn't that what all kids go through?

Susanne, a librarian in New Hampshire, says, "Banning books is like telling a person not to think. Ridiculous. Libraries are an invaluable resource and free. What else do we get for free these days?"

※※※※※※※※※※※※※※※※※※※※

Where does it end with the rules, bans, and laws? *It doesn't.* History proves that more often than not, whatever is different will be targeted. When social media is thrown into that mix, we can be left more divided than ever. And what's the difference between a good rule from a lousy rule? If it removes your constitutional rights, it's a bad one. My advice? Don't jump on the bandwagon to support something without knowing all the facts. Just because a friend shares something with you, you see it on a news channel, or you read it on social media, does not mean you're getting all the information you need to prove its validity.

In law enforcement, Officer Doug says there are *three* sides to every story: your side, their side, *and the truth*.

Wayne looks back on the rubber snake stunt and says, "Boy, I thought I was hilarious. I knew I was one of Miss Dion's favorites and thought nothing of scaring the crap out of her. But to this day, I still hear Mr. Heit saying, 'Why are you picking on that woman who cares so much for you?' He approached it from an emotional connection and hit my core." Wayne's lesson from Mr. Heit was undeniable. "At my job now, I tell kids, I was your age once. You've never been 50-something, but I've been twelve. *I get you.* But you shouldn't hurt or be mean to people who care about you."

"There are different types of rules now," David in Kentucky says. "We had rules about respecting people and property and conducting yourself. Now respect seems alien, and conduct is anything goes, yet there are absurd levels of safety protocols."

It's so easy to let accountability slide with the younger generations after what they've gone through with the COVID pandemic. They may be more informed because they can access the internet, but they are not smarter or wiser in years. They're still young and naive, navigating massive amounts of information that may not all be true. They need structure and guidance—not a bazillion rules to live by.

We Gen Xers had the flexibility to roam, earning the infamous labels of the feral generation and latchkey kids. We didn't live in a world governed by a 77-billion-page handbook of rules, GPS tracking systems, and security cameras like we do now. We had the liberty to break rules, make mistakes, *and* simply be human. We had the freedom to experience the thrill of porta-potty stunts, hold red Solo cups, and head to the beach in our bikinis to enjoy life without constantly wondering and worrying if we were being watched.

And you know what? We learned from it because we were *held accountable*. We had the free rein to break the rules, and accepting the unyielding consequences is how we learned.

One Gen Xer summarizes it perfectly: "Our childhood is illegal now."

What rules are shaping our lives now that our parents are no longer there to put the hammer down on us anymore? As adults, it's up to us to create and follow our own guidelines. But, have we established clear consequences for ourselves? If you have a regimen, say, to eat healthy but break it by indulging in carbs and sugary drinks, you're the one in control of that hammer now. It's time to reflect on where you might be conforming to external expectations and pressures. Standing up for what you believe in often means challenging norms, *aka breaking the rules*. But you also need to own the consequences. Accountability was key in shaping us into resilient, badass Gen Xers and CD-55ers, and it remains crucial today. It taught us respect—and that's something to be proud of—even if it took some of us decades to fully appreciate.

Now, go play the chapter's playlist and the banned '80s music playlist (on the next page) and jam to a little Twisted Sister and Prince while you reflect on what we've learned from not being micromanaged.

NEW BUFFALO AREA SCHOOLS
222 South Whittaker Street
New Buffalo, Michigan 49117
Telephone 616/469-2211

RICHARD L. JOHNSON, Superintendent of Schools

HIGH SCHOOL, Member N.C.A. 469-2770 • ELEMENTARY SCHOOL, 469-3410

3-10-80

Mr. & Mrs. Robert Kliss

New Buffalo, MI 49117

Dear Mr. & Mrs. Kliss,

    I have had your daughter, Becky, in my office on Friday. She has been involved in throwing food in the cafeteria. I am sure that this is not the type of activity that you allow at home and we certainly do not wish to have food thrown at school.

    I would appreciate it if you would talk to your daughter about the proper use of the school cafeteria.

Sincerely,

Andrew B. Cook

Andrew B. Cook, Principal
New Buffalo Elementary

ABC:sw

Who's with me on breaking the rules on this one? It's a good time to crank up the Invincible '80s Banned Songs playlist. You might be shocked by some of the tracks that made it onto that list!

Shortcut to Spotify Playlist: beckykliss.com/bannedsongs

Ch 14 – We're Not Gonna Take It

Chapter Rapture 14
Our childhood is illegal now

Sixth Hour Bell

As latchkey kids, Gen Xers had the freedom to break the rules, make mistakes, and learn from them—an experience that isn't as common today. We grew up roaming freely without GPS trackers, security cameras, or a thick rulebook. We were held accountable by facing the consequences of our actions, which shaped us into the independent CD-55ers we are today and instilled in us respect and accountability.

Now, as middle-aged adults, it's up to us to set our own guidelines and hold ourselves accountable. While breaking rules and challenging norms can be necessary, it also comes with responsibility—we need to own it.

Reflect on where you may be conforming to external pressures, and avoid supporting something without knowing all the facts. Remember, there are three sides to every story: yours, theirs, and the truth.

Extracurricular Activities

- Read *First, Break All the Rules* by Marcus Buckingham and Curt Coffman.

- Search for banned books from the '80s and pick one familiar to revisit, like *The Handmaid's Tale, Flowers for Algernon,* or *Are You There God? It's Me, Margaret.*

- Evaluate your daily structure and rules. Identify what's effective and make changes to better align with your values, needs, and health, such as focusing on fitness and healthy eating routines.

- Find an inspirational sign to hang in your space, such as Katharine Hepburn's quote: "If you obey all the rules, you miss all the fun."

Field Trips

- Visit the library and explore! Check out a book you loved as a child, especially those nostalgic ones like *Clifford the Big Red Dog* series by Norman Bridwell, *Ramona the Pest* by Beverly Cleary, *Cloudy with a Chance of Meatballs* by Judi Barrett, and *Gus and the Baby Ghost* by Jane Thayer.

Passing Notes in Class

"My mom always said, 'As long as you live under this roof, you'll do as told.' She was the discipline giver while my dad would sit and calmly talk about the situation and make me feel worse than being grounded about my dumb mistakes—and yes, they were dumb mistakes."

~Debbie in Ohio

"I can watch whatever TV show I want. I can stay up as late as I want. I totally run with scissors and sit too close to the TV now."

~Jennifer in Texas

"That's an attention-getter." (in reference to a kick in the ass)

~Sheriff Buford T. Justice

After-School Specials

- Watch the *PMRC Senate Hearings* on YouTube about record lyric labeling. The testimonies from John Denver, Dee Snider, and Frank Zappa are monumental.

- Watch *Footloose*, then check out the video of Kevin Bacon returning in 2024 to the iconic dance scene at Payson High School in Utah, forty years later.

- Watch Prince's interview in 1999 on *Larry King Live* for insights into his life and music, and how his upbringing contributed to his success.

- Listen to podcasts from RetroZest for engaging interviews with stars from movies such as *Footloose*, *Top Gun*, and *Better Off Dead*.

Chapter Mixtape

- "We're Not Gonna Take It" – Twisted Sister
- "Darling Nikki" – Prince
- "Breaking the Rules" – AC/DC
- "Whip It" – DEVO
- "Footloose" – Kenny Loggins
- "Be Good Johnny" – Men at Work
- "It's Not Over ('Til It's Over)" – Starship
- "Breaking the Chains" – Dokken
- "Naughty Naughty" – John Parr
- "Play the Game Tonight" – Kansas

Shortcut to Spotify Playlist: beckykliss.com/CR14

Chap. Fifteen

The Safety Dance

Risks

"I remember hearing someone say, 'That heavy metal is going to turn you into a degenerate!' And I thought, that sounds like a pretty good path, I think I'll take that one. Like, you can have Donny and Marie, or you can have Aerosmith and Sex Pistols. Hmmm, let me think about this..."

~Nikki Sixx

It was 1984, just days before the Jacksons' *Victory Tour* concert in Chicago, when my lucky rotary dialing fingers won two $28 tickets to the concert from B96 Radio. The *Victory Tour* was the only tour Michael Jackson and his six brothers, Joe, Jermaine, Marlon, Jackie, Tito, and Randy, planned together. *Thriller* was on top of the charts. They were playing at Comiskey Park, home of the Chicago White Sox, for three nights, October 12th, 13th, and 14th. I was sixteen, and luckily, my eighteen-year-old boyfriend had his own car, and off we drove to the Windy City like there was nothing to it.

When the concert ended, it was late, and somehow, we managed to get lost in an unsafe neighborhood on the south side of Chicago. There were no pay phones or cars in sight and no gas stations open. Everywhere we looked, apartment buildings were so dilapidated that they wouldn't even make the cut for *The Money Pit*. We were going to ask for help from a lone couple standing on the sidewalk, but as we came closer, it seemed we were in a scene out of *The Jerry Springer Show*. We'd watched enough '80s slasher movies to know that if we stopped to interrupt their brawl and ask for directions, it wouldn't end well for us.

We drove a little farther and pulled to the side of the road at a stoplight. Our foldout map covered the entire dash, but that dismal dome light wasn't shedding any rays on a solution. Suddenly, a large white limo with tinted windows pulled up next to us. We were the only two cars around at 1 a.m., and we had no idea at this point if this was the night our photos would end up on the back of a milk carton as two missing teens last seen at a Michael Jackson concert.

How many of us '80s kids remember predicaments similar to this when we realized the risk was greater than we bargained for? We didn't normally foresee the safety dangers involved in the things we did—the excitement of the adventure usually outweighed the what-ifs. Let's face it, Gen X has some of the best hair-raising stories *because* taking risks didn't faze us. In our defense, many of us were left unsupervised. We would have put TikTok on the map with our stunts demonstrating how invincible we *thought* we were—and why shouldn't we? We were raised with the motto "Just rub some dirt on it, and you'll be fine."

The dangers we faced at recess on the playground equipment alone were countless.

Sherri in Fresno remembers, "The metal slide that had baked in the 110-degree sun, the monkey bars that we'd spin around backwards on at warp speed built fifteen feet over concrete, or the thousand-pound wooden merry-go-round that at maximum centrifugal force would fling off the weaker kids into the giant elm tree if they let go at the wrong time."

And let's not forget the jungle gym takeover where we shoved off all invaders hard enough to their doom to cause concussions.

Playing tetherball or dodgeball was no better. The goal in each of those games was to either *smash* someone with the ball or *kill* the person who had the ball. *Classic Gen X style.*

The playground didn't pose the only danger during elementary school, though.

"Smoking Winstons stolen from my buddy's grandma's tavern behind the fence of the ballfield...just what every fifth grader should have been doing," Jason in Wisconsin says.

How many of us rode in the back of a pickup truck, hanging our heads over the sides, while the driver had a "roadie," speeding up and down the country roads without thinking twice that it could be dangerous? That was our normal.

Even the thought of using seat belts to us was outlandish. "I loved sitting in my parents' station wagon in the last row facing the rear," Julie in Chicago says. "Being the youngest of three, I had the privilege of sitting on the bump in the floor in the middle of the second row when the back seat was full, without a seat belt or anything, even on long trips."

Our "break-your-neck" behaviors didn't stop there. Danielle would put her cousin, Robin's little brother, in a sleeping bag, zip him up, and roll him down the stairs. When I asked my BFF what she was doing at that moment, she chuckled and said, "I was probably helping."

We'd swing outside like Tarzan from tree branches or vines over the crick in the ravine, waiting to see whose luck would run out when the vine finally broke. Some would sit on their skateboards at the top of the bridge over the highway and then cut loose like a bat out of hell down the hill, hoping we didn't hear our friend yell "Carrrr!" midstream.

Shaun in Kalamazoo remembers hauling ass down a deserted dirt road on his moped. When he wiped out and flew over the handlebars, he just laid there on the gravel road, trying to decide if he was okay, knowing it was very likely no one would come looking for him until dark when the streetlights came on. *Who can relate?*

Dawn in California remembers, "We were left on our own after school. We cooked pancakes, popcorn, and made popovers in the oven. Surprisingly, we never caught the kitchen on fire, but the living room carpet did go up in flames while making a campfire for our Barbies once. Luckily, we put it out, though."

And we're not even going to talk about that stupid daredevil stunt Gen Xers pulled turning Aqua Net cans into makeshift blowtorches.

Meanwhile, across the street, there were kids whose parents adhered to thicker rulebooks, preventing them from playing by the creek for fear of drowning or getting poison ivy. Some parents were so cautious and protective they didn't even want their kids getting dirty.

Remember Romper Stompers? They were two upside down plastic cups you walked on while holding a rubber rope attached to them until you fell—and it was imminent—you *would* fall. If you were like me and coupled that with a 10-cent metal wiener dog pin from a gumball machine and pinned to the front of your shirt—with the sharp needle protruding out past the dog's ass—guaranteed an unplanned trip to the emergency room for stitches after you fell and gashed your chin open.

Where were the *Danger, Will Robinson* warnings on these toys? Where were the safety regulations governing what a kid could buy in a bubble gum machine? Where were the crash dummy tests performed on Romper Stompers? Kids were busy becoming statistics for toys like lawn darts, the weighted metal-tip spikes that flew through the air. These, in particular, accounted for an estimated 675 emergency department visits per year, as reported by the National Library of Medicine in 1990. *Hmm, that stat sounds low for us Gen Xers.*

Amy in Oxford remembers Click Clacks, aka Clackers. "They were just two glass balls on strings that you beat back and forth until your arms turned black and blue with bruises."

Once when Robin was young, she was chasing the neighbor, Theresa, down the stairs at full speed just as the glass storm door at the bottom of the stairs swung shut. Robin ran right through the door, shattering it. Blood was everywhere.

Theresa turned around to her and said, *"You're gonna get in trouble."*

Robin ran to her dad at the neighbor's house. He panicked momentarily, then yanked a piece of glass out of her chin and bandaged it up with the proverbial, "I'll bet you won't do that again." Robin returned to playing, and her parents went back to socializing. *Classic '80s style.*

Our fear *wasn't* about getting hurt; it was about our parents whooping us for doing something we shouldn't. And, ironically, most of our parents didn't think twice about us getting hurt until something serious happened and we were crying, and they'd say, "Are you bleeding to death? Any broken bones? No? *Good*. Now brush it off, and next time when I tell you not to do something, you'd better listen to me!"

Nancy in Three Oaks jokingly says, "My mom didn't pay any attention to us at all. She was just keeping us alive."

"It was the 'put a little Bactine on that bullet wound, kid, and you'll be fine' mindset," Kristen in Minnesota says.

If we didn't have a limb missing or blood gushing, we followed a simple four-step protocol:

1. Run to the bathroom and get the metal BAND-AID box out.
2. Squirt Bactine, iodine, or worse, Mercurochrome on the wound.
3. Scream bloody murder since that hurt worse than the 'effin injury.
4. Slap a bandage on it and head right back out the door to double dare each other to do the same darn thing again—no stupid injury was stopping us from accomplishing our mission.

Wait a minute, did we really use *Mercurochrome*? In 1998, the Food and Drug Administration banned it due to the amount of mercury it contained. *Suuuumbitch.*

When my brother and I were little, we climbed to the very top of the tallest tree in our backyard. We looked down, then at each other, and screamed for dear life, "Mommm!" She was so perturbed that we'd interrupted her canning process in the kitchen that she scolded us from seventy-five feet below, shouting, "You got up there. Now you better get down, one branch at a time!" Today, her tune has changed. "I probably should've called the fire department. You kids could have gotten hurt if you'd fallen." *You think? Yet, we're still here.*

Our parents' view of risk was much different than ours is today.

One Gen Xer says, "They would let us do the damnedest things. They'd hand us a loaded BB gun and tell us, 'Just don't shoot at the eyes,' and then turn around and tell us not to sit too close to the TV or we'd go blind."

Many Gen Xers shared stories of times they really *were* hurt with a broken bone, a concussion, or some other injury, but their parents made them walk it off. Sometimes, it took days or weeks for the severity of their injury to surface. These stories sucked to hear, but running to the doctor or hospital wasn't the norm unless your arm was dangling by a thread.

Depending on your parents, your upbringing could vary widely with the level of safety measures you took or didn't take.

"Some of us were raised by hippies, some by military families, some by conservative Christians, and some of us raised ourselves," Sean in Georgia says.

Mikey recalls, "When I was young, I wasn't even allowed to cross the street because my mom saw a young boy get hit once. Yet, my dad was all about putting me on a dirt bike when I was six years old."

Safety to us kids of the '80s simply meant *not getting hurt.* Life was about seeing and trying things and figuring out how to make them happen with as few battle scars as possible.

"We didn't see the opportunities; *we saw the challenges*," Pat from Canada says. What a perfect summary of Gen X—it was about the experience!

Why was our generation this way? Was it because we often had no one supervising us and we were raised to figure it out ourselves without being micromanaged?

What *is* micromanaging when it comes to parenting?

Merriam-Webster defines a helicopter parent as "a parent who is overly involved in the life of a child." This term's first known use was at the *end* of the '80s—so who are they implying *are* the helicopter parents? Certainly, they weren't implying our parents' or grandparents' generations were, with the amount of freedom we had? Is it possible *we* were the first parents to start hovering over our kids because we knew the risks we took were really dangerous?

Here's my question for Gen Xers: did taking risks benefit us in some way? Has it helped us to become resilient, resourceful, and persistent? Are we the generation that jumps in to help and solve problems?

In his book *Zero Hour for Gen X*, Matthew Hennessey talks about Gen Xers riding bikes without helmets, roaming neighborhoods, climbing trees and jumping off garage roofs, riding buses and being left in cars alone while our parents grocery shopped, walking to school and baseball practice and home again unsupervised. Hennessey says, "Nobody called the cops when they saw us alone minding our own business. When it was absolutely necessary that we get in touch with our parents—or our friends—we somehow managed to do it without cell phones. All of this independence equipped us with resilience and self-reliance, characteristics that have slowly been going missing in America."

How many of us find that these characteristics continue to serve us well throughout our lives?

Today, when we think of safety though, it seems to correlate more with fear than taking risks and being self-reliant.

When I visited New Buffalo High School to conduct interviews for this book in 2021, I was blown away by the security measures in place. There was only one door designated to enter the school, and visitors were watched on camera in the vestibule while waiting to be buzzed in. An ID badge had to be worn and guests had to be escorted at all times. It didn't matter that I was a NBHS class of '86 graduate and knew Wayne, the principal. A police officer in uniform walked the halls wearing a fully stocked gun belt, and security cameras were everywhere. As a visitor, it felt more alarming than reassuring.

Sadly, it makes sense. Schools today conduct lockdown drills due to the alarming rise in mass shootings over recent years. As of 2023, there are, on average, seventeen school shootings per year in the US. According to *The Washington Post*, there have been four hundred school shootings between 1999 and 2023—since the Columbine High School horror—affecting over 370,000 children.

In 2022 alone, there were forty-six school shootings, the highest number since 1999. It's unfathomable. That's a far cry from the tornado and fire drills of the '80s.

"I was led to believe school desks were of super strength and that sitting under the desk would save me from nukes, air raids, and a host of natural disasters," James in the U.K. says.

Our worries back then couldn't hold a candle to the challenges today's kids face.

Note to my BFF:

> We have to get moved out of our locker quick because Jim H knows the number of our locker and the combination (sorry, it was an accident). So we'll have to stop at the office on the way back from lunch and get the combination straight because that look in Jim's eyes tells me that he's just dying to get in our locker.
> — Gotta go, Becky

Did my BFF and I feel "unsafe" because we were worried that Jim H might break into our locker to pilfer, *what*, our *BJ and the Bear* poster, our schoolbooks, or a note or two? I think you get my drift to how safety concerns were then compared to now in comparison.

Statistica.com reports that overall crime has significantly decreased from 1990 to 2022. Because there are so many ways to categorize crime rates—by type, state, and country—it's not easy to summarize. Trying to decipher anything more than the general trend would require an amount of in-depth research that would last an entire semester of Mr. T's English lit class. If crime rates were truly higher in the '80s, why didn't fear didn't put a damper on the risks we took? It's likely because we didn't have easy access to hearing about the dangers—not because they didn't exist.

Cricket in Michigan says, "I don't remember learning about strangers until after the abduction and murder of 6-year-old Adam Walsh in 1981 in Florida. I remember police officers coming to my elementary school and talking to us about strangers. I always felt like there was a shift after that and parents became a little bit more vigilant." And the same went for those of us who lived close to Chicago when serial killer John Wayne Gacy murdered over thirty boys throughout the '70s. That raised some concerns, *for what, a few weeks or so?*

Kris in North Dakota says, "I remember my mom would leave me and my siblings in the car in the parking lot when we were young while she went grocery shopping."

How many of us can relate to being left alone in the car, like Kris, while our parents were off shopping?

What's the title of this book again? *Oh, yeah, When We Were Invincible.*

Today, many parents use technology like GPS trackers and home camera systems to monitor their children's safety. Could this focus on security be why many kids seem less adventurous? Are these safety concerns fostering and instilling *more* fear? Or are we simply more aware of the terrible happenings via the internet, social media, and constant news coverage?

In the US, young adults can legally buy or drink alcohol at twenty-one, smoke cigarettes at twenty-one, and drive at fifteen or sixteen. Yet, as soon as kids can type, they have access to the entire internet and can search for anything on the planet.

"We don't let nine-year-olds drive cars or give them cigarettes, so why would we give young kids social media or wide-open access to Google?" Mike Gathright, lead teacher at Storyline Church, says.

But where are our kids mostly today? The answer is: *on their mobile devices.*

"My kids live in a bubble," Terry says. "In bigger cities like Chicago, kids are mugged, and their phones are stolen all the time. The struggle is real as a parent."

Robin agrees. "I wouldn't let my kids ride their bikes to your house like we did, even with a cell phone because I'm more aware of what could happen."

Jill in Benton Harbor loves that her son's friends come to her house because they do fun things like building things out of scrap wood and having campfires. She acknowledges, "As parents, we're still way more thoughtful and organized during play than when I was growing up. The boys can only play in the backyard where I can see or hear them from the kitchen window, or I get anxious. I have a burn injury kit ready, and I've used it. I guarantee we didn't have a burn kit growing up, just an aloe plant. I love sending his friends home dirty, smelling like bug spray and campfire just like we used to."

I get excited seeing Gen X parents like Jill who plan activities with their kids that remind me of how we lived in the '80s. She is letting her kids be kids while still being a mindful parent.

Are many parents overcompensating in their efforts to protect their kids now?

Could the helicopter parenting style limit kids' freedom to take risks, gain experiences, and learn? Is fear influencing the trend of young adults living at home longer? It might be worth discussing with the adolescents in your life to find out.

A Gen Zer in her early twenties from Minnesota says, "I don't take a lot of risks. I like to be safe and comfortable. I tend to stick to what I know and follow the rules."

There is no question that the terrorist attacks on September 11, 2001, were a turning point in our perception of safety and security in our country. We've been taught to fear the Boogie Man from the Middle East. The internet and 24-hour news share details of heinous crimes happening all over the world. Sitting at my computer in Michigan as I write this, in a two-minute glance at the news headlines, I learned a seven-year-old girl was kidnapped and murdered by a FedEx driver in Texas, a power outage in North Carolina was caused by gunfire in two substations, and a coyote attacked a two-year-old girl in Los Angeles. How do you "un-hear" these eerie, fear-invoking stories? It'd be easy for me to start scrutinizing FedEx drivers and buy extra flashlights in case of a power outage. I might be worried coyotes will nab my animals. *Okay, not gonna lie, I already am.* It's a lot of anxiety-driven topics to think about.

I stopped watching the news years ago for this very reason. I already know I take a risk the minute I walk out the door and get behind the wheel. The average driver is in a car crash once every 17.9 years of their life, which means "plan on being in at least three collisions during your lifetime." More than likely Gen Xers had all three in and done by the time we were twenty.

We're even at risk in our own homes. Our identity can be stolen, our accounts can get hacked, and our computers can be infected by a virus. A friend called me a while back to say, "I think your mom got hacked on Facebook because I received a strange message from her." So, I called my mom and gently explained this to her, knowing darn well she'd have a meltdown. She barely came up for air saying, "I didn't send him any messages. I haven't even logged in. Why would I send him a message? I didn't *get* any messages." *Oh, I hate it when I'm right.*

We live in a litigious society, with lawsuits that fly faster than a MiG-28. If Bob C were to pull his ex-lax stunt today—targeting Stan the Man in the NBHS cafeteria—ten bucks says he'd be facing some type of expulsion or even legal action. Remember when McDonald's was sued in 1994 for their coffee being so hot that it caused burns? Yeah, those things that gave attorneys a new purpose. That's what I'm talking about.

What's our life lesson here? For me, the answer was in that white limo that pulled up next to my boyfriend and me in Chicago. A man in the front passenger seat stuck his head out and motioned for us to (literally) roll down our window and asked, "Are you guys lost?"

Even though we were tempted to wave our big map and yell "DUH!" *this was clearly not the time.*

He asked where we were trying to go, and we told him I-94.

He replied, "Follow us, and we'll honk when you need to exit," and put his window back up. Since we had no better options, we began to follow the limo through the turns; the roads got a little bigger, busier, and began splitting off. I *thought* I heard the limo honk (*you know, concert ear-ringing aftermath*) so we abruptly exited to the right as the limo bore left. Then the limo suddenly stopped, so we stopped, too. We were directly across from them.

The man jumped out of the limo and ran over to my passenger window and said, "Man, we didn't honk. This isn't your exit." As I was giving him some lame deaf excuse, he interrupted and said, "How'd you like the concert tonight?"

We both looked at each other and back at him and said, "How'd you know we were at the concert?"

The man replied, "Michael's *in* the car," then, he bolted back to the limo yelling, "Just follow us."

As my boyfriend cranked the steering wheel left—faster than the Bandit in his black Trans Am—our minds were racing. I grabbed my little 110 Kodak camera and took a picture of the limo's back bumper but because I was so excited, I couldn't hold the camera still. Eventually, the limo slowed down and honked because we were at our exit. As we veered off, we drove beside the limo, and the tinted back window glided down. Michael Jackson, sitting in the back seat, turned to us, smiled slightly, and waved goodbye, wearing his big dark sunglasses and signature sparkly white glove.

After you digest that story, think of situations you've been in. Could stepping out of our comfort zone and taking risks lead to more experiences and adventures? Embracing risks and taking chances can open the door to new opportunities.

I took a chance by calling the radio station to win tickets. Our parents took a chance by letting their children drive to Chicago. We took a chance by following the limo.

I've told this story many times, some believe me, and some don't. What can't be disputed is that someone in that limo directed the driver to stop and help us to safety. Two teenagers in the wrong place at the wrong time could've ended badly.

Michael Jackson may have gotten a bad rap later in life, but in 1984 he was only twenty-five and already famous. Ironically, he had just suffered his own trauma eight months earlier when his hair caught on fire during the filming of a Pepsi commercial. Six people ran to his rescue to save his life. In my mind, I believe this was MJ's way of paying it forward.

It also could have been that cruising around in the limo was his way of interacting with society incognito, especially since we were near his hometown of Gary, Indiana. In a 1997 interview with Barbara Walters after Princess Diana died, he talked about the tabloids and paparazzi. "I go around the world dealing with running and hiding. I can't go to the store; I can't take a walk in the park. I have to hide in the room. I feel like I'm in prison." Was this MJ's way of taking a chance and collecting experiences? *I think so.*

Do you consider yourself a risk-taker? Or are you more cautious than you used to be?

How many of us have stopped roller skating, jumping off roofs, or opted for shorter heels? Many Gen Xers shared random things they've stopped doing, such as dropping acid, hitchhiking, cartwheels, consuming dairy, drinking, partying, getting out of bed quickly, going to Tijuana, climbing ladders, having one-night stands, driving 120 mph, riding roller coasters, skateboarding, and my favorite, prank calling. *Damn Caller ID.*

Remember when the value of getting a good night's sleep didn't matter whatsoever? When we'd stay up all night and then drag ass to work the next morning?

Jerry, a Gen Xer, says, "I remember in high school, I had to go take my SAT test on a Saturday morning. I went out Friday night partying; I got in at 6 a.m. and had just enough time to change my shirt and brush my teeth before I had to leave to be there."

What CD-55ers still do shit like that? Maybe you do when you're on the '80s Cruise or at '80s in the Sand, pretending you're back in the '80s! Most of us are probably in bed before 11 p.m. now.

As we age, our decisions often become more conservative, driven by fear of risk and harm. While stepping out of our comfort zone can become more challenging, isn't it really about being smarter with our risks?

To stop taking any risks is not the answer.

How *do* we take leaps of faith and step out of our comfort zones, whether it's traveling abroad, leaving a toxic relationship, or exploring new destinations?

Mike in Lakeland says, "Back in the '80s, the movie *The Day After* freaked me out. I was always worrying we'd have a nuclear war. Now, all the craziness, stupidity, and asinine behavior of many people make me more aware of my surroundings because who knows what the hell could happen."

Having a sense of personal safety and security is central to our health and well-being and helps us enjoy the present with peace of mind. When we don't feel safe, or someone we love is at risk, anxiety and worry can overwhelm us.

So, what is really within our control? Truthfully, not much, except how we engage with risk. Our choices should focus on living life fully, not on potential pitfalls. We need to use our '80s adventurous spirit with learned wisdom to balance our current physical limitations. After all, our bodies don't recover as quickly as they used to.

We already have to do damage control with everyday challenges—like coughing, laughing, sneezing, bending over, and even sex that can pull muscles or knock our backs out. And those things alone can make us hesitant to take risks.

"I don't remember the ground hurting as much at twenty," Eric in Sacramento notes. "I've learned there is no shame in bailing instead of powering through a probable slam. I still ski but avoid the steep technical runs. I still go mountaineering, but I only do the easy scrambles now. I make better choices."

Other Gen Xers see it differently. Tony in New York, says, "I still take risks like mountain climbing just to stay feeling alive."

Are we like Tony, embracing risks, or do we pass up opportunities because they threaten to push us out of our comfort zone? Have our fears made us overly cautious? Have we become a society that is afraid to roll down the windows and help someone in need?

There'd be no Michael Jackson story to tell a million times over if we hadn't ventured out of our comfort zone and jumped in the car, headed to a city of seven million with just a paper map and every ounce of our risk-taking, teenage inexperience.

My mom reflected on that night, saying, "I always worried about you until you got home. I lived a sheltered life growing up and always told myself I was going to let you kids go and do things. If you're going to be afraid all your life, you'll never achieve anything."

Mike Gathright of Storyline Church puts it well: "Life isn't about avoiding risks. Without challenges and adversity, we lose our purpose. Without purpose, our life becomes less meaningful." Mike also shared one of his favorite quotes from J.R.R. Tolkien: "It simply isn't an adventure worth telling if there aren't any dragons."

Experiences—and risk—build knowledge and confidence. Embrace them, and don't shy away from adventure—roll down the window and invite them in.

Chapter Rapture 15
Life begins where comfort ends

Sixth Hour Bell

Our childhoods were filled with carefree risks. We were raised with a "rub some dirt on it and you'll be fine" mentality. This risk-taking made us resilient, resourceful, and persistent—traits that have served us well.

Today, safety often feels more tied to fear than self-reliance, as news coverage and social media have heightened our awareness. Avoiding risks isn't the answer. Our '80s adventurous spirit can help us balance our learned wisdom with the realities of aging. Embracing opportunities outside our comfort zone can lead to new experiences.

While personal safety is essential, we shouldn't let fear hold us back. Gen X has some of the best stories because we took risks. Let's keep that spirit alive by inviting adventure into our lives!

Extracurricular Activities

- Enter a contest or competition to challenge yourself, whether it's cooking, sports, a marathon, or an art contest. Competing can be a great way to push your limits and grow.
- Commit to a passion project you've always wanted to pursue, like writing a book, creating music, or teaching a class. Invest time and energy into something that truly excites you.
- Enjoy some classic lawn games by setting up your backyard for '80s favorites like horseshoes, badminton, or even a game of hacky sack.

After-School Specials

- Discover where it all started, from age five to having the best-selling album in the world, in *Michael Jackson's Journey from Motown to Off the Wall*.
- Watch *Risky Business* and appreciate the line "You gotta risk it to get the biscuit." — Tom Cruise as Joel Goodson.
- Watch *Evel Knievel: The ULTIMATE Daredevil the FULL Documentary* on YouTube, where Evel says, "People come to see me die."
- Watch *Pee-wee's Big Adventure*, the "Bike Chain" scene, on YouTube for a hilarious take on safety.

Passing Notes in Class

"Growing up, all the kids and parents in my small town would tube down the river a couple times a year together. My college friends and our families went tubing last summer—the kids had a blast—it was kind of risky but it was outside and hard to have your nose in a phone while you are floating on water."

~Jill in Benton Harbor

"I could make just about any toy dangerous, but Jarts, it had to be Jarts. I still have a set and got them out for our kid's grad parties and even strung out some police caution tape around it."

~Steve in Minnesota

"Do epic shit."

~Ken M in Virginia

Field Trips

- Visit a theme park or fair with someone and enjoy a ride that provides the "thrill" factor, but not necessarily the "sick" factor.
- Consider taking a first aid or CPR class to proactively manage risks and stay prepared for emergencies at this stage in life.

Chapter Mixtape

- "The Safety Dance" – Men Without Hats
- "Danger Zone" – Kenny Loggins
- "Let It Whip" – Dazz Band
- "Tarzan Boy" – Baltimora
- "In the Dark" – Billy Squier
- "Burning Down the House" – Talking Heads
- "Kickstart My Heart" – Mötley Crüe
- "Shot in the Dark" – Ozzy Osbourne
- "On the Loose" – Saga
- "Jump" – Van Halen

Shortcut to Spotify Playlist: beckykliss.com/CR15

Chap. Sixteen

Somebody's Watching Me

▭

Fears

> *"We are made up of two contrasting ideals: love and fear. Pick one, and live."*
>
> ~Axl Rose

At fourteen, I'd hang out with my cousin, Theresa, who was a few years older than me and hearing impaired. She drove the coolest car—a dark-green 1979 Thunderbird with raised letter tires. With our hair feathered perfectly, braces on our teeth, and our gaudy, big, plastic sunglasses on, Robin and I would go cruising with her, and we became the elusive badass older girls like Theresa that we envisioned ourselves to be.

One day, our destination was McDonald's in Michigan City, Indiana, fifteen minutes away. We were sitting in a booth by the window, eating our Chicken McNuggets and people-watching. Across the parking lot and heading toward the entrance came two older girls—one was blond and had embraced the new trend of punk hairdos.

Now, *had* my parents been cable subscribers and *had* I watched MTV, this whole incident could've been avoided, but because I'd never seen this hairstyle before, I stared at her out the window. Miss Cutting Edge's hair resembled David Bowie's from his *Aladdin Sane* album; it was spiked on top and straight on the sides, down to the top of her shoulders. I believe she recognized my gawking as youthful ignorance and spared me her retaliation because the two girls came in, took their food to go, and walked out.

As they left, I couldn't help myself. My stare progressed to one that clearly declared, *"Your hairdo looks so stupid."* And that was all it took. Any grace she was giving me was gone. She gave me back the bug eyes with the full-on *"fuck you"* face. Despite Robin muttering "stop staring" to me the whole time, and without any thought of ramifications, it happened. My middle finger surfaced. It didn't matter that I was a newbie at flipping people off. Hovering my hand behind the window frame and pushing up my middle finger a couple of inches above the glass *counted*. That was all it took. The punk girls did a one-eighty back into McDonald's straight for us.

This is the point where fear can suck the blood out of you.

Theresa, who was sitting across from us with her back to the door, asked, "What's going on?" Because of her hearing impairment, she didn't completely understand I was about to die.

My BFF and I had mere seconds to come up with a plan. It went like this: "Robin, you have to save me," I said frantically, knowing of the two of us, I charted way higher on the wimp scale than she did.

We've all felt fear in our lives for various things—it's an awful feeling. According to FearlessLiving.org, some of the most common fears are snakes, spiders, heights, public speaking, and needles.

They also reported the top five emotional fears are:

1. Fear of failure (not believing in ourselves and our capabilities)
2. Fear of loss (income, home, relationships, identity, health, power, youth, etc.)
3. Fear of change (the what-ifs holding us back)
4. Fear of intimacy (revealing our inner selves, thoughts, feelings, and vulnerabilities to others)
5. Fear of being judged (hiding from who we really are to avoid being embarrassed or feeling foolish)

I think they forgot the "wait 'til your father gets home" or "getting beaten to a pulp over giving the bird" fear on the damn list.

The fears that most of us experience are emotional—ones we can't see or readily recognize. With those, there's no spider to squash.

If deep-rooted fears are not addressed, they can turn into phobias that bring on anxiety and panic attacks.

Most Gen Xers say their top fears in the '80s were fighting and getting their asses kicked, getting ousted from the click, getting busted, getting in trouble, getting grounded, speaking in public, or contracting AIDS like young Ryan White.

And who was worried they'd be diagnosed with scoliosis in elementary school?

"I remember going into a classroom one at a time and the teacher and a nurse had us take our shirts off, put our hands above our heads, and lean over while the nurse ran two fingers down our spine and said if it was good or bad," Matt K in New Buffalo says.

Selwyn, a NBHS graduate who is 6-foot-5, recalls, "I was nervously waiting for my turn to give my oral book report in Mr. T's class my senior year. When it was finally my turn, I was so nervous, I locked my knees and gripped the podium a little too hard. They say when I blacked out, the stand went down with me." Selwyn, who has a solid athletic build and was a defensive tackle on the football team, let his fear of giving an oral book report literally take him D-O-W-N. Public speaking can be a powerful phobia no matter how tough *or tall* you are.

And let's not forget the fear our parents instilled in us about microwaves.

"My uncle bought a Geiger counter to detect radiation to use with his first microwave because he was convinced he could get exposure from it," Eric in Canada says.

Most of us girls were more worried about heating things up with *boys* than we ever were with what we were heating up our food with.

Robin and I went from having a fear of catching cooties from a boy to the fear that if the boys we liked found out were into them, we would die. *Seems to be a theme here so far.*

Note from my BFF to me:

> This is a subject I don't want to talk about but I'll say it anyway. Oscar. What is it you like so much about him? And why is your future ruined because you think he knows you like him? That's a good sign because he'll think about you more. When I found out Wayne liked me, I started liking him because I thought about him more. It all goes to show that you have some hope. I don't want you to ruin your life you shouldn't give up hope.
>   -Rob (p.s. Call me.)

Of course, that didn't stop us. We wrote notes and passed them back and forth every day at school, talking about all our secret boy crushes. The top two note thieves, Tommy and Bret *(aka Guppy and Salmon)*, were obsessed with knowing what we were writing about and went to great lengths to intercept our notes. Obviously, we had to outsmart them, so we went to the school library and checked out a book listing all the types of fish. We assigned alias fish names for every boy *and* their evil girlfriends weren't spared, either (names like *Piranha, Parasite, Snail, Crab,* and *Seaweed*). Then, we created a secret decoder sheet to help us remember them all, which I still have—and, *yes,* there *really* were fifty-five names on the list.

It worked perfectly until the decoder sheet was intercepted. When the list became compromised, it was a Code Red, and the process started all over with ice cream flavors, tree types, or candy bar names like *O'Henry, Raisinet, Charleston Chew,* and *Milk Dud.*

There is no question we meant business when it came to boys. But why did we have this much fear? It's not like we would *literally die* if someone knew we liked them.

I've carried fears related to worrying about what others think of me forever. In my fifties, I'm pushing through it. If you don't face the fears dragging you down, they will compound until they change your habits and your life, and not for the better. That fear factor continued into my relationships over the years. Yet, I appeared fearless because I ran a successful business.

The thing is, fear can be a huge motivator.

My fear of what others thought about me drove me to become *fearless*. I led my business to almost two million dollars in sales—statistically, only 1 percent of companies in my industry achieve that amount of success. I never realized that it was because I wanted to prove that I was competent, rather than simply wanting to run a successful business.

Here's a note from my BFF to me when we were sixteen:

> You may really like him, but not as much as you say you do. If Catfish broke up with you today, you'd go home and cry. 70% because of failure and 30% because you liked him.

My BFF was on to something. Her diagnosis was right on the money.

Understanding the role fear plays in our lives is complicated. Do you worry about change, loneliness, rejection, uncertainty, or inadequacy? Are your fears crippling you from getting out of your comfort zone, trying new things, and moving forward? What *are* your fears?

Do you fear getting dementia or cancer? Do you fear not having enough money to live the rest of your life? Do you not like to drive at night because you are fearful of getting in an accident? Do you have parents—like my mom—who have a fear of online banking, because they're worried that someone will steal their account numbers or money? We all have a list when we really think about it.

It's so easy to make a quick decision *not* to do something without understanding the underlying reason and how it might be related to fear.

When this happens, a certified hypnotist in Michigan advises, "Ask yourself, 'Why *can't* I do this?'" She suggests that if you find yourself asking the proverbial "What-ifs," you should finish the sentence. Acknowledge the worst that could happen and consider how you would recover and move on. This process can lead you on a soul-searching journey to uncover the true source of your fears, but it works.

FOMO – *FEAR OF MISSING OUT*

FOMO (fear of missing out) wasn't a term we used in the '80s. However, when I asked Gen Xers if they experienced FOMO back then, I found they actually did! Maybe they were anxious they weren't keeping up with the fad or fashion trends, fretful about missing a TV show, afraid of finding out about a party they missed or weren't invited to, or experiencing utter anguish over missing concerts.

"When I was eleven," Mina in Houston says, "Cyndi Lauper was performing at the Houston Summit in 1984 but my parents wouldn't let me go because I was too young. Everyone in the audience was told to wear white because she was filming the video for 'Money Changes Everything.' I'm still bitter."

Eric in Canada says, "I remember telling my mom I had to have Converse attire for phys ed. Of course, she got me knockoff 'converted' pants. The ridicule I had to endure!"

Today, FOMO is something we all deal with more than ever through our exposure to social media—and it's felt most severely by the younger generations.

Teens I interviewed for this book talked about a common theme: how their images and statuses on social media affect them. They want to know who is being included and excluded. What are people I know doing? Are people having more fun than I am? Why am I being left out? Why does it feel like everyone else's lives are better than mine? Feeling the pressure to check social media and constantly compare your life to others is FOMO, and it's real. It can be considered a form of bullying if someone is posting purposely to make others feel excluded.

When I asked a 10th grader what her dream was, she answered, "To be content in life and stop constantly feeling like I can be better." Weren't our dreams at that age about having money and fun, along with a car with a kick-ass Pioneer stereo?

When asked about her biggest challenge, another student answered "to fit in." Did she want to fit in with her clothes, sense of humor, or her likes and dislikes? Are we being audited for acceptance through social media today? For the younger generations, it seems so.

One student has a Facebook account only to make sure her parents don't post anything embarrassing about her. We know we can't control what others post. Social media can feel like gossip when we watch it to see if something is posted or mentioned about us.

Ultimately, many versions of FOMO on social media exist. No one likes the feeling of being left out. But, when lonely, what do we turn to? Often, social media—the digital pacifier. Ironically, seeking comfort and acceptance through social media can have the opposite effect.

Retired NBHS PE teacher and baseball coach Roger Vink passed away as I was wrapping up final edits on this book. I was traveling at the time of his funeral and knew his celebration of life services would be filled with stories of his involvement at NBHS and of opening Oink's Ice Cream Shop in town after he left teaching. I found myself feeling guilty for not being there, to the point of having "funeral FOMO" *(if there is such a thing.)* It was easy to want to turn to social media to see the homage of what I missed, but instead, I picked up the phone and called one of the baseball players who was a pallbearer. I explained how I felt bad that I was absent from Mr. Vink's services and asked him how it went. It felt so heartwarming to hear him share the story of the gathering and tribute to Mr. Vink's life that I ended up feeling like I *had* been there. Isn't that the solution for FOMO—to diffuse that feeling that you weren't really isolated from something?

Terry remembers wanting to see Loverboy in concert so badly he could taste it. When Mikey showed up to school wearing Loverboy's concert T-shirt, Terry was envious.

"At first, I was jealous and mad at Mikey for getting to do something I wanted to. But then I realized, if I wanted to see Loverboy, I needed to be the one to make that happen, not sit around and sulk at Mikey over it."

Fiona in Florida may have the FOMO battle dialed in the best. She says, "For me, overcoming FOMO starts with living in gratitude for what you have, gratitude for the people who care about you, and focusing your energy on that instead of what you don't have or are missing out on in life. Perspective matters."

I believe FOMO can be offset if you tackle it head-on. Whether you use Fiona's method of gratitude, Terry's approach of creating your own experiences, or my way of hitting it head-on and talking to people about their experiences—find what works for you and ditch that draining process of ruminating about what you missed that adds no value to your life.

Looking back on his speech collapse, Selwyn said, "Later in life, I became football head coach and had to speak to thirty to forty young men who played for me. I had to overcome the fear of speaking in front of groups of people. I still don't like it, but I can do it. A mentor once told me I had to learn to 'get comfortable being uncomfortable.'"

Wow. For only four words, that is a powerful statement and mantra to live by: "Get comfortable being uncomfortable."

For me, I now realize that my fish-name note-writing strategy wasn't about worrying what the boys thought of me. It had everything to do with what I thought of myself, my confidence, and my fear of others not liking me.

Mike in Tulsa says, "As a young boy, I feared what my peers thought of me because I had epilepsy. I was teased, avoided, and judged by my classmates and even teachers. I was scared, but over the years I accepted the fact that I was different due to a factor that I couldn't control or change. The only thing I could do is adapt. Turns out, I have motivated others by accepting and being myself and letting go of my fears."

A therapist once told me, "The reality is not everyone is going to like us. We should expect that one-third of the people will like us, one-third of the people won't, and one-third of them won't think about it either way." Why give those two-thirds the power to intimidate us, especially on social media?

Today, Gen Xers' fears have changed to a list they shared that looks like this: outliving the people we love, our parents' declining health, being old enough to join AARP, losing our jobs, having another heart attack, the toll of arthritis, the taxman, being alone, government decisions, social alienation, bullying on social media, what's in the water we are drinking, if our Amazon package is going to arrive on time, the internet going down, getting a DUI, that our '80s bands won't be around to keep playing, mass shootings, and, of course, getting terrible diseases such as dementia or cancer.

"My biggest fear is my mind dying before my body," David in Kentucky says. "I'm an only child and had to watch dementia take my mother." Isn't David's worry about poor health a fear we all are faced with now—one that didn't cross our minds in our youth?

After attending three funerals in a week, Terry said to me, "We're getting to that age where God is taking away more things than He's giving us." That'll scare the hell out of you if you think about it.

Does that snake or spider still foster the same amount of fear it used to compared to the worry of disease or losing our parents? Probably not. Our fears are far more emotionally based now. *Okay, for real though, I still hate spiders.*

Jackie in Chicago says, "Fear and worry are two feelings I try to avoid. You are what you think."

Ironically, I was editing this chapter on a plane flying home in the worst turbulence I've ever experienced. Sitting over the wing looking out, watching the wing bounce us around, and gripping my water bottle, I felt waves of panic.

Like Jackie, I had to shift my mindset. There's nothing I can do to change the situation but have faith that the plane is strong, and the pilots are skilled. Silently sending good vibes to them in the form of "you've got this" helped me transfer my fear to faith.

Terry's son was avoiding applying for jobs because he feared rejection. Terry's encouraging words to his son can apply to all of us, "What's the worst thing that can happen?" *You have to try, or you'll never know.*

The exciting lottery-winning story my family experienced (detailed in Chapter 13) actually had an element of fear that I didn't share. It was a Friday night when our family won the $10,000 instant lottery. The ticket needed to be driven to Lansing, Michigan, the following Monday. My parents were so fearful something might happen to the ticket—like two kids excited to get bikes losing it—that they came up with a plan to hide it inside the frame of their wedding picture, placed high on their dresser. You'd think with just the four of us living there it'd have been safe, but my mom recalls, "We kept going back all weekend long and opening the frame to make sure the ticket was still there." Fear spares no one, regardless of age. *And, doesn't it always seem to creep back to the what-ifs?*

<hr />

Looking back at that day at McDonald's, I went from *bad-ass* to *meek-ass* in seconds as fear raced through my entire being. Who would explain to my parents why my cousin brought me home, beaten to a pulp? Why had I put Theresa and Robin in this situation? And, of course, the self-reproach: "What was I thinking?"

But in a matter of minutes, it was over. I stammered through a lame apology, "It was an accident. I didn't mean to…" Miss Cutting Edge instructed me never to let that happen again. And that was it—other than our Chicken McNuggets being permanently stuck in the top of our throats for the remainder of the week. It was a fear that turned into embarrassment, which became a lesson learned—and one we've had a good laugh about over the years.

Theresa says today, "We were lucky. Holy shit—that girl was crazy—I thought she was going to hit one of us. Now, I think it was so funny."

To this day, I will never give "the bird" to anyone I *don't* know, and I scold anyone I'm around who flips the bird to strangers because I'll always associate that with the fear of getting my face kicked in.

And what a simple fear to have—one that will likely keep my middle finger out of trouble for the rest of my life. Use fear to protect yourself, but *don't* let it paralyze you. Don't use fear to avoid the discomfort of making difficult decisions. Instead, let it help you pause and think those decisions through—*just don't make it too long of a pause.*

Whether it's fear of failure, loss, change, intimacy, being judged, or any other deeply rooted emotional issue, it's time to squash them like we would that spider.

Get comfortable being uncomfortable. Replace your fears with faith.

Author Judy Blume sums it up best: "How we handle our fears will determine where we go with the rest of our lives."

Chapter Rapture 16
Faith over fear

Sixth Hour Bell

Understanding the role fear plays in our lives is complex. Are your fears keeping you from getting out of your comfort zone, trying new things, and moving forward? Fear has power only if we allow it to. It can also be a motivator. Don't make quick decisions to avoid something when fear might be the real reason.

Expect that one-third of the people will like you, one-third won't, and one-third won't care either way. Why give power to those who don't matter, especially on social media?

Fear can protect us and allow us to think decisions through, but it shouldn't stop us. Get comfortable with being uncomfortable. Replace fear with faith, and take control of your life.

Extracurricular Activities

- What gives you FOMO? Have a strategy to work around it. For insights, check out *The Fear of Missing Out: Practical Decision-Making in a World of Overwhelming Choice* by Patrick J. McGinnis.

- What are your "what-if's"? Are they related to failure, loss, change, intimacy, or judgment? Ask yourself, "Why can't I do this?" Confront the worst-case scenario by answering, "If it happens, I will…" Think about how you'd recover with confidence and faith and move forward.

- Master your fears by reading books like *Rejection Proof*, *The Solution to Social Anxiety*, *Do It Scared*, *Feel the Fear… and Do It Anyway* by Susan Jeffers and *The Art of Fear: Why Conquering Fear Won't Work and What to Do Instead* by Kristen Ulmer.

Field Trips

- Take a spontaneous road trip without a planned route, using just maps and intuition, inspired by the adventurous spirit of '80s road movies such as the *National Lampoon's Vacation* series.

- Explore breathtaking quaint Estes Park in Colorado and tour the Stanley Hotel, where parts of *The Shining* were filmed. Or head to New York City to visit locations where scenes of *Ghostbusters* were shot.

Passing Notes in Class

"I loved going on supernatural hunts in the '80s. We'd all meet at the pizza place and then pile into cars and trucks and drive to the boonies to look for abandoned churches, houses, graveyards, or anything spooky."

~Kristin in Ohio

"I don't need to say 'hold my beer...' before doing dumb stuff because now I have the confidence and courage to try. Sometimes it works out, sometimes it doesn't, either way, I had a great time trying."

~Sandra in Tucson

After-School Specials

- For a night of frights, have a Stephen King movie marathon with '80s classics like *The Shining, Creepshow, Cujo, The Dead Zone, Christine, Children of the Corn, Firestarter, Cat's Eye, Silver Bullet, Maximum Overdrive, The Running Man,* and *Pet Sematary*.
- Rewatch *Ghostbusters* to remind yourself that you can conquer your fears! Just say, "I ain't afraid of no ghost!"
- Watch *Peanuts* reruns on YouTube, especially the episode on Snoopy: Nights Watch "Snoopy is Scared of the Dark." Let Charlie Brown lift your spirits with his line, "Don't worry about the world coming to an end today. It's already tomorrow in Australia."

Chapter Mixtape

- "Somebody's Watching Me" – Rockwell
- "Ghostbusters" – Ray Parker Jr.
- "Silent Running" – Mike & The Mechanics
- "I Ran (So Far Away)" – A Flock of Seagulls
- "Hysteria" – Def Leppard
- "On The Dark Side" – John Cafferty
- "Nothing to Fear (But Fear Itself)" – Oingo Boingo
- "Shadows of the Night" – Pat Benatar
- "Renegade" – Styx
- "It Can Happen" – Yes

Shortcut to Spotify Playlist: beckykliss.com/CR16

Chap. Seventeen

Invincible

Perseverance

"I do count my lucky stars. I don't know why I'm still here and I do sometimes think I'm on borrowed time... What a great fucking life we've had and what a great fucking experience."

~Ozzy Osbourne

In 1983, Tink, 16, and his good friend, Mark, 17, hopped in Mark's bright-red beater Mustang-2 hatchback in Union Pier, Michigan, and headed south for three hours. They had the radio cranked, an atlas, and a few bucks in their pockets. They were on their way to the bustling metropolis of Indianapolis, a city they'd never seen. They were psyched to visit their neighborhood friend, Bruce *(Miss Pretty in Pink's ex)*, who'd moved there. They planned to party together and see Quiet Riot and Whitesnake in concert.

None of them were of legal age to buy alcohol, so they concocted a plan. The oldest looking one would go into the liquor store, walk up to the counter with a case of beer, and act as guiltless as possible. At eighteen, Bruce was the oldest; however, Tink was voted to go inside, despite being the youngest. They reasoned the plush *'fro hair* on Tink's upper lip—his jet-black mustache—would make him look old enough.

Tink strutted into the liquor store—five years *under* the legal age—and set the case of beer on the counter, laid the money down, and smiled innocently while making small talk with the older male clerk. His beer was rung up without question. The three teens couldn't high-five and fist-bump their illegal accomplishment enough. But then they did the math: twenty-four beers divided by three meant only eight beers each. Clearly, that wasn't enough for partying all night. So, they decided to do the same thing all over again. However, purchasing an additional case would cut into their gas money to get home. They had to prioritize. Beer was needed *now,* and gas money was needed *later*. In no time, Tink emerged from the store grinning wide, carrying a second case of beer.

They partied for the next eight hours, scoped out chicks, jammed at the concert, and drank all their brewskies. In addition, somewhere between "Here I Go Again" and "Cum on Feel the Noize," they *inadvertently* became stoned. The three weren't into pot, but weed was being smoked everywhere at the concert. The skunky odor in the air gifted them with a contact buzz.

It was 3 a.m. before they knew it and time to make the long drive home. Tink and Mark, wiped out from the evening festivities, slid into the car homeward bound with Tink driving. After two hours, the arrow on the gas gauge was pointing to 'E' and there was still an hour to go, so Tink wheeled into a gas station. They went inside to negotiate their predicament with the clerk for the twenty dollars of gas money they had spent on whooping it up. A deal was cut. Mark would leave his New Buffalo Bison school letterman jacket with the clerk as an agreement they'd return tomorrow with the cash and get his coat back.

As promised, they headed back the next day with their twenty bucks. Tink and Mark spent hours driving all over, looking for the gas station, but they couldn't find it. They couldn't remember which one they stopped at in the wee hours of the morning. Mark's cherished letterman jacket, a symbol of his love and high achievement in basketball, was gone. His parents were furious because they didn't have the money to replace the jacket. Replacing an item may not seem like a big deal today, but it often was back then. One of anything was usually all you got.

Tink reflects, "The excitement of road-trippin' in Mark's little shitbox Mustang that he was so proud of, to see a rock concert and party with long-time neighborhood buddies, was all we were focused on, even though the night didn't end as planned."

This story captures so many of the life lessons in this book: enjoying moments, collecting experiences, taking risks, and making choices based on our values. It highlights our relationship to money and our deep connection to music. But, more importantly, it reflects what life was like when technology didn't dominate our every move. Isn't this how many of us rolled back then? We chased fun, embraced the moment, and didn't get caught up on the *what-ifs*, even when we were pushing the boundaries. You might call it perseverance, but did we see it that way? Maybe we were simply plowing through challenges, turning them into adventures, and not seeing them as obstacles at all.

Joe M in Texas remembers, "Our neighborhood was like a small army of kids. We'd play cops and robbers with BB guns and make bow and arrow contraptions with sharpened points. We'd have fights where we'd find any throwable rock and try to hit someone. We also shot Roman candles at each other. Many kids weren't allowed to play with us because we were dangerous, but these were some of the greatest moments of my childhood, even though we could've really gotten hurt."

Christopher in Michigan reinforces this. "I'd jump on a passing freight train to hitch a ride to McDonald's. No, I am not brain damaged, but probably should be. Or dead."

Denise from Las Vegas recalls driving under the influence of alcohol many times, but she never had an accident. She says, "God had to be driving the car."

Think of everything we've been through. How many of us have defied the odds or had Jesus at the wheel when we ended up in bad situations? I've heard Gen Xers' stories from across the world describing being bullied at school, surviving accidents, growing up in a dysfunctional household, having unloving parents, experiencing anger, heartbreak, or loss, and being abused, harmed, or put in dangerous situations.

But yet, we are still here.

All of our life experiences have brought us to right here, right now, sitting with this book in our hands.

A year and a half after Mark lost his letterman jacket, sadly, he lost his life. He was only eighteen. After graduation, he enlisted in the Navy and was stationed in California. He died in a motorcycle accident pulling out of the base. The picture on the cover of this book of the carefree, vibrant kid in red with his arms stretched overhead *is* Mark. It was taken at New Buffalo Beach hanging out with friends the year before he died—just a cool kid who loved basketball and felt on top of the world in this picture.

Couldn't that picture of Mark have been any of us back then? How many of us have a photo or a memory like this that screams, *"I'm Invincible"?*

The truth is, we're *not*. We're human. We can strive to be invincible, but there's no getting around the fact that we all have an expiration date. When we hear about bad things happening to others, it's common to analyze their circumstances. How many times have we thought, "If they had only eaten better, their health wouldn't have given out," "If they hadn't smoked, they wouldn't have developed cancer," or "If they weren't drinking, that accident might not have happened?" When I catch myself doing this, I stop and ask why. Am I avoiding confronting my *own* vulnerabilities or trying to rationalize why misfortunes happen to others? Are we attempting to distance ourselves from reality and our own invincibility to ward off fear? Or, worse, do these *what-ifs*—like car accidents, losing a loved one, cancer diagnosis, or illness—start to feel more imminent to us?

The truth is anything can happen at any time, but until something does, we can't fully comprehend the outcome. In the meantime, counting our blessings and being grateful are much better things to think about.

Juan, a Gen Xer in Bridgman, Michigan, says, "My *abuela* (grandma) recently turned 102. I know she's mindful of her mortality, but doesn't focus on death, nor is she afraid of it. Her zest for life, passion, and optimism tells me that's what keeps her going. In fact, when I left from visiting her in Argentina on her birthday, she said, 'See you next year!'"

How do we get a mentality like that? One like Juan's *abuela* has—living each day with an optimistic outlook? How many of us live our lives today like Mark did, in the pursuit of adventure, joy, and friendship? His close friends believe if he had known his life would end in eighteen months and was offered a do-over on the Indy trip, he would have chosen to do the same darn thing again because for him, adventure was the epitome of living life to the fullest.

So how do we make the changes before we have a meltdown like the one I had sitting in my sunroom? Let's face it, we don't just get out of bed one morning and find all our painful baggage and bad habits have disappeared. For some of us, it takes hitting rock bottom, or dealing with a health setback or other trauma, before we decide to make a change.

We've all been faced with challenges and adversity. We're at that age where we see wrinkles and gray hair and feel our aches and pains more often. We've run households, had careers, raised families, and dealt with sickness, sadness, and grief. We've had a ton of curve balls thrown at us. We've learned many life lessons and we are all survivors in some way, whether we realize it or not.

When we were young and lacked experience, we made choices like Mark and Tink did that could've ended much worse than with a lost coat. So, what does being invincible look like now that we're not out jumping on moving trains and slingshotting each other with rocks? Could it be as simple as "not thinking about it" anymore, like Juan's grandma?

Dave, Mr. Quality of Life who you met in Chapter 13, is a walking answer to that question. At fifty-nine, he was cutting clients, gearing up for retirement, and spending time doing what he loved most: playing golf. Then one morning he woke up and couldn't talk right. Within an hour, he was airlifted to a specialty hospital for emergency surgery to remove a blood clot from his brain. His wife's quick action along with the medical know-how of today saved his life.

After his stroke, Dave couldn't read, write, or remember people's names. He'd call me Benjamin instead of Becky. What used to take him a minute to read or write now takes hours. He is unable to process things like he used to. But that doesn't stop him. Every day, he pushes forward. He was a great golfer and won a tournament the day before his stroke but had to learn how to chip a golf ball again. He continues progressing ahead one day at a time. He is persevering.

Isn't that the key for us CD-55ers now? Accepting the cards we're dealt, continuing to move forward, and being grateful for the positives? Could being invincible really be more about eliminating the stress in our lives and *persevering*? Dave would probably agree.

Screw all the unimportant ruckus and ignore all the noise that gets in your way. *Pick your battles and let the rest of that shit go.*

This is what we know: Tomorrow doesn't necessarily get easier. We just become stronger, wiser, and more experienced. We have so much to look forward to, including retirement, grandchildren, bucket list checkmarks, travel, Friday night poker nights, roller skating, jumping in the car and going to concerts, and starting new hobbies.

Remember, when it's all said and done, what really matters is that the people we care for are by our sides and we have peace in our hearts. It took me a long time to realize this.

The airlines tell you to put your oxygen mask on before the person next to you for a reason. You can't help anyone else if you aren't functioning first—which leads me to an important question: **What is in your oxygen mask?** What are the daily items that feed your soul? Maybe they are simple things like bird watching, practicing yoga, volunteering, going to the beach, crafting, playing music, dancing, or spending time with people you love and your fur babies.

Those are the things that need to be in our oxygen masks.

Our once-in-a-lifetime bucket list items need to fill our oxygen masks, too: a road trip to Rocky Mountain National Park, a concert at Wembley Stadium, a river cruise in Europe, an adventure in Iceland watching the aurora borealis from a natural hot spring, a meet-and-greet with Jon Bon Jovi, or a ride on your

Harley down the Pacific Coast Highway. They're all important, but the daily, soulful ones that quiet our minds are the ones that keep us most content.

It's time to fill your inner bucket before anything else. It may sound selfish, *but it's not*.

Ask yourself, How often do you turn down opportunities? Do you respond automatically with, "I've got too much going on, maybe next time," or "I have to work," or "I'd like to, *but…*"?

Yes, we were raised to work our asses off, but that can't be the excuse holding us back anymore. We've all paid our dues, and we've earned this time for ourselves. In our youth, we rarely let time, risk, or fear stop us from chasing joy. Sure, our parents pushed us to get outside, and that did help us to explore and be innovative. But let's be real—we'd have done it anyway—*we're Gen X, after all*. No one handed us the solutions or coddled us. **We figured shit out and made things happen.**

Nathaniel in Louisiana sums it up nicely. "We were latchkey kids. We learned to function on our own. We have the best ride-or-die friends any generation could ever hope for. When shit hits the fan, we will know how to survive."

He's right; we didn't focus on the excuses. Gen Xers came to adolescence fast and furious with our left-to-our-own-devices upbringing, and most of us experienced a shorter childhood because of it. We focused on how to remove our obstacles and make shit happen.

Chris Clews, '80s keynote speaker and author of the book series *The Ultimate Series on Essential Work & Life Lessons from '80s Pop Culture*, says, "What I truly appreciate about so much of '80s pop culture is that it didn't try to hide what it was or try to vanilla it up. In movies like *The Breakfast Club, St. Elmo's Fire,* and *The Big Chill* the character's lives were messy, just like our lives can be messy."

Gen Xers are one tenacious and resilient generation. And it's far from over—we have so many places to go, cool people to see (and meet), and fun things to do! Take a good look at your life now. What makes you laugh? What makes your energy level soar? What makes you feel like you are still in your twenties?

The '80s Cruise I went on in 2023 was sold out. Some three thousand people were onboard. Cruisers invested their hard-earned money and took a week off work just to be there. I talked to random CD-55ers on the cruise and asked them, "How old do you feel *mentally*?" Most answered that they felt like they were in their twenties. Not one person answered that they felt over thirty. Cognitively, they felt *half* their age. Morris Day was performing on the cruise, and I asked him the same question, and without hesitation, he blurted out, "Twenty!" When you watch Morris on stage dancing and singing "Jungle Love," loving what he does at sixty-five, he looks like he feels twenty.

However, when I asked the same question to CD-55ers when they weren't on vacation and at their daily grind of work and routines, the answers were not the same; their mental age went up drastically.

When you're engaged in activities you love, such as being on a cruise with great music and fun people, you'll feel younger and more vibrant than in your day-to-day work life. What does that suggest? That you need to incorporate those joyful experiences into your oxygen mask *daily*.

Courtney Benson, an entertainment talent manager in California, used to be a workaholic. But now that he's turned fifty-two, he says, "Work for my client comes first each day, but at 3:00 p.m., it becomes 'Courtney Time.' If I don't make time for myself, it won't happen because no one else will do it for me."

I had a meeting with a financial planner last fall. He presented me with a fancy report, mapping out my living expenses until I'm 100 years old. My immediate response was, "I won't live to 100—we need to drop that number down by ten years."

A few days later, I was in a hotel room in Nashville with my parents. My dad was channel surfing and clicked on a show called *Talking in Circles*. Clint Black was interviewing Sammy Hagar.

Sammy was telling Clint how much he loves walking on the beach with his wife and dog. He spoke about what inspires him and what it's like playing in a band. Then the interview ended with Hagar saying: "I plan to live to a 100, so, *you know…*"

Whoa! That hit me like a gut punch. Before that day in my sunroom, I would've missed the sign, but now I'm living in the moment. I'm more receptive to the universe's *(and, apparently, Sammy's)* messages saying, "Why shouldn't you plan on living to one hundred?"

Imagine us old and sassy Gen Xers in a retirement home with someone bringing us Tombstone pizzas and mac and cheese, while we're playing Monopoly or Uno, drinking Dr. Pepper, and sucking on Doritos with the few teeth we have left. Next, we'll be pushing each other around in our wheelchairs while we sing Salt-n-Pepa's "Push It," bouncing our walkers to the beat of Beastie Boys' "No

Sleep Till Brooklyn," and listening to our 65-year-old mixtapes. And we don't have to worry, because the '80s invented "I've fallen and I can't get up" by LifeCall. *Something we can finally put to use instead of making fun of, like we used to.*

What's stopping us from envisioning the best possible outcome for ourselves? We absolutely deserve it.

I've always believed in the adage "when one door closes, another one opens" because I believe it's true.

Miss Pretty in Pink lost her husband of thirty-three years to cancer as I was finishing this book. Our close five friends (aka The Girl Squad) would do anything to take her pain and sorrow away, but we can't. Like any of us dealing with a tragedy, it just takes time. What do we do instead? We create things to look forward to and opportunities to replace the pain with laughter—even if temporary or in small doses. We've been able to look forward to bingo at the brewery, taking walks together out to the pier, Girl Squad dinners, going to see a parade, and yes, even a Night Ranger concert. Whether you have adversity in your life currently or not, always have something to look forward to. There are open doors waiting somewhere, even when others are closing—be open to seeing them.

The *abuela* who tells her nephew, "See you next year," on her 102nd birthday—*that's* what I'm talking about.

Colleen, an older cashier at a resale store in Minneapolis, was checking out my purchases and asked me why I was buying a bunch of crazy hats. I laughed and told her it was for a fun party I throw called "BecFest" for people my age. *Did I really just say "my age"? Lord!*

Her reply was matter-of-fact: "Most adults don't know how to play."

Think about that. *Most adults don't know how to play.* It's no different than the '80s Cruisers saying they felt like they were in their twenties on the ship. Days without joy will age you mentally more than you realize—who says we have to become old, cantankerous people when we could keep our twenties mentality, add in our CD-55 wisdom, and enjoy our second youth?

Did you love practical jokes as a kid? Bring them back! Did you always want to take guitar lessons? Take them! Get back to the things you used to love to do, and new ones. And, of course, adapt them accordingly to your current risk factors. Build a fort with your grandkids, get on a bike again and ride—even if it's a three-wheeler—or make a path in the woods and hike down to the crick to check out the fish. Have a backyard you hardly use? Set up the badminton net or go buy a Wiffle ball set and have your crazy friends over and play (*notice I didn't say dodgeball*).

"For my 48th birthday present, I am purchasing a backyard swing set for myself," Shelly in Texas says. "Am I going to look strange, a grown woman swinging on a swing set in a backyard? Probably. Do I give a rat's ass? Clearly not. Swinging has always been one of my favorite activities."

Kristen in Minnesota recounts, "I traveled to my hometown to a classmate's father's funeral. My friend Jeff lived there, and knew I was feeling down so he said, 'Let's go roller skating!' And, at fifty-five years old, we did! It took us back to a time when we were kids. We laughed so hard. I was forced to get out of my head and focus on something else, like just trying to stay standing up and save my kneecaps."

Sometimes, impulse decisions, as simple as they may be, are what takes your mind off the weight of your troubles and lower the stress in your life: jumping in the car to go play a round of golf, hiking a new trail, shelling on the beach after a storm, heading out listening to live music, taking your dog for a car ride, reading a good book, gardening in the mornings, or sitting on the park bench watching the sunset.

You don't have to be on a cruise with other CD-55ers to accomplish this (*although I guarantee it'll do the job*).

Create your own opportunities like we used to and let the "old-people" excuses go.

At seventy-five, my mom, Bonnie, was diagnosed with lymphoma. Then she was cursed with a brutal case of Lyme disease *twice*. Then after her cancer treatments were finished, she was hit with macular degeneration. After all this, she said to me in dismay, "Whoever said these are the golden years was wrong. I can't do what I used to do." But her philosophy is, "When I wake up each morning, I open the window, and stick my head out to the sun coming up and thank God for another day because I don't know what tomorrow will bring." She's filling her oxygen mask with nature and gratitude the minute her day starts.

At Dave's follow-up appointment after his stroke, the doctor told him, "Dave, you're the luckiest guy I know. You had a 95 percent chance of *not* making it out of this hospital, and here you are."

I asked Dave, "Do you remember the three questions you gave me for my book about being happy?" With his memory loss from the stroke, he didn't, so I read them to him from Chapter 13.

1. What made you happy in the '70s and '80s?
2. What makes you happy now?
3. What do you think will make you happy five to ten years from now?

He replied, "Oh, nice! You gotta be happy." He joked about his brain being like scrambled eggs at times, but went on to say, "I refuse to argue or let any stress in my life get to me again."

Dave finds humor in life despite his challenges. When you're true to your situation, it's freeing.

There is a saying, "The only BS I need in my life is 'beach' and 'sunshine.'" Health statistics tell you, medical and holistic doctors tell you, and now *I'm telling you*: Get rid of the wrong type of BS in your life.

Reconsider your choices, how you spend your time, and pay attention to what gives you stress. How have you changed over the past twenty-some years? Are you making time for yourself, finding laughter in your day, and making choices to spend quality moments in nature filling your lungs with fresh air, and spending time with people who bring out the best in you?

If not, what the hell is holding you back?

Imagine starting and ending your day with something simple—yet powerful—as gratitude that replenishes and fills your heart. Being grateful is sustainable food for your soul.

I love being a Gen Xer. We grew up in the best decades—the '70s and '80s. Being in the CD-55 Club empowers me. Knowing we all have similar shit going on, and we're all in this together, feels encouraging, inspiring, and uplifting. I may still have to remind myself not to overthink things and worry about the what-ifs. To accept it's okay for me to be a dork. It's okay for me to be who I am. *Screw the two-thirds who don't really care about you!*

Let's get out of our own way. Don't worry about jumping on your swing set in your backyard like a crazy person or roller skating like a cautious three-year-old when you're fifty-five. It doesn't matter what we look like or what people think as long as we're experiencing joy.

Staying young at heart will add time to your life. Go play golf, fish, write that book, walk the trails, and, most definitely, jump in that red Mustang and live with the mindset we did in the '80s: carefree and excited about our opportunities. You know what's best for you. No one else does. Look inward and find what those things are.

Remember the question I asked you early on: "When do you feel your best?" *Incorporate those things into your oxygen mask daily.*

If there's one thing I've learned through this journey of writing and interacting with CD-55ers, it's we'll *never* figure everything out.

It's *never* too late to make changes—stop a bad habit, start a new venture, seek new relationships, or focus on your health. When one door closes, another one will open.

Courtney Benson says, "We get smart too late and we get old too soon. The only thing that matters is what happens in the middle."

That *is* us. We are in the middle—right here, right now. We are Gen X strong, halfway through this thing called life.

Our story has had *so* many chapters leading up to this moment and now it's time for us to be intentional about writing what comes next. Let's pursue the things that light a fire inside of us, bring us inner peace, and allow our laughter to shine through.

That's perseverance.

It's *our* time to be invincible again.

Chapter Rapture 17
Jump in the red Mustang and go

Sixth Hour Bell

Remember when we chased fun, embraced the moment, and plowed through obstacles? We need to still do that as we face more challenges and adversity now! Along with counting our blessings and being grateful for what we have. It's never too late to change—stop a bad habit or start something new. Let's get out of our own way and figure our shit out!

Being invincible is about reducing stress, having the people we care about by our sides, and peace in our hearts. What feeds your soul? Those are the things to focus on to persevere. Prioritize your inner well-being. Focus on what brings joy and embrace your inner child. Staying young at heart adds years to your life and life to your years.

Extracurricular Activities

- Master a challenging skill, whether it's playing a song on the piano, learning to sew, growing your own herbs, or going retro and solving the Rubik's Cube!

- What's in your oxygen mask? Create a bucket list of adventures you want to do and include things you look forward to daily. Choose activities that make you feel mentally alive and young again.

- Start a daily gratitude practice, including appreciating those who bring out the best in you.

After-School Specials

- Watch *St. Elmo's Fire* to reflect on how far you've come and the challenges you've conquered. Rob Lowe said, "My issue isn't about physical aging; my issue is about wanting to remain vigorous and youthful in my spirit."

- The movie *The Legend of Billie Jean* is a hidden '80s gem, but it's an impactful reminder to stand up for what you believe in. Its motto, "Fair is fair," embodies the spirit of resilience and being invincible!

- Watch *Rocky IV* or any *Rocky* film to fuel your fight for your dreams.

Passing Notes in Class

"I wear a bracelet with 'it is what it is' stamped on it; I get tons of compliments on it."
~Nancy in South Carolina

"Peace and progress."
~Alan Hunter, MTV VJ and host of *'80s on 8*

"I travel solo fairly often. Every time I learn something new. Sometimes about myself or sometimes it's something weird. Like, mountain goats have square pupils (I've been that close). It all changes my perspective on life."
~Steve in Minnesota

Field Trips

- Embark on a road trip on the western stretch of the iconic Route 66. Experience the nostalgic charm of this famous highway, stopping at quirky diners, vintage motels, and unique roadside attractions that capture the spirit of a bygone era.

- For more travel ideas, check out travel groups. The Facebook group "Roadside America-Offbeat Quirky Tourist Attractions" offers some adventurous insights!

- Reconnect with your inner child by visiting a playground or a toy store like Toys "R" Us or a LEGO store. Enjoy the liberating feeling of jumping on a swing or sliding down the slide, just like you did as a kid.

Chapter Mixtape

- "Invincible" – Pat Benatar
- "Things Can Only Get Better" – Howard Jones
- "Magic Power" – Triumph
- "Never Surrender" – Corey Hart
- "I'm Still Standing" – Elton John
- "Baby I'm a Star" – Prince
- "Here I Go Again" – Whitesnake
- "St. Elmo's Fire (Man in Motion)" – John Parr
- "Eye of the Tiger" – Survivor
- "No Sleep Till Brooklyn" – Beastie Boys

Shortcut to Spotify Playlist: beckykliss.com/CR17

Crystal Ball

That's all she wrote...for now...

My quest in writing this book was to help CD-55ers get a jump on finding our Holy Grail in life—hopefully, easier than it was for Indiana Jones! It was to guide you in exploring a path to what's important in life. If we want a happy ending, it's on us to make it happen. I hope I encouraged you to reflect on your past—when life was simple and more carefree—and inspired a desire to get out of your comfort zone. To use the past to pave your future to an uncomplicated, rewarding lifestyle that's more enjoyable.

When writing *When We Were Invincible*, I kept thinking of all the things we CD-55ers are going through in life. It's way too much to fit into one book! I started a plan four years ago, and already have stories, quotes, and a layout for book 2 and even book 3.

Book 2 in *The Invincible '80s* series will take a trip down memory lane back to the '80s, where friendships, parents, love, communication, trust, anger, and disappointment shaped us. We'll talk about finding inner peace and accepting who we are—and who we've become—while exploring relationships. What have we learned about these things? Are we happy, still trying to figure it out, or chalking it up? We'll also dive into how we "expressed ourselves" with epic outfits and hairdos that could defy gravity. And, yes, we'll cringe (and laugh) at those awkward puberty moments we all went through. We'll rediscover what makes us the bold, resilient Gen Xers we've always been!

Book 3 of *The Invincible '80s* series brings it all home. It's about staying healthy, having fun, and living your best life, Gen X style. We'll tackle anxiety, remember the junk we used to eat, get "Physical" (cue Olivia Newton-John), sleep better, and laugh through the ups and downs of aging—especially as we try to figure out what the H-E-L-L happened to our hormones! We'll relive those epic '80s parties—you know, the keggers—and celebrate our ingenuity, travels, and troubles, both then and now. What does the future hold? Retirement, chasing your dreams, and living life on your terms. I'll have you jumping back in your first car, Mountain Dew and a bag of Doritos in hand, cruising down Nostalgia Lane to arcades, concerts, and those unforgettable first road trips.

"Crystal Ball" by Styx is one of my favorite songs, probably because it reminds me there is so much to look forward to. *The Invincible '80s* has plenty more coming your way, so I hope you sign up for the email list and join the Facebook group to stay in the loop!

To all you Gen Xers and CD-55ers, you're not alone in navigating "this thing called life" past the halfway point. We're all in this together. Supporting each other to be invincible—mentally and emotionally—is what will keep us resilient and strong.

Let's keep the connection going. This book isn't the end, it's just the beginning! Join our *Invincible '80s* Facebook community and discuss the chapters you've read. Our shared experiences will shine and unite us like never before as more Gen Xers and CD-55ers join the conversation.

Share the book and group with your friends, spark those nostalgic chats, and let's pump up the volume like its 1984!

In the meantime…

Play More, Worry Less, & Rock On!

~ XOXO

Becky

Shortcut to the When We Were Invincible Soundtrack on Spotify: beckykliss.com/ost

The Author

'80s   Now

Becky Kliss is just a small-town girl, livin' in an ever-changing world. She took the midnight train to a life-long love of all things Gen X, along with an endless curiosity for culture, how it changes, and how it has changed *us* throughout the decades. Whether it is diving into communication styles, trends, social structures, societal issues, technology, or music (oh, yes, the music!), Becky's zeal goes far beyond just nostalgia. Her interest is in what made Gen X (i.e., The Slackers, The Forgotten Generation, The Latchkey Kids) into the self-reliant generation that we've become today.

Becky is also a passionate environmentalist. A mixture of her love of nature and her entrepreneurial talents led her to start a sustainable commercial cleaning company. Something started with a bucket, mop, broom, and idea grew into a staff of 180 employees across six counties.

After selling her business, Becky started a nonprofit dedicated to helping businesses and schools become more sustainable. She also opened *Re-Imagine*, a gallery that showcased and sold upcycled art, and held sustainable art workshops.

Now in her mid-50s, Becky is living her best life with her two four-legged children, Scrappy and Murphy. Her never-ending curiosity has her reflecting on and divining the lessons and values that were instilled in us as Gen X, what we've learned along the way, and how it's shaped us into who we are.

Invincible '80s Backers Club

Amy Wright	Michael A. Burstein
Bev Shembarger	Michelle Fairley
Bob Cooley	Mike Palmer
Chandra Kendall	Mike Rand
Danielle Landron	Nancy Przybylinski
David Christopherson	Randy James
Deb & Jeff	Rennie Burian
Ed Bennett	Robin Galloway
Emanuele Iacono	Roger Paradiso
Jan Green	Roman Coloma
JoJo Burns	Steve Branstrom
Kai Wright	Terri Malerbi
Lisa Siebenmark	Terry Frye
Lori Berman	Trish (McGinnis) Basinger
Mark Wilkey	

Colophon:

Cover/Book design and production by Bob Cooley

The text of this book is set in Baskerville, designed by John Baskerville, Bohemian Typewriter, designed by Lukas Krakora and Architect's Daughter, designed by Kimberly Geswein

Photos provided by: Rob Huber, Beverly Prillwitz-Shembarger, Wendy (Lubke) Smith, Paula Wilkey, Terry Frye, The Kliss Family, The Cooley Family, The Burian family, and the Bartos family

Author photo by Scott Gain

Acknowledgements

This book began as a tribute to the '80s, but transformed into something far more meaningful and life-changing. Many people joined me on this journey—some from the beginning, others along the way, and a few jumped in at the end for the save. If your name isn't listed here, please know you're still in my heart, even when my memory fails me!

To my *Invincible 80s* Facebook group peeps: Your time and loyalty inspired me to keep "telling the story." To my beta readers: My mom, Robin Galloway, Terry Frye, Ken Kozminski, Steve Branstrom, Kerrie Douglas, Ross Maroney, Mike Palmer, Amy Wright, Brooke Steinberg, and Fiona Hayward—your feedback was invaluable. To all the Kickstarter supporters who believed in the project: I'm deeply grateful.

To my creative team: Denise M. Michaels, my book coach the first year; Jules, my incredible "I don't buy it" editor, who challenged me to think bigger; and Matthew O'Brien, my line editor who spit-shined the last of it. To Bob Cooley, my creative director and talented photographer friend: Your design, layout, and unwavering support through thick and thin have taught me so much! I couldn't have done this without you!

A heartfelt thank you to my Girl Squad: Deb, Lisa, Nancy, and Robin. And to my best buds, the Class of '86: Mikey, Lisa, Terry, Wayne, Rennie, Tink, and Robin. To Dave Montayne, whose "Quality of Life" talks finally worked! To Becky Laney for pushing me out of my comfort zone; Courtney Benson, for your encouragement and words of wisdom; Steve Branstrom, for your loyalty and damn-good Gen X stories; and my treasured book group, Kristen and June, aka my "Vegas Girls." Special thanks to Chandra Kendall, my '80s partner in crime, for your passion and friendship.

To the New Buffalo Area Schools, the New Buffalo Township Library, and the New Buffalo American Legion, where many of my stories came from and my favorite cheerleaders can be found—You all are the best.

To my mom, thank you for my smarts and for teaching me to value memories and cherish family; to my dad, for teaching me how to have fun and the get-out-of-jail-free card that I'm *still* saving; and to my brother Jeff, for always being there for me.

Above all, thank you to the universe for opening my eyes so I could see the bigger picture. You made a believer out of me!

www.ingramcontent.com/pod-product-compliance
Lightning Source LLC
Chambersburg PA
CBHW070611030426
42337CB00020B/3748